C000157348

The Speos Artemidos Inscription of Hatshepsut and Related Discussions

The Speos Artemidos Inscription of Hatshepsut and Related Discussions

Hans Goedicke

HALGO, INC.

©2004 by HALGO, INC.
All Rights reserved
Prinbted in the United States of America

HALGO, INC., PO Box 511, Oakville CT 06779

Library of Congress Cataloging-in-Publication Data

Goedicke, Hans.
The Speos Artemidos inscription of Hatshepsut and related discussions / Hans Goedicke.
p. cm.
Includes bibliographical references and index.
ISBN 1-892840-02-2 (alk. paper)
1. Egypt—History—Eighteenth dynasty, ca. 1570–1320 B.C. 2. Hatshepsut, Queen of Egypt. 3. Egyptian language—Inscriptions. I. Title.
DT87.15.G64 2003
932´.014—dc22 2003021324

Contents

Preface

Hatshepsut's inscription on the Speos Artemidos has been known for more than 120 years. Its first copy was provided by Golenishchev[1] followed by Sethe's[2] edition, which really introduced the long text to Egyptological studies. Because of its unique nature and the difficulties it contains, the text, aside from certain parts, did not gain the attention it should have deserved. It was Gardiner, whose curiosity was awakened by the numerous questions the earlier readings held, who then decided to tackle the text again. He was greatly helped by a new epigraphic copy made by Norman de Garis Davies in 1931 and which he had further collated by B. Grdseloff and H. W. Fairman.[3] Despite later efforts[4] Davies' copy can be considered as definite as presently possible and is used as the basis for the study presented in this volume. Its publication by Gardiner[5] is also the matrix from which the enclosed text copy was made, which is not an independent one.

Gardiner upon reflecting on his study emphasized the unusual difficulties of the text, an opinion everybody who has seriously dealt with it will confirm. However, Gardiner also promulgated the challenge that "scholars should not shrink from translating difficult texts. At the best they may be lucky enough to hit upon the right renderings. At the worst they will have given the critics a target to tilt at." It is in this spirit that the present study is presented. It began many years ago when I thought the passage "that the earth had removed their foot-prints" could be elucidated. It was from this starting point that the text gradually made sense as a very personal but also extremely revealing historical account. It required some difficult adjustments in the approach to appreciate the individuality which shaped the text, beginning with the particular style to the degree of self reflection to the complexity of the underlying political processes. If these afforts are at least partly successful, the aim to envision ancient Egypt as a human drama was worth the effort.

[1] Vladimir Golenishchev, "Notice sur un texte hiéroglyphique de Stabel Antar," *RT* 3 (1882), 13; *RT* 6 (1885), 20.

[2] Kurt Sethe, *Urkunden der 18. Dynastie* (IV 383-391), based on extensive collation by Georg Möller.

[3] See *JEA* 33 (1947), 12.

[4] See Susanne Bickel and Jean-Luc Chappaz, "Missions épigraphiques du fonds de l'Egyptologie de Genève au Speos Artemidos," *BSEG* 12 (1988), 9-24.

[5] Alan H. Gardiner, "Davies' Copy of the Great Speos Artemidos Inscription," *JEA* 32 (1946), 43-56.

The Speos Artemidos Text of Hatshepsut

General Discussion

The translation offered here is based on the hieroglyphic text as established by N. de G. Davies with additions by H. W. Fairman as published by Alan H. (Sir) Gardiner in 1946. Only in one minor point has the text been changed, as will be pointed out. The translation itself is based on repeated and extensive study, however, without an opportunity to inspect the original. Later translations than that by Gardiner have been consulted and as far as necessary integrated into this study. The translation tries to stay as close as possible to the Egyptian text. This is bound to impede the clarity of the English wording. On the other hand, it will, I hope, convey some of the specifically ancient Egyptian flavor. Thus, the translation tries to attain a compromise between English idiomatics and the way Hatshepsut formulated approximately 3500 years ago.

The long text, comprising 42 vertical lines, can be divided into nine sections plus an introduction and conclusion. The account of Hatshepsut's deeds opens with the description of an event and its consequences which happened early in her carrier when she had not achieved her ambition to be king in Egypt. The main part is introduced by her elevation to sole rule. It is cast as musing at this occasion about the future. As demonstration of her success as ruler a number of religious deeds in Middle Egypt are mentioned. In addition, it emphasizes her efforts for gaining support by the professional military. This acceptance is contrasted in the closing sections with an account involving opponents of her reign.

The Introduction

As is to be expected, the text opens with Hatshepsut's royal protocol. It is, however, not in the customary form, but has instead of the royal prenomen the designation *nb-tꜣwy*. What might be considered a stylistic variant is, however, a reflection of the particular political situation prevailing during Hatshepsut's early years. While later in the text (l. 35)[1] mention is made that "Amun had made her appear as permanent king on the throne of Horus" the title *nswt-bit(yw)* is nowhere mentioned. The latter reflects

[1] See below, p. 76.

the constitutional acceptance by the society,[2] a fact which did not apply to Hatshepsut who had become "king" (*nswt*) on account of a (staged) divine oracle.[3] The designation which is instead listed in the protocol specifies the bearer as descendant of the/a past king,[4] in this case Thutmosis I, whose fatherhood she emphasizes especially in the earlier part of her sole reign.[5] That the *nswt-bit(yw)* title is avoided, which she sports later without any discernable hesitation, points to a degree of political insecurity which is later overcome.[6]

Beyond a general attribution to the early part of her life, a more specific date is difficult to establish because of the absence of any direct date in the text. There are, however, some indicators which allow some suggestions for it. It is clear that the text was written after her elevation to be "king" (*nswt*), which is directly mentioned in line 35, but also in line 8.[7] This event, though not fixed chronologically by a text, has been assigned to her 7th regnal year.[8] In connection with her reach for power, Hatshepsut delineates her ideas of planting myrrh trees like they grow in Punt. This plan was carried out in her 9th regnal year by the well documented expedition there.[9] All other events mentioned in the text lack any basis for assigning a date to them and it is even uncertain if they are all mentioned in chronological order. This is all the more regrettable as some of the events mentioned have ramification far beyond the limits of Egypt.

[2] 2Although there are serious misgivings concerning the traditional rendering of the royal designation as "king of Upper Egypt and King of Lower Egypt" it is not the place to delve into this complex problem. As for the particular occurrence the traditional rendering as "King"suffices.

[3] Aside of the later concerted efforts by Hatshepsut to claim predestinatiuon for the office intended or inaugurated by her father Thutmosis I, the political realities are quite different. It is the event during the great feast of Amun that propelled her into the position of King after Thutmosis III had ruled for several years. That the divine "oracle"could not have happened without the collution of the Theban Amun priesthood requires hardly any comment. The principal question who was the driving force leading to this development, was it Hatshepsut excessive drive for power or was it the design of the Theban priesthood using Hatshepsut as a tool for gaining their aims, is not elucidated by the information to be gained from this text. The possibility that both parties were ultimately responsible for the development avoids assigning exclusive responsibility. This would seem to serve best the efforts to understand the text and the specific political motives behind it.

[4] The designation is traditionally rendered *nṯr-nfr* "good god," as if the notion of a bad god is a likely one. In addition, it presumes a divinity of the ruling king, which, despite frequent insistance, is an untenable axiom. The designation, which is paralleled by *Nfr-tm* and *nfr-Ḥr*, rather emphasizes lineage, i.e., descent from a *nṯr*, i.e., a ritually buried former king.; cf. Hans Goedicke, "God," *JSSEA* XVI (1988), 57-62.

[5] For Hatshepsut's relation to her father, cf. Suzanne Ratié, *La Reine Hatchepsout: sources et problèmes*, Orientalia Monspeliensia I, (1979), 49 ff.; 93 ff. It is impossible to decide when the (political) myth of her divine descent, that Amun took on the appearance of Thutmosis I to engender her was promulgated. It is certainly not a traditional idea as Hellmut Brunner, *Die Geburt des Gottkönigs*, Äg.Abh. 10 (1964), 194 ff. claims, but rather an individual creation by her or for her. Its codification in her memorial temple at Deir el Bahari suggests rather a later than an early date for it.

[6] The earliest datable occurrence of this title is year 9 (= Urk. IV 349,10).

[7] See below, pp. 44 f.

[8] Suzanne Ratié, *La Reine Hatchepsout:Sources et Problèmes*, (1979), 83 f.; The proposal of Year 2 by Siegfried Schott, *Zum Krönungstag der Königin Hatschepsut*, NGAW 1955, 6, 212 f. has been decidedly disproven by Jean Yoyotte, "La date supposé du couronnement d'Hatshepsout," *Kêmi* XVIII (1968), 85-91; see also Roland Tefnin, "L'an 7 de Touthmosis III et d'Hatshepsout," *CdE* 48 (1973), 232-242; Jürgen von Beckerath, *Chronologie des pharaonischen Ägypten*, MÄS 46 (1997), 109; Peter F. Dorman, *The Monuments of Senenmut*, (1988), 43-45.

[9] *Urk* IV 349-354; S. Ratié, op. cit. 139-161.

The topic of the introduction, aside of listing Hatshepsut's protocol, is the desire for three things: one is permanence,[10] second is historic recognition and third, the wish "to prevail over the region of the 'mountain-mistress' eastwards." The first two make it clear that the inscription was written at a time when Hatshepsut was "king," because only then did she hold a "great name" and would have been noted in the "annals."[11] The prevailing anxiety about her fame would seem to point to a time in her reign, when her antagonist Thutmosis III was not an insignificant or marginal figure, but rather a political player to be reckoned with. When this happened is difficult to decide but almost certainly prior to the reconciliation between the two at the occasion of the "first jubilee" in Year 15.[12]

The wish for recognition is matched with the desire to be "always powerful over the region of the mountain-goddess eastwards."[13] Two things are noteworthy: the verb *qnn* expresses forceful control, while the area concerned has no qualification which would explain this desire, especially as there is no limit specified. Its attribution to the "mountain-mistress" is curious for its omission of a divine name; the anonymity might be due to the desire to keep the claim as open-ended as possible in case more than one regional deity would be affected. Specifically, the "mountain-mistress" is identical with Pakhet, whose home is indicated at Beni Hasan as *Z(ri)t*, the "sheep-country".[14] The wish for political control over the territory to the East of Egypt, including the Sinai Peninsula, implies a high degree of interest on the part of Hatshepsut. It is further demonstrated by the fact that a claim to the "precious steppe which is in the area of the East" is found three times in her reign.[15] This claim was first formulated under Sesostris I, who established control over the western Sinai and its mines.[16] After Hatshepsut, this particular claim is not stated again until Psammeticus I[17] who reestablished control over the region after it had collapsed for half a millennium. If it would concern the resources of the region the wish for forceful control would be out of place, just as the center of the mineral exploration is fairly circumscribed. In other words, the reason for Hatshepsut's interest in the area should be different in nature. It might have something to do with the

[10]The wish for permannence is taken up again in the text's conclusion; see below, pp. 88 f.

[11]Cf. Donald B. Redford, *Pharaonic King-lists,Annals and Day-books* (1986), 70.

[12]The "jubilee"which was celebrated in year 15 is the occasion when Thutmosis III appears next to Hatshepsut in an almost equal role. It would seem that it was celebrated as a political attempt to come to some form of a reconciliation between the two contenders for the throne. When seen in this light, the complex explanation for the fact that the celebration was in Year 16 would become unncessary. For Hatshepsut's "jubilee,"see S. Ratié, op. cit. 201-04; Erik Hornung undElisabeth Staehelin, *Studien zum Sedfest*, Aegyptiaca Helvetica I (1974), 54; J.v. Beckerath, 73; 121; E.P. Uphill, "A joint Sed-Festival of Thutmosis III and Queen Hatshepsut," *JNES* 20 (1961), 248-251.

[13]See further below, pp. 58 f.

[14]P.E. Newberry, *Beni Hasan* I, pl. 24;cf. also A. H. Gardiner, *Ancient Egyptian Onomastica*, II, 90*. Her earliest attestation is on a coffin from north of Antinoe; see Pierre Lacau, *Mél. Maspero* I (1935), 929-37; she is mentioned *CT* V 399 a, where it might be a secondary interpretation of a misreading of *pꜣwt*.

[15]Edouard Naville, *Deir el Bahari* IV (1890), pls. 112/13; N. de Garis Davies, *The Tomb of Puyemre'* (1922), pl. 50; see also Hermann Kees, *ZÄS* 57 (1922), 99.

[16]Cf. Jaroslav Černý, *Inscriptions from Sinai*, II (1955), 34; 36.

[17]Hans Goedicke, "An Egyptian Claim to Asia," *JARCE* 8 (1969-1970), 13.

expulsion of the opponents mentioned in the nineth section of the text.[18] A definite answer is unfortunately impossible.

Section One

The section deals with a number of deeds affecting cults carried out under Hatshepsut. No particular deity is singled out as beneficiary of her actions, nor is there any indication about the exact date or the duration of them. The nature of the actions taken, however, suggest some duration of cause and consequence. They are unusual in their nature and can be summarized as extensive restorations, from emergency measures to fashioning divine statues to fixing religious feasts by the civil calender and those determined by seasonal events.

The description focuses on the sanctuaries and the deities dwelling in them. Two statements express their satisfaction about what had been done for them during extraordinary circumstances. One concerns their "hiding places," the other some makeshift appointments to carry out the ritual for them. Connected with it is the indication that the divine dwellings were strengthened up to a point specified as "the place (of the rite) of removing the footstep."[19] This refers to the closing act in a ritual when the officiant, after completing his performances for the deity, moved backwards towards the door while sweeping away his own footprints.[20] When the rite thus came to a close the dwelling place of the deity was pristine again. The fact that the deities needed a "hiding place" indicates conditions quite extraordinary.[21] The other statement supports this idea: the deity, i.e., its image, apparently had to be removed from its usual setting.

The extraordinary circumstances that led to the measures indicated as necessary in some cults are specified in the opening statement. "The Lord [of the glow] over the coast-line—his flames were outside the Two Mountain-ranges" describes a divine power and its effect. This divine power has no name and is identified solely by the features conspicuous to men. One a "glow" or "shine" (Egyptian *iꜣḫw*),[22] the other its visibility "over the coast-line." As the Red Sea coast is unconnected with any settled area of Egypt, the shore-line referred to has to be seen as the Mediterranean coast-line. The "glow" or "shine" which is observed there is not a deity itself, but rather its reflection. To be described in this fashion is an indication that Egyptians were unfamiliar with the identity of the power which they saw reflected "over the coast-line." Although the "glow" is only its reflection, the power is creating "flames." These "flames," i.e., the manifestations of destructive force, were "outside the Two Mountain-ranges." The latter describes the

[18] See below, p. 80.

[19] See further p. 40.

[20] For this ritual, cf. Hermann Junker, *Gîza* III 110; J. J. Clère, *JEA* 25 (1939), 215 f.; Harold H. Nelson, "The Rite of 'Bringing the Foot' as Portrayed in Temple Reliefs," *JEA* 35 (1949), 82-86; Eberhard Otto, *Das ägyptische Mundöffnungsritual*, Äg.Abh. 3 (1960), 157 f.; cf. also Hans Fischer-Elfert, *Die Vision von der Statue im Stein* (1998), 7, note 14.

[21] See below, p. 37.

[22] For this reading, see pp. 35 f.

geographical particularity of the Nile Valley, south of modern Cairo, which is lined on either side by the desert edge.[23] In other words, the "Two Mountain-ranges" is a pictorial expression for the southern part of Egypt, but does not necessarily include the Delta. During the time when the burning impact of the distant divinity was felt outside of Upper Egypt, "braziers were distributed."[24] This action or reaction would seem senseless except when darkness prevailed. "Braziers" were first of all vehicles to provide artificial light. In a society which followed closely the natural cycle of day and night, the first for activity, the latter for rest, artificial illumination was practically unknown and also unnecessary. It was only under exceptional circumstances that darkness had to be responded to with artificial light.[25]

The distribution of braziers was caused by the impact of "the Lord [of the glow] over the coast-line," i.e., a distant power which was perceived in the reflection visible over the Mediterranean. The seeming dichotomy of distant glow and fiery impact necessitating the distribution of braziers for artificial lighting can be reduced to a fiery cause happening outside of Egypt across the Mediterranean with darkness in Egypt as its result. The only natural explanation for this dichotomy is volcanic activity and its consequences, such as ash clouds blocking out the sun.

There is no volcano in Egypt, nor does the text allow for one, as the reflection is seen "over the coast-line." North of Egypt, i.e., beyond the "coast-line," lies the island of Thera/Santorin in a distance of 750 kilometers.[26]

That darkness was the affliction is corroborated by the statement about the effects the distribution of braziers had for the deities. They "enlarged the shrines into favorite places."[27] The Egyptians envisioned their deities as being quite similar to themselves in their living patterns. People had a place to spend the night that was, of course, dark and confined, and another place that was light and open.[28] The same holds true for the sanctuaries. The inner shrine, where the deity spent the night, was in total darkness. It was part of the daily ritual that the shrine was opened, the divine statue cleansed, and finally an offering provided.[29] The "favorite place" denotes the choice accomodation for the day time for human and deities alike.[30]

[23]The term occurs already in the Pyramid Texts (Pyr. 2064), although its limitation to Upper Egypt has not been recognized; see Adelheid Schlott-Schwab, *Die Ausmasse Ägyptens nach altägyptischen Texten*, ÄAT 3 (1981), 89 f.

[24]See further, p. 37.

[25]Another case of reference to artificial illumination is contained on the stela of a certain *Ꞽppi* found at Tell ed-Dabʿa. The man brags about having provided light for king Apophis and the King's sister Taʿo. Again the circumstances are extraordinary; they were due to a natural disaster which also brought an intrusion of the Mediterranean as far as Avaris; see Hans Goedicke, "Two Inscriptions from Tell ed-Daba," *BACE* 13 (2002), 57-70.

[26]For the impact of volcanic activity of Thera/Santorin on Egypt, see Hans Goedicke, "The End of the Hyksos in Egypt," L. H. Lesko, ed., *Egyptological Studies in Honor of Richard A. Parker*, 1986, 37-47; idem, "The Northeastern Delta and the Mediterranean," in *Archaeology of the Nile Delta, Problems and Priorities* (1987), 165-175; idem, "The Chronology of the Thera/Santorin Explosion," *Ä&L* III (1992), 57-62.

[27]See below, p. 38.

[28]The wish for a light and lofty place is a recurrent theme in the funerary wishes; e.g., *Urk.* IV 117, 1; 148, 12; 499, 7; etc.

[29]For the opening events of the daily ritual performed for deities, see especially the p.Berlin 3014, 3053 and 3055; *Hieratische Papyrus aus den königlichen Museen zu Berlin*, I (1901), Tf. 1 ff. Alexandre Moret, *Le rituel du culte divin journalier en Égypte* (1902), passim.

[30]Cf. Dieter Arnold, *Wandrelief und Raumfunktion in ägyptischen Tempeln des Neuen Reiches*, MÄS 2 (1962), 7 ff.

In addition to the illumination, "every single god who was away from the sanctuary which he had loved—his *ka* was satisfied about the places, which I have assigned as residence."[31] While in the initial case the distribution of braziers sufficed to make gods content, the second one is more serious. It concerns such instances where the sanctuary had to be abandoned and where substitute arrangements had to be made.[32] Although no cause is specified, there can be no doubt that it is the same cause that led to the darkness and the need for illumination; in other words, established cult-places had to be abandoned and the cults transfered to other places.

Not in all cases was a re-assignment necessary. In some it sufficed to reinforce "the hiding place inside the house", a praxis seemingly prefered for pillard halls (*iwnyt*).[33] The need for this kind of reinforcement would seem to suggest major structural damage, which ought to have reasons others than natural decay. It conforms with the prevailing of darkness (during daytime), for which volcanic activity was proposed as cause. Structural damage that required reinforcement would also be a likely consequence of an earthquake accompanying a volvanic outbrake.

During the natural disaster and its aftermath, not every cult could receive the same attention. As a feature of distinction in the awarded care, the existence of an image made of "electrum of *ʿmꜣw*" is mentioned; in those cases one would continue to have their calendrical as well as seasonal celebrations.[34] The distinction that "the body be made of electrum" might seem surprising, because it indicates categories among the "gods" by material distinctions.[35] The Egyptian term *nṯr* does not only apply to a "god" in the theistic sense, but also to anyone expected to have attained permanence, especially ritually buried dead ones.[36] While the latter might receive veneration, they are not object to worship and thus have not their own feasts etc. In other words, only recipients of an organized cult are meant here, whose service was continued despite prevailing adversity.

Because of the implicit references to a natural disaster and the havoc it created in the part of Egypt not lined by the two mountain ranges, it would be especially important to establish it chronologically. This task is, unfortunately, hampered by the lack of any direct date in the text. However, the fact that these allusions are followed by the description of events associated with Hatshepsut's becoming "king" makes it virtually certain that they occurred during the time when she apired to become king, i.e., prior to Year 7.[37]

[31] See further below, p. 38.

[32] While gods, like humans, traveled, I am not aware of another occasion telling specifically about temporary shelter for a displaced cult.

[33] See further, p. 40.

[34] The performance of the feast associated with a particular cult are an essential part of its existence. They are not only the highlights of religious activity, in all likelihood attracting people from a wider area, but were also essential for the material sustaining of any religious activity.

[35] That not all gods were equal applies not only to the local arrangements, but has also its reflection in the fundamental evaluation of the different numina. The distinction between "great" and "minor ennead" is a case in question; for them, see Wilfried Barta, *Untersuchungen zum Götterkreis der Neunheit*, MÄS 28 (1973), 53 ff.

[36] See Hans Goedicke, "God," *JSSEA* XVI (1988), 57-62; idem, *GM* 172 (1999), 23-26.

[37] For this date, see Roland Tefnin, "L'an 7 de Touthmosis III et d'Hatshepsut," *CdE* 48 (1973), 232-42; S. Ratié, op. cit. 83 f.; Jürgen von Beckerath, *Chronologie des pharaonischen Ägypten*, MÄS 46 (1997), 108 f.

Section Two

In this section Hatshepsut speaks about reflections at the time she reached for the kingship in the country. The partisans of her predecessor and official mate Thutmosis II (1492-1479 B.C.) had seen to it that his son from another wife named Isis would be appointed to succeed him. Already upon her mate's early death, Hatshepsut had ambitions to gain political control and in the seventh year of Thutmosis III she had herself crowned king of Egypt.[38] The setting for this takeover was the great feast of the god Amun celebrated in Thebes.[39] It was then that Hatshepsut prostrated herself before the advancing deity, promising to do what the god desired. After this she was taken into a nearby chapel, from which she emerged wearing the crown of Egypt. The attending people were taken by surprise, but Hatshepsut's guards made sure that everybody reacted properly in the situation. This transpires even from the "official" inscription where it says:[40] "The entire land was taken by silence 'One does not understand' the royal noblemen said and the great ones of the palace turned the face to the one behind saying 'why?' The weak-of-heart turned into frustration, as their hearts trembled under its (unexpected) event."

Hatshepsut's decision to reach for the supreme power in the country is widely interpreted as a political move inspired by her unbridled drive for power.[41] In her own statements Hatshepsut always emphasizes the religious motive, in particular her love and support for Amun.[42] Her close association with his cult and his priesthood is the frame of her actions, especially in her earlier years.[43] With this as general background, the section becomes more transparent. It states her reflections about the meaning of life. Although she held the reins of the country, her main concern remains constant. It is, in her words, "Amun, Lord-of-Millions." Her religious orientation is exclusively directed towards this one god, whom she sees as the ultimate *raison d'être*. All political advance does not diminish for her this central conviction of her being.

The opening statement, juxtaposing the "divine heart" with the "heart of the noble-person" (*ḥit*), stresses the uniformity of her aspiration. The "heart" is for the Egyptians the seat of all emotions and

[38]See below, Hans Goedicke, "Thutmosis III's early years," pp. 107 ff.

[39]Pierre Lacau et Henri Chevrier, *Une chapelle d'Hatchepsout à Karnak* (1977), 97-153.

[40]P. Lacau–H. Chevrier, op. cit., 98; 100.

[41]E.g. William C. Hayes, *The Scepter of Egypt*, II (1959), 82 "it was not long before this vain, ambitious, and unscrupulous woman showed herself in her true colors"; Sir Alan Gardiner, *Egypt of the Pharaohs* (1961), 183 ". . . her ambition was by no means dormant, and not many years had passed before she had taken the momentous step of herself assuming the Double Crown"; Jacques Vadier, *L'Égypte* (1962), 338 ". . . En fait, elle usurpa le pouvoir . . ."; Eberhard Otto, *Ägypten* (1953), 146 "Die Leidenschaftlichkeit des Herrschenwollens drückt sich . . . auch darin aus, daß in bilderreicher pathetischer Sprache die Berufung auf den Thron durch den Wunsch des Gottes Amun . . ."; John A. Wilson, *The Culture of Ancient Egypt* (1951)," the rule was usurped by his (scil. Thutmosis III) aunt and stepmother Hat-shepsut"; Donald B. Redford, *History and Chronology of the Eighteenth Dynasty of Egypt* (1967),77 "as soon as Hatshepsut achieved her coop, all Egypt came over to her . . . She had a circle of favourites, a motley collection of individuals with no common background and little reason to share political goals."

[42]E.g., in her claim that Amun was her actual father having taken on the form of Thutmosis I the lengthy text in which Thutmosis I expresses his gratitude to the Theban gods for the elevation of Hatshepsut to kingship (*Urk.* IV 266-274), certainly composed by her or in the numerous epitheta, as collected in *Urk.* IV 274-76; cf.also S. Ratié, op. cit. 93 ff.

[43]It is, of course, in her earlier years that Senenmut plays a dominant role, not only as tutor of the *Nfrw-Rʿ* but in the running of the country as well; cf.S.Ratié, op. cit., 243 ff., Peter F. Dorman, *The Monuments of Senenmut* (1988), 22 f.

thoughts.[44] The "divine heart," a term otherwise not attested in this form before the Ptolemaic Period,[45] should be understood as the "holy heart," i.e., the reflections on an ultimate goal. Hatshepsut might have used this formulation to reflect the double nature she felt she had as child of the god Amun and as human being.[46] The "divine heart" can thus be seen as divine inspiritaion, which she held because of her proclaimed descent from Amun. It is this aspect of her that is "searching about the future" in her political role as king. The "heart of the noble-person (*bit*)," likewise an unparalleled Hatshepsut formulation, denotes her frame of mind prior to her elevation to kingship. It too is directed towards eternity inspired by the pronouncement of her elevation. The latter is expressed in the mythological phrase "the pronouncement of 'Him-who-splits-the-*ished*-tree.'" Although there is the motive of having the name of the newly crowned king inscribed on its leaves, the metaphor is rooted in political reality.[47] The Egyptians were neither in the habit of inscribing tree-leaves, because they had papyrus as writing material, nor did they have the idea of a sacred tree, just as splitting wood is not a significant activity. The *ished*-tree is rather a metaphor for the process by which somebody became king in ancient Egypt, and "the one who splits the *ished*-tree" is the official who pronounces the result, a role mythologically assigned to the god Thoth, in the physical world of politics most probably the vizier.[48]

Hatshepsut's thoughts upon becoming king center on the god Amun. She apparently perceives her elevation as the consequence of the deeds she had carried out previously: "I magnified the order which is desired for him."[49] She also indicates by these words her intentions to expand the "order of Amun" during her regency. In numerous inscriptions she states her devotion for Amun, whom she considered her spiritual and genetic father.[50]

This "order of Amun" she professes as the basis of her existence, comparing it with bread as basic sustenance.[51] Not satisfied with her present religious commitment, she anticipates an even greater degree of closeness to the god after her earthly existence. To become "one flesh with him" is a recurrent idiom used concerning the demise of a king in the wish that"he ascends to heaven and mingles with the one who had

[44]Alexandre Piankoff, *Le «coeur» dans les textes Égyptiens* (1930), does not include the expression; but cf. Adriaan de Buck, *JEOL* 9 (1944), 9-24.

[45]Cf. Penelope Wilson, *A Ptolemaic Lexicon*, OLA 78 (1997), 559.

[46]This double nature is the basis for her promulgation of a divine procreation by Amun taking on the physical appearance of her father Thutmosis I. This earliest attestation of the motif better known in the Greek version of Amphytrion was either her personal invention or was promulgated for her. There is no basis to project this notion of divine origin back before her as H. Brunner, op. cit. 188 f. has proposed.

[47]For the mythological aspect of the ceremony see Wolfgang Helck, *ZÄS* 82 (1957), 117-140.; also Donald B. Redford, *Pharaonic King-Lists, Annals and Day-Books*, (1986), 66.

[48]The claim, that "her father Amun had placed her great name on the *išd*-tree" (*Urk.* IV 358, 14) credits Amun with planning her ascent before the constitutional processes had actually occurred.

[49]For this interpretation, see below, p. 45.

[50]See above, note 40.

[51]Bread as metaphor is not common, but does occur; cf. Hermann Grapow, *Die bildlichen Ausdrücke des Aegyptischen* (1924), 143.

created him."[52] While she anticipates this ultimate apotheosis, she sees her role as appointee of Amun to spread the god's fame in the land.[53] Therefore Hatshepsut views herself not as accomplishing political ambitions but as acting as a tool of Amun. This religious activity for one god is in her words the single motive for her actions.[54]

The allusion to her ascent to power at this point in the long text can serve as a chronological indicator. Hatshepsut most probably became king in her 7th year (1473 B.C.). The events described in Section One apparently occurred before this time.[55]

Section Three

While in the previous section Hatshepsut emphasizes her special devotion to Amun this section does not concern personal religiosity, but rather her role in the divinely conceived kingship. Amun at the time of Hatshepsut was first of all the local god of Thebes.[56] It is in part due to Hatshepsut's efforts that Amun became the divine patron of kingship in his role of Amun-Reᶜ. The divine power which kingship represented on earth was conceived by the Egyptian theologians from ca. 2400 B.C. onwards as Atum.[57] As transcendental godhead he is beyond human comprehension. In his manifest form he is denoted as Kheperi, i.e., "being," to whom creation is assigned. What Kheperi made is under the sway of the sun-god Reᶜ, whom the Egyptians considered a form of Kheperi. Reᶜ is the ruler of the world, whom the early king represents and serves. In other words, the Pharaoh carries out the plans of Reᶜ.

Hatshepsut claims that she is respected in the Black Land and the Red Land.[58] The former is a metaphor for Egypt because of its black soil, the latter for the desert and by extension any territory outside of Egypt. Her superiority is expressed not only in geographical but also in social terms. The "foreigners," literally "hill-dwellers," are juxtaposed with the flat-land dwellers, the agrarian population. Both, the land

[52]The earliest occurrence is in Sinuhe R 7 f.; for the formulation, cf. Hermann Grapow, *Anreden . . .* IV (1943), 142 ff.; Elke Blumenthal, *Untersuchungen zum ägyptischen Königtum des Mittleren Reiches*, AAWLeipzig 61,1 (1970), 53 ff.

[53]In this missionary zeal she anticipates the attitude permiating Wenamun's conviction of Amun's universal grandeur as expressed to the Chief of Byblos; see, Hans Goedicke, *The Report of Wenamun* (1975), 87 ff.

[54]See further, p. 46.

[55]Although there is some uncertainty, the fact that there is an inscription still dated to the 7th year of Thutmosis III basically confirms that her ascent did not occur substantially earlier.

Unfortunately the different sections of the text do not reflect a clear chronological order. This applies especially to the events mentioned in Section Nine, which apparently occurred also during the time prior to becoming king; see further, p. 84.

[56]Eberhard Otto, *Amun und Osiris* (1966), 117; what might seem to reflect a supreme role of Amun during the reign of Thutmosis I, on closer inspection turns out to be due to Hatshepsut's crediting her father. The elevation of Amun to "king of the gods" (*nswt-nṯrw*) is first attested in the inscription of Thutmosis I's second year at Tombos; cf. also Kurt Sethe, *Amun und die Acht Urgötter von Hermopolis*, AAWBerlin, 1929, 4 (1929, 12 f.

[57]Hans Goedicke, "Unity and Diversity in the Oldest Religion of Ancient Egypt," in H. Goedicke, ed., *Unity and Diversity* (1975), 201-217.

[58]E.g., *Urk.* IV 283, 17.

and the people, should be seen in political terms as directly under the authority of Hatshepsut as king of Egypt. Added to this is the description of her influence beyond the political borders of the Pharaonic realm. Three areas are specified as the main contacts abroad. El-Shawat[59] is attested since the Middle Kingdom as a region which in particular produces turquois, but also antimony. It was inhabited by Semites who traded with Egypt. All this suggests that el-Shawat should be seen as the designation of the central and northeastern Sinai Peninsula. As a trading partner the region was significant for Egypt's economy in supplying turquois, antimony, and probably also some copper. *[M]iww*, as the term is most likely to be read, is attested since the reign of Kamose (ca. 1554-1550 B.C.) and is especially during the Eighteenth Dynasty mentioned quite frequently.[60] The area to which it applies is in the southern Nile Valley; Thutmosis III (1479-1425 B.C.) had hunted a rhinoceros there.[61] A likely identification has been suggested by Karola Zibelius[62] as the Nile bent between the Third and Fourth Cataract. The area, which originally had Kerma as its political and economic center, came under full Pharaonic control only during Hatshepsut's successor Thutmosis III.[63] Located to the south of the Pharaonic empire at the time, it was the natural commercial bridge to Africa.

That el-Shawat and *[M]iww* did not "hide" from Hatshepsut indicates that the commercial contacts prevailed in their usual form. The third area with which Hatshepsut conducts business is Punt. It is the general term for the region which produced the myrrh used extensively in any form of religious cult. In her 9th year (1470 B.C.) Hatshepsut sent out a major trading expedition to Punt, about which she gives a detailed report on the walls of her mortuary temple at Deir el-Bahari.[64] The exact goal of the expedition is not certain. Myrrh grows even now on both shores of the lower Red Sea, so that her venture went either to south Yemen or possibly as far as the Somali coast on the Horn of Africa.[65] She not only imported large quantities of myrrh but also myrrh trees, which were planted in front of her mortuary temple.[66] Her motives were probably shrewdly commercial. By eliminating the intermediaries Hatshepsut apparently tried to establish a royal monopoly which would control the needs not only within the Pharaonic domain, but also in the Levant and the Mediterranean basin.[67] The reference can serve as a chronological indicator, establishing the commercial links for the time before the 9th year.[68]

This date is particularly important for the remaining statement in this section. The "desert tracks"

[59]For this reading of the term, see below, p. 50.

[60]Cf.Hans Goedicke, *Studies about Kamose and Ahmose* (1995), 20.

[61]*Urk.* IV 1246.

[62]Karola Zibelius, *Afrikanische Orts- und Völkernamen in hieroglyphischen und hieratischen Texten*, TAVO B/1 (1972), 118-120;

[63]Torgny Säve-Söderbergh, *Ägypten und Nubien* (1941), 153 f.; William Y. Adams, *Nubia:Corridor to Africa* (1977), 218-220.

[64]Edouard Naville, *The Temple of Deir el Bahari*, III, pls. LXIX ff., (1897); S. Ratié, op. cit. 139-162.

[65]The location of Punt is the topic of much debate, although the term is most probably not to be understood as a specific geographic label denoting a defined area, but rather as a general term of reference to myrrh producing land.

[66]Cf. S. Ratié, op. cit. 167; the actual pits for the planting of the trees can not be ascertained.

[67]One could see it as an early forerunner to the monopoly on pepper by Venice during the Middle Ages; for the latter, cf. Frederic C. Lane, *Venice.A Maritime Republic* (1973), 287 ff.

[68]See also, p. 51.

which had been closed are not identified. As far as is known, Egypt did not trade overland to the west, but only to the east and northeast.[69] The reason that these trade-routes had not been used by commercial or military expeditions was the closing of something called the "Two Roads." This seemingly ambiguous identification becomes clearer by taking into consideration that there was a place called *Rꜣ-wꜣty*, i.e., the "Beginning of the Two Roads," in the northeastern Delta.[70] It was apparently the starting point of two tracks both leading eventually to the trading areas east of the Isthmus of Suez. On the map published by the expedition Napoleon had brought to Egypt, two tracks are indicated leading from the northeastern Delta, approximately from modern Sharkiyeh, to come together in the neighborhood of modern Qantarah.[71] The reason for these double tracks is the different geographical areas they transgress: The northern one runs directly south of the Pelusian branch of the Nile; the southern one follows the edge of the elevated desert ground; it is longer but is safe from any impact by the nearby Mediterranean Sea.[72] What caused the closing of both tracks is not stated, nor is the duration of the disruption. The context mentioning commercial contacts with Punt suggests that the disruption occurred prior to the trading expedition of Hatshepsut's 9th year.

In connection with the disruption of the tracks to the east, Hatshepsut mentions an adverse economic impact on her troops. Military activity brought the participants the chance to enhance their status, socially and economically. It is not clear if Hatshepsut refers here to military operations or if she has in mind economic ventures, which could involve military assignments as in the case of the expedition to Punt. Although Hatshepsut repeatedly depicts troops in her mortuary temple,[73] information about actual military campaigns, particularly in the Levante, is minute. Some of her officials speak of military actions in the north, e.g., Inebni, the overseer of the royal armors.[74] However, these were probably limited military operations and certainly not a large-scale campaign. At any rate, Hatshepsut's years before becoming king saw no military action, while after her ascent to kingship the lot of the military improved. It is nowhere said that the military activity was against Asia, so that one against Nubia is more likely. A military campaign against the south in which Hatshepsut possibly took part personally has been established from a graffito left by an official named Tiy on the island of Sehel in the First Cataract which says,[75] "I followed the 'Good-

[69]Wolfgang Helck, *Wirtschaftsgeschichte des Alten Ägypten* (1975), 259 ff.

[70]Hermann Kees, "Ein Handelsplatz des MR im Nordostdelta," *MDIAK* 18 (1962), 1-11; Manfred Bietak, *Ä&L* VIII (1998), 12 ff.; cf. also Hans Goedicke, "Two Inscriptions from Tell ed-Dabʿa, *BACE* 13 (2002), 57-70.

[71]*Description de l'Egypte, État moderne*, pl. 31.

[72]Manfred Bietak, *Tell ed Dabaʿ*, II, AAWWien, 1975, 130 ff.; it has to be stressed that the configuration of the Mediterranean littoral has changed substantially since Hatshepsut's days. As far as can be ascertained, the Lake Menzaleh was still open water, i.e. part of the Mediterranean, at this time. It was probably not before sometimes in the Nineteenth Dynasty that the hydrography of the Delta changed when the Damiettana became the main drain which produced the spit which eventually closed in the area which became the Lake Menzaleh.

[73]E. Naville, op. cit., pls. 88; 89; 91.

[74]*Urk.* IV 465, 2; because there is no specific geographic reference it could be that the claim to have served his lord on the southern and northern foreign territory might be a stock phrase.

[75]Labib Habachi, "Two Graffiti at Sehel from the Reign of Queen Hatshepsut," *JNES* 16 (1857), 88-104; Wolfgang Helck, *Zur Verwaltung des Mittleren und Neuen Reichs* (1958), 351 f., D. B. Redford, *History and Chronology*, 57 f.

god', the King *K3-m3ʿt-Rʿ*, may she live! I saw when he (sic) overthrew the Nubian bowmen, and when their chiefs were brought to him as living captives." Allusions to this military activity in the tomb of Senenmut, and in Hatshepsut's mortuary temple at Deir el-Bahari make it likely that it happened before the 11th year.[76] This would agree with the statement that the economic conditions of Hatshepsut's military improved after her ascent to kingship. The re-opening of the "Two Roads," however, does not necessarily have anything to do with this.

Section Four

After having talked about events in her early years leading up to her assuming the role of king and the religious and international implications of it, Hatshepsut turns next to specific projects done in Middle Egypt under her rule. It would seem that Sections One to Three were part of a fundamental decree, which was expanded by incorporating issues of local or regional nature taken from other annalistic records.[77]

The Lady of Qusae is a local form of the goddess Hathor. The cult is attested since the Sixth Dynasty (± 2200 B.C.) and in the Middle Kingdom.[78] Of the ancient town of Qusae (Qis) or the temple of the goddess, nothing is preserved. It is generally identified with the modern settlement of el-Qusiya, some 60 kilometers south of Beni Hasan on the western bank of the Nile.[79] The cult enjoyed considerable esteem during the Middle Kingdom, as indicated in the tombs of the local dignitaries at Meïr. The main festivities were marked by music and dance in honor of the goddess and women played a major role in them. There are no references to Qusae from the early Eighteenth Dynasty after it had marked the demarcation line between the Hyksos realm and the Theban Seventeenth Dynasty.[80] The earliest New Kingdom mention is in the tomb of the chief-treasurer Djehuty who lived under Hatshepsut.[81]

According to our text, the temple had fallen into disuse and the divine shrine was covered with earth. No reason is given for this decay. It is certainly not to be attributed to any "Hyksos" destruction, which would have to have occurred at the beginning of the Hyksos-rule, i.e., around 1650 B.C. It would seem more likely that Qusae was destroyed by the advancing Theban Kamose (± 1551 B.C.) for its resistance.[82]

[76]D. B. Redford, op. cit. 58 f.

[77]Although nothing is left of the records of Hatshepsut's reign, probably due to Thutmosis III's later prosecution of her memory, there can be no doubt that such records once existed; for royal annalistic records, cf. D.B. Redford, *Pharaonic King-Lists, Annals and Day-Books*, 165 ff.

[78]Schafik Allam, *Beiträge zum Hathorkult*, MÄS 4 (1963), 23-41.

[79]Dieter Kessler, *Historische Topographie der Region zwischen Mallawi und Salamut*, TAVO B/30 (1981) 54; 118; 240; Farouk Gomaà, *Die Besiedlung Ägyptens während des Mittleres Reiches*, TAVO B/66, 1 (986), 281 f.

[80]Hans Goedicke, *Studies about Kamose and Ahmose* (1995), 36; 42; 43 f.

[81]*Urk*. IV 441, 6.

[82]Although there is no direct report available about any destruction during the campaign of Kamose, the significance of the place as border between the two political domains would make such an action very probable. That the Theban advance north was not carried by a wave of national feeling is well demonstrated by the resistance Kamose met at Nefrusi; cf. H. Goedicke, op. cit. 50 ff.

This would explain why the sancturay had remained unrestored for over 70 years in addition to having lost its significance as demarkarion between a northern and a southern political setup. The appealing picture of the child frolicing over the grounds covering the former sanctuary is used once more a thousand years later concerning Edfu.[83] It might serve here as an expression of total disregard for the sanctity of the religious edifice, but it could also have a political meaning due to Qusae's role demarcating the northern realm from the Theban interests. The disregard for the sanctuary is blamed on a single child, which opens the possibility of being a political reference, namely to the early years of Thutmosis III, when he was not only young of years but probably resided in the North. During these years Hatshepsut controlled the South, aspiring for an eventual takeover of the kingship of all of Egypt. The reason that things had remained in such bad straits Hatshepsut attributes to dishonest people in charge of the damage evaluation. When this occurred remains unspecified. The statement that "there were not its dates of appearances" is rather obscure; it might refer to the discontinuation of any public functions in connection with the cult, such as processions.

Hatshepsut claims that she had the sanctuary rebuilt and that she personally consecrated it. Probably at this occasion she donated a specific statuette made of gold. It represented a uraeus snake and was apparently mounted in the ark in which the idol of the mistress of Qusae was carried during processions on land.[84] Such additional votives to be mounted in the processional arks are found with many cults and at different times. They served as a token of the donating ruler's personal interest and devotion.[85]

Section Five

The second Middle Egyptian deity to receive support from Hatshepsut is Pakhet. For her she has a rock-shrine excavated. It is clearly a new project and not merely an embellishment of an already existing cult-place as was the case in the previous section. Pakhet has two rock-cut shrines in the wadi Batn el-Bakara near Beni Hasan.[86] Both bear the name of Hatshepsut. The larger, the so-called Speos Artemidos, is the place where the long text studied here is inscribed. The other, smaller one, is located at the end of the wadi. It also bears the name of Thutmosis III and of Nofru-reᶜ, the daughter of Hatshepsut.[87] It is not clear which of the two shrines is meant in the great inscription. The likelihood is that the passage refers to the

[83] *Edfu* I 211.

[84] For the description of a bark of Hathor of Old Kingdom date, see Paule Posener-Krieger, *Les Archives du Temple Funéraire de Néferirkarê-Kakaï*, BdE LXV/1 (1976), 99 ff. The particular aspect of the uraeus as "guide-serpant"(*sšmw·t*), attested first in Pyr.396 c, might be the cause for the inclusion.

[85] For this and similar embellishments of divine arks, the bark of Amun is a good illustration; cf. *LÄ* I 248-251.

[86] D. Kessler, op. cit. 63; PM IV 163 ff.; Alan H. Gardiner, *Ancient Egyptian Onomastica*,II (1947), 88* ff.

[87] Ahmed Fakhry, "A New Speos from the Reign of Hatshepsut and Thutmosis III at Beni-Hasan," ASAE 39 (1939), 709-723. The mention of Thutmosis III and of Nofru-reᶜ can be taken as an indication that it was made before Hatshepsut had become king.

smaller one, which was named *Ḥwt-mn*.[88] According to the text the shrine was not to serve as a site of worship the year round, but only for the performance of a specific feast that was not fixed by the civil calender but had to be computed.[89] This is a sign that the celebration had to take place on a specific day. As the Egyptian calendar had exactly 365 days and did not include leap-years, the year would move one day every four years.[90] In cases where emphasis was given to the celebration on a fixed day it had to be established anew every four years. Aside from this celebration the shrine was to be closed.[91]

The shrine was made "for the ennead of her (i.e., Pakhet's) gods." The term might suggest a group of nine gods but is actually an idiom denoting the totality of deities combined into one cult.[92] In the minor shrine Pakhet is sharing the worship with Hathor, mistress of Nefrusi and with Harakhty. In the Speos Artemidos, Pakhet, honored as the "One-great-of-Magic," is the sole recipient of worship.[93] In the portico of the shrine is also a representation of the god Thoth informing the ennead of Karnak that Hatshepsut had become king.[94] This event is certainly the one alluded to here, so that the shrine referred to here is most probably the small one at the end of the wadi.[95]

The making of the shrine Hatshepsut set up originally was apparently instigated by actions attributed to the goddess Pakhet from which she had profited. Pakhet is normally identified as "Mistress of the Sheep-country"[96] or as "Mistress of Heaven, Lady of the gods" in her specific role as patroness of the cemetery located near the Speos Artemidos.[97] In our text, however, Pakhet has the epithet "the Great who roams the wadis" emphasizing her domain in the desert valleys. Her cult-place in the wadi Batn el-Bakara is a reflection of this desert dominance. This is additionally specified by the second epithet "who resides in the East(ern desert)," indicating that her domain is, at least in this case, specifically the desert to the east of Egypt.

[88]The name is specified in a small inscription on the face of the rock into which the shrine is set: *rn n ḥwt-nṯr Ḥwt-mn*: A. Fakhry, op. cit. 716.

[89]See below, p. 61.

[90]Richard A. Parker, *The Calendars of Ancient Egypt*, SAOC 26 (1950), § 254; Christian Leitz, *Studien zur Ägyptischen Astronomie*, Äg.Abh. 49 (1989), 24:, J. v. Beckerath, *Chronologie des pharaonischen Ägypten*, 7 ff.

[91]Other shrines which were closed except for special celebrations are to be envisioned in out of the way places, such as Gebel es-Silsilah and most probably also Serabit el Khadim.

[92]Winfried Barta, *Untersuchungen zum Götterkreis der Neunheit*, MÄS 28 (1973), 59 f.;

[93]The "worship" should be as limited to what appears to have been a single occasion. How long it was maintained is another uncertainty about the particular cult. At the same time another effort was made under Seti I and it is not clear what motivated this "revival."

[94]*Urk.* IV 289 f. = *LD* III 26, 7. It should be noted that the "great ennead of gods resident in Karnak" consists of twelve members. The wording is curious, because Thoth addresses the gods with the words "Hear this great matter, which Amun-Reʿ lord of *Nswt-tꜣwy* has decreed to all gods: *Kꜣ-mꜣʿt-Rʿ*, who is King, has appeared on the throne of Horus permanently and the [great] god, lord of the Great temple, wishes that she leads all living ones" as if the gods required this notification.

[95]See also pp. 93 f.

[96]Alan H. Gardiner, *Ancient Egyptian Onomastica*, II (1947), 90*

[97]For cemeteries beginning with the Old Kingdom, see D. Kessler, op. cit. 63. The frequently occurring epithet *nb-pt* or *nbt-pt* would appear to mean "lord or mistress of heaven" although it is held by deities who have no celestial aspects. This seeming contradiction disappears when recognizing *pt* "heaven"as a metaphor for "cemetery."

The deed credited to the goddess for which Hatshepsut made her a rock-cut shrine is described in the words "[she opened] the roads of the water-torrent without drenching me, in order to catch the water."[98] "To open roads" is a recurrent idiom in Egyptian and expresses any trail-blazing activity. It can be applied to military movements, but in most cases its use is peaceful and conveys the notion of "leading the way." In processions the divine emblems carried at the head are said "to open the road," as does the royal standard carried in front of the king. "Pakhet, who roams the wadis" is said to have led the ways of the "water-torrent." The word rendered "water-torrent" (*snmw*) occurs only once more as a simile for the carnage done among enemies in the 2nd year of Thutmosis I (1502 B.C.).[99] The use here indicates that it should be understood primarily as a devastating wave. To have it associated with a goddess whose domain is the Eastern Desert would seem incoherent. Cloudbursts occur occasionally in the desert leading to short-lived torrents.[100] They run off normally in the desert where they evaporate and form no threat to the inhabited Nile Valley. It would be curious that Hatshepsut should show gratitude to the goddess Pakhet for something that would not have been a potential danger for her and her subjects.

The torrent which the goddess led away was obviously not caused by rain. The Nile is not known for torrential actions, nor would the goddess Pakhet have been a likely patroness for an event involving the Nile. Her domain is specifically the Eastern Desert, i.e., the area east of the Nile Valley, and it is there that the "water-torrent" has to be envisaged. The only other cause for the occurrence of a "water-torrent" in the Eastern Desert would be a massive incursion of the Mediterranean Sea, especially in the area east of the Delta. Two details in the formulation support such a thesis. Hatshepsut is grateful to the goddess for leading the "water-torrent" away "in order to catch the water." She also indicates the potential danger for her and her country, which could have been "drenched" by the "water-torrent." No hydrographic phenomenon is known that would suit the indications in the text except a torrential wave of the Mediterranean Sea rolling across the shore inland.[101] From the specification that it occurred mostly east of Hatshepsut's domain it results that it rolled off into the Eastern Desert at the Isthmus of Suez. That Hatshepsut was grateful to the goddess for averting this disaster is natural. That it led to making a shrine for Pakhet in Middle Egypt is, however, only indirectly linked with the divine deed. Pakhet had a cult in the Beni Hasan region already in the early Twelfth Dynasty.[102] Hatshepsut's deed was apparently motivated by her general gratitude to the goddess which led to a revival of worship that had been discontinued for several centuries. The origins of the cult of Pakhet at Beni Hasan and the reason leading to Hatshepsut's making of a rock-cut shrine for the goddess are totally different.

[98]See further, pp. 59 f.

[99]*Urk*. IV 84, 9:"their blood was like a torrent of rain."

[100]Cf. Alain-Pierre Zivie, *LÄ* V 201-206.

[101]There is written evidence for at least one intrusion of the Mediterranean into the eastern Delta as far as Avaris. This event occurred prior to Amenophis I and is to be equated with the natural disaster that happened very soon after the violent death of Kamose; see H. Goedicke, *Studies Studies about Kamose and Ahmose*, 121 ff; now also idem, "The Chronology of the Thera/Santorin Explosion," *Ä&L* III (1992), 57-62.

[102]D. Kessler, op. cit. 134 f.

Section Six

The three places "Hor-wer, Wenu and She[-ʿaa]" are known in close connection with Hermopolis. Hor-wer is attested since the Fourth Dynasty, but its localization is still somewhat uncertain[103] after the identification with modern Hur, ten kilometers west of Beni Hasan, has recently been questioned.[104] The place was certainly one of the major population centers in the 15th District of Upper Egypt, which included the tombs of Beni Hasan and the Speos Artemidos. The second place, Wenu, was somewhat further south. It probably denoted a part, possibly the oldest, of the town which the Greeks called Hermopolis.[105] It is identical with modern Ashmunein. The deity worshiped there was Thoth. About a restoration of the temple there Hatshepsut speaks in the next section of the text. The reading of the third place-name is not obsolutely certain, because of its partial obliteration. Gardiner has proposed the restoration Sha-ʿaa which is followed here.[106] No identification is possible. It was probably a place with some population concentration in the general vicinity of modern Ashmunein.

Hatshepsut's actions discussed in this section concern primarily the civil population.[107] Two measures are singled out, namely the distribution of provisions and the consecrating of sanctuaries.[108] The first refers to emergency measures to sustain people. The second does not concern opening new places of worship, but rather restoring and re-consecrating existing ones to their proper functions. It implies that they had been desecrated by improper use.

The reason which necessitated Hatshepsut's measures is given as "their towns were settled with unwelcomed ones from . . . ." The implication is that the places had experienced an influx of people from elsewhere. Unfortunately the origin of this people cannot be determined, since the text is broken in this vital place. Nevertheless, the character of those people transpires from their description as "he who came up—may he go down" when rendered literally.[109] It not only indicates that the people had come upstream from somewhere in the North; it also conveys the fact that they were thoroughly unwelcome. It seems justified to see them as refugees, who are never welcome to an indigenous population. This identification of the people is corroborated by their remaining description "[they went to] the store-room while begging 'Give!'"[110] The few words invoke the misery of refugees who hang around the places where they imagine food while

[103]See the exhaustive discussion by D. Kessler, op. cit. 120; 185.

[104]Wolfgang Helck, *Die altägyptischen Gaue*, TAVO B/5 (1974), 108.

[105]W. Helck, op. cit. 107; A. H. Gardiner, *Ancient Egyptian Onomastica*, II 81* f.; D. Kessler, op. cit. 83 ff.

[106]D. Kessler, op. cit. 89 mentions a *mr*-canal with this name, but considers it rather a mythological than a geographical term.

[107]Hatshepsut's interest in Middle Egypt is curious, especially when taking into account that there are no attestations of her further north. Could it be that the 15th/16th Upper Egyptian district was the northernmost area under her direct rule and that the North was *de facto* the domain of Thutmosis III, i.e. that the country had been partitioned along the same line as during the late Hyksos and Kamose. Such a possibility would agree well with the emphasis assigned to the sanctuary of Hathor of Qusae, which seems to have served as marker of the division during the later Second Intermediate Period.

[108]See the detailed discussion, pp. 61 f.

[109]For the descriptive designation and its implication, see further, p. 62.

[110]Despite the paucity of words, the prevailing situation is quite clearly conveyed. For this form of including a verbatim quote, see further, p. 62.

begging for it to keep alive. Hatshepsut's measures were apparently designed to bring relief to the population centers in Middle Egypt from the burden of refugees gathered there. To alleviate the situation she provides "provisions," primarily food, and returns the temples, which apparently had been used by refugees as shelter,[111] to their proper religious functions. It implies that the refugees were removed but without giving an indication what happened to them.

Section Seven

The mention of relief measures taken by Hatshepsut to help the settlements in Middle Egypt about the refugees living there, are followed by a detailed description of her intended actions for the temple of Thoth. He was the main god of the capital of the 15th district, modern Ashmunein. In the mention of the settling of the towns with unwelcome people it was implied that they had taken shelter in the sanctuaries, which Hatshepsut eventually re-consecrated. Thoth's temple had apparently suffered badly on account of those adverse conditions. They affected the furnishings of the temple, but also the priests assigned to it.

Hatshepsut formulates the deplored misery as a rhetorical question directed to the god to tell her where all his belongings were. Among the furnishings she wonders about is "the altar of silver and gold" apparently the main place to present offerings to the god.[112] Having been made of precious metals, it had disappeared—presumably used as "money."[113] The other furnishings she inquires about, namely linen and vessels, are of obvious practical use. The implication is that they had been taken by the refugees squatting in the temple. Hatshepsut explains her inquiry to the god about the whereabouts of those objects with the fact that not even the high-priest, i.e., the one who faces the deity eye-to-eye, knew about them.

The pilfering of the sanctuary was paralleled by a lack of attendance of religious services. That neither "gods nor men" were "familiar with the house" of the god means that they stayed away and that no religious services were conducted. For the temple this meant lack of any income, which in turn left the personnel of the temple in bad straits. Eventually they turned to Hatshepsut asking for her help.[114]

It is against this backbround of past impoverishment and desolation that Hatshepsut tells about her deeds for the cult of Thoth. They are of three kinds. First, she plans to rebuild the god's main temple, i.e., the sanctuary itself. She intends the most lavish materials for it, such as the fine limestone from the quarries at Tura, just south of modern Cairo;[115] the gateways were to be made of alabaster from the quarries in the

[111]The use of temples to quarter substantial numbers of transient people might not be limited to this particular instance. In connection with major religious feast the gathering of large crowds can be envisioned who had to be sheltered in some fashion. I wonder if the large spaces inside some of the temple pylons were not used for this particular purpose.

[112]For a special offering place made of precious metal, see *Urk.* IV 629; 636; 867, 11-12; 869, 17; 870, 8.

[113]For the notion of money in ancient Egypt, though not in the sense of coinage, see Jac.J. Janssen, *Commodity Prices from the Ramesside Period* (1975), 101-111.

[114]For the temple economy and its relation to the crown, see W. Helck, *Wirtschaftsgeschichte des Alten Ägypten*, 201 ff.

[115]There is no indication about the way this material is to be procured. The mention of material from the Memphite region does not necessarily constitute proof of political or administrative control over that area. The amount of stone for the temple whose size is

nearby Hatnub.[116] The gates themselves were sheathed with imported copper inlaid in gold.[117] The second deed is her personal participation in the consecration of the temple. This is to be done during a double festival when Hatshepsut herself, under the guidance of Amun, introduces the cult-statue of the god Thoth into his renewed and refurbished temple.[118] The double feast is the result of her reinstating an old feast, the Thoth-feast.[119] It had been celebrated as a "seasonal feast", i.e., it followed the natural year and not the civil calender.[120] As a result, it had become separated from the *nḥb-k3w*-feast, i.e., the social aspect of the New-Year festival.[121] Hatshepsut joined them again and had them celebrated as one calender feast.

Her third, and in some ways most consequential deed, is the doubling of the royal subsidy to the temple. The sanctuary, as was customary, was financed in a complex fashion.[122] The temple had an endowment which produced income. In addition it received donations from the worshipers attending the services. Finally, the cult was subsidized by the Crown in return for performing religious services for its benefit. Hatshepsut claims that she doubles the subsidy for the temple. It is to be used for "divine offerings" for a number of divine beneficiaries. They were: 1) the Ogdoad, i.e., the group of eight deities who in Egyptian mythology represented the constituents of matter.[123] 2) the god Khnum, whom the Egyptians saw as a demiurg, fashoning men on his potter's wheel.[124] 3) The three goddesses Heqat, Renenet and Meskhenet, who are all connected with childbirth. They are depicted in the representation of Hatshepsut's divine birth,[125] but are also attested otherwise as helpers during the delivery.[126] Together with Khnum the three goddesses form a team. Hatshepsut explains their receipt of a "divine offering" for their cooperation in fashioning her bodily. The last two in whose honor offerings are performed, are not regular members of

unknown, is impossible to estimate; nevertheless, it should involve a considerable amount of labor that had to be paid in some form. An additional uncertainty is the status of the quarry operations, if they had been a royal enterprise or if they were run on a kind of commercial basis.

[116] It is curious to note that only one inscription dating to the New Kingdom is recorded in Hatnub; see Rudolf Anthes, *Die Felseninschriften von Hatnub*, UGAÄ 9 (1928), 17 f. (Inschr. XIV).

[117] For this form of decoration, cf.*Urk*. IV 53, 15-17; 56, 0-10; etc.

[118] The personal participation of the ruler in the opening of a temple is especially emphasized for the opening of the temple of Soleb by Amenophis III; cf.Hans Goedicke, *Problems concerning Amenophis III* (1992), 17 ff.

[119] For the "Thoth-feast, "see Anthony Spalinger, *Three Studies on Egyptian Feasts and their Chronological Implications* (1992), VIII, 6. It is not clear if the "Thoth-feast" re-instated by Hatshepsut is the same as the one mentioned in the Old Kingdom listings of funerary celebration, or if its denotes here a specific, local celebration.

[120] For the distinction between natural and civil calender, cf. R. A. Parker, op. cit. §§ 282-305.

[121] The *nḥb-k3w* is primarily a social occasion rather than a religiously motivated celebration; Siegfried Schott, *Altägyptische Festdaten*, AAWMain 1950, 10 (1950), 93 f. Literally "the tying on (scil. awarding) of honors" it should be recognized as the official celebration of the social order, comparable to the New Year's reception celebrated in various monarchies of recent date. Schott's (op. cit. 37) rendering "Empfang im Königshaus" reflects a similar line.

[122] W. Helck, *Wirtschaftsgeschichte des Alten Ägypten*, 239 ff.

[123] Kurt Sethe, *Amun und die Acht Urgötter von Hermopolis*, §§ 63 ff.;Siegfried Morenz, *Ägyptische Religion*, (1960), 184 f.;

[124] He plays a major role in the series depicting Hatshepsut's divine birth. After Amun had fallen in love with Hatshepsut's mother Ahmose and had spent the night with her, he instructs Khnum to fashion a child, Hatshepsut. He sits down at his potter's wheel and makes the child and its *ka*; cf. H.Brunner, op. cit., 68-74; Taf.6.

[125] H. Brunner, op. cit., 90-106.

[126] In Egyptian custom the delivering woman was assisted by three women, one holding her on either side, while the third received the child; see F.Weindler, *Geburts- und Wochenbettsdarstellungen auf altägyptischen Tempelreliefs* (1915), 27 ff.

the Egyptian religious worship. Neḥmet-ʿway might best be rendered "she who saves the bereft one."[127] It appears to be a personification of Hatshepsut's conviction of having improperly been bypassed as daughter of Thutmosis I in her ambition to rule.[128] Nekhbet-ka, on the other hand, could be understood as Hatshepsut's personal fate.[129] It is to it that Hashepsut credits her role as king, controlling "heaven and earth." In other words, the last recipients of divine offerings are deifications of roles carried out by Hatshepsut, namely her aspirations and her royal fate. To both she expresses gratitude.

Section Eight

The reading of the section is marred by some serious weathering of the inscribed surface. This concerns especially the nature of the subjects Hatshepsut is talking about. Despite the uncertainties, the general drift of the section seems clear. She apparently refers to people in the military line since she mentions "battlements."

Little is known about the organization of the military forces during the early Eighteenth Dynasty.[130] It is tempting to think of military units garrisoned in barracks; and when war happened, they marched out from their camp with music and flying colors. The picture might be appealing, but it is certainly an inappropriate application of modern military romance to ancient Egypt. There is every reason to believe that the majority of members in the military establishment of ancient Egypt were either foreigners or of foreign extraction.[131] The latter had come to Egypt in search of military employ and settled there without becoming members of the indigenous population, whose main occupation was agriculture. In general, those people, who made up the backbone of the military establishment, were living on their own and were persuing their own livelihood, except in case of military emergency. They seem to have formed a kind of military class somewhat similar to the Mameluks in the late Turkish Empire.[132] There were, however,

[127]Alan H. Gardiner, *Notes on the Story of Sinuhe* (1916), 42; Jacques Parlebas, *Die Göttin Nehmet-awaj* (Diss. Tübingen) (1984), 22-25; 41 f. where he discusses the association of the goddess with Hermopolis.

[128]It should be noted that the mention in the Speos Artemidos text is the ealiest occurrence; cf. J. Parlebas, op. cit. 6; 8; 25.

[129]Cf. Alan W. Shorter, *JEA* 21 (1935), 41-48; *Wb.* II 392, 6 considers it "weibliche Schutzschlange der Königin" which, however, disregards the direct link between it and Hatshepsut.

[130]Andrea Maria Gnirs, *Militär und Gesellschaft*, SAGA 17, (1996), 17 ff.

[131]The role of foreigners as professional fighters in the Nile Valley might have its beginning as early as Naqqada II. In the late Old Kingdom and the period following it, the presence of foreigners in the military service is well documented; cf. e.g. Henry G. Fischer, "The Nubian Mercenaries of Gebelein during the First Intermediate Period," *Kush* 9 (1961), 44-80. The situation is less pronounced as far as the Middle Kingdom is concerned with the possible exception of Beni Hasan where military professionals were buried in the early Twelfth Dynasty; cf. Hans Goedicke, *JARCE* XXI (1984), 203-6. While the situation is quite obvious in the Second Intermediate Period as far as people from the South are concerned (Torgny Säve-Söderbergh, *Ägypten und Nubien*, 1941, 135-140; William C. Hayes, "The Pangrave People," *CAH*[3] II, 74-76; W.Y. Adams, op. cit. 215), it is less transparent for the Eighteenth Dynasty in part due to a rapid acculturation of the people concerned. This applies especially to people with Levantine background; e.g., it is tempting to assume Ahmose, son of Eban to have been of foreign extraction.

[132]See Thomas Phillip and Ulrich Haarmaan, *The Mamlukes in Egyptian Politics and Society* (1997).

recurrent attempts by the Crown to exert greater control over this military class by forcing them to live in garrisons and on the income provided for them by the Crown.[133] Although the military would receive their support, the quartering in garrisons was apparently not a desirable situation, especially when compared with the possibility of living independently and pursuing their own livelihood. It is unknown to what extent the discontent arose from family separation, from economic factors, or from the less tangible issue of "freedom."

The persons Hatshepsut talks about in this section are to be recognized as members of the military establishment, who had been moved into garrisons. The reasons which had led to this move are not specified. It transpires, however, that the military were not happy with their present situation. In order to meet this discontent, Hatshepsut indicates that she does not intend to keep them in garrisons. In a truly political fashion she promises "I don't know battlements in my design!"[134]. This means that in her plans for the future there were no fortified garrisons for her mercenaries. This promise was obviously highly welcome and put those concerned into a festive mood.[135]

Hatshepsut's political gesture has specific terms. She promises an individual abode to everyone who voluntarily accepts her as king on the throne of Horus.[136] In the required promise of loyalty[137] she makes a reference to her choice by the god Amun. This is another demonstration of her strong religious motivation focusing on one specific god, the one of Thebes. In the demanded formulation of loyalty the definition of her status as "permanent king" is striking.[138] It reflects her concern that her political achievement to ascend the throne of Horus be not curtailed. The worry might have something to do with the potential threat posed by her competitor Thutmosis III, who at the time was taking steps to assert his control over Thebes and Egypt's south, the bailiwick of Hatshepsut, as demonstrated by his appointment of Useramun as southern Vizier in Year 5. Thus the section was apparently formulated prior to the time that a compromise was worked out between Hatshepsut and Thutmosis III by making them full co-regents. According to the available evidence, Thutmosis III begun playing a somewhat more visible political role around Hatshepsut's 13th year, i.e. 1466 B.C.[139]

[133]While little is known about the time of the earlier Eighteenth Dynasty, a particularly informative case of this nature is well documented for the reign of Ramesses III. In the review of his reign, the Papyrus Harris I (76, 8-10), the Pharaoh recalls how he reduced the status of mercenaries to "non-existing ones" and then he "settled them in strongholds bound in my name: numerous were their recuits like hundred thousands. I awarded them all with clothes and rations from the treasury and the granery every year."

[134]See further below, p. 74.

[135]See especially p. 73. The reference to "festive mood" does not necessarily include celebration and might be used here in a more general fashion.

[136]It is difficult to grasp the full weight of this promise in its material but also in its social aspect. Although remunerations of soldiers in the form of valuables, land and servants are well known throughout the early Eighteenth Dynasty, I am not aware of another case of housing as a reward.

[137]It is not clear if the required promise of loyalty had a set traditional wording or if it was up to the individual to express his intention.

[138]The unusual notion of "permanent king," i.e. king for life, is a reflection of the particular situation in which Hatshepsut became king; see further below, p. 76.

[139]The actual reconciliation between the two contestants for ruling Egypt apparently happened in Year 15 and was the cause for

Section Nine

In the last section Hatshepsut recounts an event which she considers a demonstration of the special divine protection she enjoys. It is directed to the totality of her subjects, encompassing both social strata, namely the "nobility" (*pꜥt*) and the "commoners" (*rḫyt*). Although it follows the topic of the last section, namely her graciousness toward her military personnel, this specific group is not addressed here. This break suggests that Section Nine was not part of the text composed especially for Middle Egypt, but was from a more general statement. That it was included here can be taken as an indication of its importance for Hatshepsut in her political pursuit.

That this part of the Speos Artemidos inscription is taken from another more general text is also indicated by the ambiguity of the opening statement "I did these things by the design of my heart."[140] As a matter of fact, no reference to any specific deed of Hatshepsut precedes this section. Consequently, it should be taken as a general attitude held by Hatshepsut, which applies also to the second statement "no neglectful one shall sleep for me," as there is no reference to any tasks she had specifically assigned to anyone.[141] It is only after these two general statements that Hatshepsut tells the episode which she apparently considered of great importance and which has practically nothing to do with the concerns of the rest of her inscription left at the Speos Artemidos. The only link might be the similarity between the people concerned. The previous section stated a political deal proposed by Hatshepsut to her military to provide them with individual housing in return for unwavering loyalty. The episode stated in this section concerns people indicated only as "resident aliens" who also followed the military profession.[142] The reason for the inclusion was possibly the fact that the Pakhet sanctuary served people of foreign extraction who were professionally part of the military establishment.[143]

The geographical setting of the episode is the north-eastern Delta, with the "region of Avaris" serving as general reference. As will be discussed later, Avaris had become the center of settlement for immigrants from the Levant in the Eighteenth Century B.C.[144] As Avaris can now be definitely identified with the Tell ed-Dabaᶜ region, the available archaeological record shows that the presence of Levantines was fluctuating.[145] Their background was partly Syrian, partly Palestinian. One of the periods of dense

---

the celebration of a "jubilee"(*ḥb-sd*); see further pp. 127 f. The political consequences are, however, obscure in detail, including the question of a possible division of the country by the two contestants.

[140]See further, p. 78.

[141]In order to deny sleep to anyone, it requires the specification of such an attitude, i.e. the circumstance for which unrestricted effort is required.

[142]For this people, specified as *šmꜣw*, see further pp. 80 f.

[143]Such a notion is supported by the only geographical epithet of Pakhet specifying her as "mistress of sheep-country"; see above note 96 and also pp. 93 f.

[144]For the geography of the region, see M. Bietak, *Tell ed-Dabaᶜ*, II, 179 ff.; idem, *Avaris. The Capitol of the Hyksos* (1996), 1-9.

[145]Cf. Manfred Bietak, "Egypt and Canaan during the Middle Bronze Age," *BASOR* 281 (1991), 27 ff.; idem, "Canaanites in the Eastern Nile Delta," in Anson F. Rainey, ed., *Egypt, Israel, Sinai* (1987), 41-56; idem, "Avaris, Capitol of the Hyksos Kingdom: New Results of Excavastions," in Eliezer D. Oren, ed., *The Hyksos: New Historical and Archaeological Perspectives* (1997), 87-139.

population is around 1500 B.C. Although Avaris was certainly their center, Levantines (or, for the Egyptians, "Asiatics") were not limited to this place. In recent years their presence has also been established in the Wadi Tumilat, specifically at Tell el-Mashkhuta and Tell el-Rataba.[146] The specific term used in the text in reference to them, namely *ʿ3mw*, identifies those people as Semitic-speaking settled inhabitants of Syro-Palestine.[147] The term is not used in reference to nomads or bedouins in the Sinai Peninsula.

Although the people involved in the episode Hatshepsut recounts are not specifically identified, they can be seen as identical or associated with those *ʿ3mw*-Asiatics. Consequently they ought to be envisaged as coming from a Semitic speaking Syro-Palestinian background. Their place of residence is not delineated, but they should be equated with the "Asiatics . . . in the region of Avaris of Lower Egypt" and thus located in the northeastern Delta.[148]

The time of the episode Hatshepsut considers so important occurred "while I restored what had decayed."[149] Two points are important in this statement. First, that her activity lasted over an extended period of time, and second, that it concerned something that was generally known. A minor reconstruction project would not have provided the frame for an event which Hatshepsut considered of major significance. Because of the subsequent reference to "the Asiatics in the region of Avaris," "what had decayed" apparently applies to the northeastern Delta.[150] The same wording occurs in an inscription which has been found at Abydos: "I made monuments for the gods: I consecrated their shrines for the future, I improved their temples. When I restored what had decayed, I surpassed the deeds of before."[151] It is commonly assigned to Thutmosis I, the revered father of Hatshepsut, but was actually written by her in favor of her deceased father.

[146]John S. Holladay, Jr., "The Eastern Nile Delta During the Hyksos and Pre-Hyksos Periods: Toward a Systematic/Socioeconomic Understanding," in E. D. Oren, ed., op. cit. 183-252.

[147]Donald B. Redford, "Egypt and Western Asia in the Old Kingdom," *JARCE* XXIII (1986), 126-130, who rightly points out that *ʿ3mw* is not confined to a specific geographical area, but emphasizes their speaking a Semitic language; cf. also Raphael Giveon, *Les bédouins Shosou des documents égyptiens* (1971), 170; Hans Goedicke, *The Protocol of Neferyt* (1977), 92; idem, *Ä&L* VII (1998), 35.

[148]The passage has long been considered a reference to the "Hyksos" despite their defeat almost 70 years earlier during which Thutmosis I had advanced from a ruler of Egypt to sovereign of the Levant. Egypt was externally secure and there was no external power threatening the Egyptian social order. As Hatshepsut's text is principally a political document there is no reason to assume here a reflection of xenophobian motives as Antonio Loprieno, *Topos und Mimesis*, ÄgAbh 48 (1988), 28 suspects. It should rather be taken as a reference to a political reality which happened against Hatshepsut. See further, pp. 101 ff.

[149]There is no reason to attribute the destructions to the Hyksos of two generations before, especially as there is ample mention of destruction in Lower Egypt, caused, however, not by men but by nature.

[150]The notion of Hatshepsut finding things in decay outside the impact of a natural disaster would put her predecessors, especially Thutmosis I in a bad light. To connect any destruction with the Hyksos would not only open chronological problems, but would also have geographical consequences. While the Fifteenth Dynasty rulers in all likelihood controlled only the northern part of Egypt, they do not seem to have caused any havoc in southern Upper Egypt, especially not in the Thebais.

[151]*Urk.* IV 102, 3. The text is commonly assigned to Thutmosis I, but the retrospective references to his reign make it clear that it was subsequently predated. The *post mortem* date is confirmed by the lack of a life-oriented epithet after the king's name (*Urk.* IV 102, 17).

While the nature of the devastation Hatshepsut claims to have restored remains obscure, the measure taken by her to cope with it is clear: "I levied the first draft since Asiatics have been at Avaris of the North Land."[152] In ancient Egypt the obligation to the society was mostly in the form of taxes, usually paid in kind.[153] As an additional obligation personal service for the common good could be required, especially in connectcion with large work projects.[154] This obligation, often labeled corvée, has a long history in Egypt. It was a major way to recruit the work forces needed for such projects as building the pyramids or installing irrigation.[155] The corvée continued to exist in Egypt, even long after the Pharaohs had gone.[156]

The labor service had apparently not been called up for a long time, as Hatshepsut says that the one she marshalled was "the first" one of its kind "since Asiatics were in the region of Avaris." This rather general reference to a long period of time covers more than 200 years when interpreted extensively or a minimum of 70 years.[157] If no *corvee* had been requested in all this time, it is only logical that this burden had been forgotten for all practical purposes. Anybody living at the time and particularly foreigners could not have any recollection of this administrative burden, and to some its institution must have been an unbearable imposition. Those opposing the *corvee* would simply try to disregard the task.

According to the inscription the assigning of the *corvee* met opposition from a specific group of people. The implication is that the majority of people accepted the royal orders and carried out their assignments. The disobedients are denoted as *shemau* (*šmꜣw*). This is not an ethnic designation in so far as it does not serve as identification of an established group, either 'nation' or tribe.[158] Its implication is rather socio-ethnical. It is attested since the late Old Kingdom, ca. 2200 B.C., in reference to people of foreign extraction who enjoyed the privilege of being allowed to dwell in Egypt.[159] They were not integrated into the basically agrarian society of the Nile Valley, but apparently pursued their livelihood at the fringe of it. Their predominant social feature was that of pasturer, or holders of mostly small cattle, which they grazed in a defined circle of perigrinations. The designation is derived from the word "to wander"[160] and it can be

[152] This passage, which is crucial for the understanding of the text, was taken differently by Gardiner as "I have raised up what was dismembered, (even) from the first time when the Asiatices were in Avaris of the North Land." Aside from textual improbabilities, as discussed in detail (pp. 79 f.),this rendering leads to a redundancy inasfar as Hatshepsut's restorative activity has already been stated.

[153] Cf. W. Helck, *Wirtschaftsgeschichte des Alten Ägypten*, 246-8.

[154] W. Helck, op. cit, 220; 231 ff.

[155] For the situation in the Old Kingdom, cf. Hans Goedicke, *Königliche Dokumente aus dem Alten Reich*, ÄgAbh 14 (1967), 244-247.

[156] It should not be overlooked that the latest call-up of the *corvée* was for digging the sweet-water canal in connection with the construction of the Suez Canal; cf.e.g., Karl Baedeker, *Egypt and the Sudan*^{8} (1929), 195.

[157] It would seem appropriate to take the reference to the presence of Asiatics in a political and not in an ethnic way. Asiatics settled in the Avaris region long before the Hyksos Fifteenth Dynasty, but their presence is unlikely to have had any administrative consequences; for their presence, see above notes 150 and 151.

[158] *Shemau* like later *shosu* are descriptive designations based on the conspicuous habits of the people concerned. To consider them as ethnic identifications means projecting modern notions on the ancient Egyptian terms.

[159] It is attested first in connection with a childrens' game (see *Wb*. IV 470, 7) in which it is used in the same way as "Indian and scout"or "Räuber und Gendarm," refering to the "alien."

[160] *Wb*. IV 470, 2; Pyr. 551; cf. Kurt Sethe, *Übersetzung und Kommentar zu den altägyptischen Pyramidentexten*, III, 36.

applied to any people who met this characteristic. If those people pursued any particular profession in addition to being pasturers, it cannot be established with certainty. Since they were not part of the settled agrarian society their responsibility to the society was probably different from its full members, particularly in regard to taxes and especially concerning the performance of labor in the public interest.

What tasks were assigned to them is not defined, but they were probably within the framework of the general levy. They were assigned by administrative measure,[161] a sign that they were not part of an established routine of obligations. The word used to describe the reaction of the *shemau*-people has the specific connotation of "overthrowing" either of structures or of abstracts, such as plans.[162] If it was chosen here for any particular reason, it eludes me.

The obstruction by the *shemau*-people is not random, but has a specific cause. Hatshepsut says, that they assumed that "Reᶜ would not be blind when the god assigned the steering-rope to my Majesty."[163] The pivotal moment in Hatshepsut's life was when she became king because of a divine oracle of Amun.[164] What might appear at a supperficial reading as a disagreement in the circle of the gods, becomes clearer when it is recognized that the word "god" refers here to Hatshepsut's deceased father, Thutmosis I.[165] This also clarifies why the assigning of the rulership is assumed to require the consent of the god Reᶜ as the highest divine authority.[166] Although the *shemau*-people had apparently learned about Hatshepsut's elevation to the position of King, they believed that the superior sun-god would not accept this political development. History proved them wrong, but it explains why those people were in opposition to the ruler. It also illustrates the importance of religious motives in the political process of that time.

To demonstrate the fallacy of the *shemau*-people's expectation, Hatshepsut summarizes her political success. She divides her political role into two phases. The first one, "when I was established over the seats of Reᶜ,"[167] refers to the time when she more or less controlled the South in a fairly independent fashion, while Thutmosis III, still rather young, was officially king, however, largely restricted to the North. This period lasted for more than six years, since according to recent studies Hatshepsut was crowned as king in her seventh year, 1472 B.C.[168] While the constitutional implications of being "over the seats of Reᶜ" are

[161] See further, pp. 79 f.

[162] See below, p. 81.

[163] The metapher of the steering rope is paralleled for Hatshepsut's role as early as Inana's text; cf. *Urk.* IV 60, 6, 8; H. Goedicke, "Thutmosis III's ascent," p. ; H. Grapow, *Die bildlichen Ausdrücke*, 155.

[164] See above, pp. 9 ff.

[165] The term *nṯr*, commonly rendered "god" is the original term for the ritually buried dead who is envisioned to exist beyond the physical demise. It is from this application that the application to *numina* in the theistic sense is derived; see Hans Goedicke, "God," *JSSEA* XVI (1988), 576-62.

[166] It is feasable that the reference to Reᶜ also reflects a religious orientation on the part of the *shasu*-people to a solar deity, but there is no way to corroborate this.

[167] For the "seats of Reᶜ" which could also be interpretetd as "property-holders of Reᶜ" in the sense of free men religiously acknowleding Reᶜ, see further the similar formulation concerning Amun-Reᶜ as discussed by Hans Goedicke, *Ỉmn-Rᶜ nb-nswt-tꜣwy*, U. Luft, ed., *The Intellectual Heritage of Egypt, Studies Kakosy*, Studia Aegyptiaca 14 (1992), 197-203.

[168] S. Ratié, op. cit. 83 f.; P. Dorman, *The Monuments of Senenmut*, 43 ff.; this date follows the "middle chronology" while J. v.

somewhat unclear, her reputation during this time as being successful is justly emphasized.[169] This phase of her career ended when Hatshepsut "came as Horus."[170] This idiom means that she became king herself and refers obviously to her ascent to the throne on account of the divine interference during the festival of Amun. For the chronological attribution of the events related in the text the mention of her ascent is of vital importance.

The differentiation between the two phases of her exercise of authority corresponds to developments in her career, with the crucial event in the seventh year (1472 B.C.). The change in her status was paralleled by an alteration in Hatshepsut's attitude towards her opponents. The metaphor "my uraeus threw fire against my opponents"[171] expresses an increase of the pressure Hatshepsut as newly ascended ruler exerted against those who did not accept the political change in the country. The uraeus, the curling cobra on the king's forehead, is the symbol of the power held by the king. It is repeatedly compared with the throwing of fire in its painfulness. Hatshepsut's increased pressure is directed against "opponents" in general, but applies, of course, specifically to those who "disregarded the tasks which were assigned to them."[172]

Despite this scenario of conflict and prosecution, Hatshepsut either did not attempt or did not manage to squelch those in opposition inside the country. By describing them as "abomination of the gods," she indicates that they were to be considered as criminals and treated as such. The term is the usual expression for denoting criminals, especially those deserving or receiving the death penalty.[173] Instead of executing them Hatshepsut let them live, but not in Egypt. The word used means literally "to make distant" and is normally used for forceful removal, i.e., "to expell," but without necessarily implying the use of force.[174] The administrative term might in praxis mean little more than the request that the undesirable people leave the country. Whichever its meaning, the statement is unusual for an Egyptian king. Opponents are normally to face the law in its fullness and no other case of similar leniency when a Pharaoh only expelled instead of prosecute opponents is known earlier.[175]

No reason for this exceptional moderation is given. It plays some role in the way the arguments are put together in the inscription. The expression of lenience is juxtaposed with the fact that this did not mean the

---

Beckerath, op. cit. 103, takes 1479 as the beginning of the reign of Thutmosis III/Hatshepsut. On this basis, the Hatshepsut coronation should be dated 1472 B.C.

[169]The Egyptian describes her with the words "as she exists, she seizes"; cf. below, p. 84.

[170]Her claim of a Horus-name established by Thutmosis I (*Urk.* IV 261, 14) is, of course, part of the political legend of her divine elevation. The formulation is as unusual as her becoming king. Her role as "Horus" is emphasized again at the very end of the text.

[171]For this metaphor, see below, p. 84.

[172]See above, p. 85.

[173]Wolfgang Boochs, *Strafrechtliche Aspekte im altägyptischen Recht* (1993), 88; David Lorton, "The Treatment of Criminals in Ancient Egypt" (1977), 29.

[174]Cf. D. Lorton, op. cit. 17.

[175]Sinuhe cannot be considered for comparison because he left Egypt on his volition (cf. Hans Goedicke, "The Riddle of Sinuhe's Flight," *RdE* 35, 1984, 95-103). That Egyptians were expelled from their country for political reasons is particularly demonstrated by the stela C. 256 in the Louvre; see Jürgen von Beckerath, "Die 'Stele der Verbannten' im Museum des Louvre," *RdE* 20 (1968), 7-36.

opponents' difficulties were over. In the end, "the earth removed their footprints."[176] The wording uses an idiom "to bring the footprint" which denotes the closing rite after performing an offering before a deity, when the celebrant moved backwards from the room sweeping the footprints as he leaves.[177] It obviously refers here not to a religious deed, and thus should be taken literally. Upon casual reading the impression might be that the departing people were completely annihilated so that not the slightest trace remained. However, Egyptian texts are much more detailed than the modern reader is commonly used to. In order to do it justice the minutiae of the wording have to be taken into consideration. A literal translation would be "the (flat) land removed their sandal imprints."[178] Three points of interest result from it. First, "the (flat) land" is in Egyptian distinguished from "(hilly) land." The latter denotes foreign territory, the former Egyptian soil or land under the Pharaoh's authority. This suggests that the event described here happened inside the Egyptian border, i.e., before reaching the border fortress of Sile, the modern Qantara.[179] Second, the people were shod, an indication of traveling rather than of a local movement.[180] Third, only the footprints were removed. There is no indication whatsoever that the people themselves were physically affected, although it might be tempting to insinuate this. In other words, the text emphasizes that all traces of the people were extinguished within the area of Egypt and does not concern itself with the fate of the people beyond this point.

The removal of the footprints by the (flat) land requires for the Egyptians an agent instigating it, since the land is not usually in the habit of doing it. The act is attributed to the "directive of the father-of-fathers."[181] The wording is extremely concise at this point. "Directive" is an individual instruction based neither on established authority nor on precedence.[182] The term is used when specific situations for which no commands have been issued are being dealt with.

The directive is attributed to the "father-of-fathers." Despite a small break in this designation comprising the singular and plural of the word "father," its restoration is beyond doubt. The particular application of the term "father-of- fathers" transpires from its occurrence between two references to Reʿ as refering to the latter. He is additionally specified as "who comes at his times," which emphasizes the freedom to chose the moment of arrival. It might have the additional connotation of the unexpected nature of the event as well as the willingness to interfere in human matters when necessary.

[176] See below, p. 85.

[177] For this rite, see above, note 19.

[178] The literal translation, awkwards as it is in English, opens the implicit details of the text and thus helps towards a real understanding.

[179] For the location of Egypt's eastern border, see Adelheid Schlott-Schwab, *Die Ausmasse Ägyptens nach altägyptischen Texten*, ÄAT 3 (1981), 95 ff.

[180] For the use of sandals in desert travel, see J. Couyat–P. Montet, *Inscriptions du Ouadi Hammamat*, MIFAO 34 (1912), no. 114, line 13; Jean C. Goyon, *Nouvelles Inscriptions rupestres du Wadi Hammamat* (1957), no 61, line 20.

[181] The designation is attested for several gods in the cosmic but also the chthonic realm; see Wolfgang Helck, "*Vater der Väter*", NAWG 1965, 9.

[182] See below, pp. 85 f.

Conclusion

The account of her deeds for the cults in Middle Egypt Hatshepsut closes with recounting the fate of those who had opposed her by the intervention of the "father-of-fathers." She sees in it a confirmation of her role as king and the assurance of continued authority. She casts it into two double clauses which she addresses to Reʿ. In the first, she asks that her inscription be as permanent as the mountain rock on which it is written.[183] The basis for this assertion is the belief that a command of the god Amun could not collapse.[184] The command she alludes to is, of course, her elevation to the royal throne by Amun's intervention. The second statement concerns the symbol of her being king, namely the "falcon-over-the-palace," which expresses the role of the king as representative or embodiment of the god Horus. The derived designation, often refered to as "Horus-name," is the most sacred in the usually five-part royal titulary. Its holding might also have a physical reflection in the form of a standard planted on top of the royal palace.[185] Hatshepsut desires that it be "elevated" continuously, just as the sun illuminates her name inscribed on the shrine.

The conclusion reveals a burning concern of Hatshepsut to retain the position as king to which she had ascended. Already in the text she had requested loyalty to her as "permanent king."[186] The worries obviously sprung from the way she shoved Thutmosis III aside and made herself the supreme power in the land. It is quite clear that her move did not meet universal approval, and opposition, open or hidden, apparently followed her ascent. In that time of uncertainty she threatened any opposition. In the words attributed to her father her political philosophy of this period of her reign is summarized as "he who praises her—he will live. He who says something evil in rebellion to her Majesty—he will die."[187]

[183]The metaphor makes sense only when associated with the rock into which the shrine for Pakhet was carved. The comparison with the "mountain of ore" (*Wb.* I 436, 10) is a particularity of the reign of Ramesses III which has a military background.

[184]Sethe's reading (*Urk.* IV 391, 1) *wḏi.n.i, which has been followed by Redford, leads to a hybris not in accord with any reasonable attitude. The "decree of Amun," i.e., the act by which Hatshepsut claims to have become king, is so much in the center of her political acting that Gardiner's reading can not be doubted.

[185]Similarly *Urk.* IV 160, 12; see also P. Lacau–H.Chevrier, op. cit. 143 f.

[186]See above p. 22 and also p. 89.

[187]*Urk.* IV 257, 14-15; cf. also *Urk.* IV 260, 13.

Commentary

Introduction

"[Life to[a)] the Horus:[b)] 'Powerful of Attributes'; the Two Goddesses: 'Flourishing of] Years'; Horus-of-Gold: 'Divine of Appearances'; the 'Good-God' Lord of the [Two] Land]s *K3-M3ʿt-Rʿ*; Offspring of Reʿ [Companion of Amun Hatshepsut, given life. She made this] lasting [monument] of perpetuating her great name like heaven,[c)] as she graces the annals, and as she prevails over the region of the Mountain-mistress eastwards.[d)]"

a) For *ʿnḫ* preceding the Horus name, see H. Goedicke, *Studies about Kamose and Ahmose*, 189-196.

b) The royal protocol of Hatshepsut is, like that of all other Egyptian rulers, the equivalent of a political program adopted at the time of the ascent.[1] Although the listing in this particular inscription is suffering from numerous lacunae, the restoration does not cause any major problems. It is more difficult to translate the Egyptian formulations into modern political concepts which they are after all.

The Horus name *Wsrt k3w* has found various renderings over the years. Breasted, Ancient Records, II, § 239, note b gave for it "Mighty of doubles," Gardiner, *JEA* 32 (1946), 45 has "Powerful of Attributes," S. Ratié, op. cit. 114 "Puissant de kas," A. Burkhardt, op. cit. 24 "Stark (durch ihre) Kas," Barta, *ZÄS* 116 (1989), 118 "Der nach Art der Ka Kräfte Starke," and Redford, The Hyksos, 16 "with mighty kau's." These renderings would seem to convey a religious role rather than a political one. Considering the fact that the Horus name is the most important indicator of the authority held by an Egyptian ruler, one would expect special emphasis on the intended political role to be expressed by this name. The designation is composed of two elements of which *wsrt* obviously concerns Hatshepsut personally because of the term's feminine gender. The notion that the holder of kingship is *wsr* is reflected in a number of royal names, such as *Wsr-k3.f* or *Wsr-k3-Rʿ* of Dynasty V (and others).[2] It would appear that the second element in such

[1]Although Hatshepsut's royal protocol is attributed to an act of Thutmosis I (*Urk*. IV 261, 12-17), the fictitious nature of this claim is impossible to overlook. As with other *post festum* steps to justify her reach for power, this proclamation inscribed in Deir el-Bahari was promulgated long after she had become king.

[2]Cf. W. Barta, "Zur Konstruktion der ägyptischen Königsnamen," *ZÄS* 114, 1987, 4; 115, 1988, 1 ff.

compounds, i.e., *ka*, concerns either a quality of the king or of a deity. Its interpretation determines also the meaning of *wsr*.

The *k3w* of Hatshepsut are also mentioned in the story about her divine origin (*Urk.* IV 230, 15) and in the account of her youth and elevation (*Urk.* IV 255, 14). Especially the latter mention helps somewhat towards its understanding. It is part of an (alleged) speech to her by her father Thutmosis I (*Urk.* IV 255,13-14): "you shall observe your instruction in the palace and the doing of your noble *k3w*." It would seem that *k3w* summarizes the deeds reflecting personality. If this is correct the Horus name could be rendered as "rich/mighty in personality."

The *Nbty* name has been rendered "Fresh in years" (Breasted), "Flourishing of Years" (Gardiner), "Florissante d'années" (S. Ratié), "Frisch an Jahren" (A. Burkhardt), "Die an Jahren Frische" (Barta), "with prosperous years" (Redford). Here too, the feminie form *W3ḏt rnpwt* makes it clear that the name pertains to Hatshepsut directly. The emphasis on the "prosperity" of her times is, of course, a sign that the prevailing conditions inspired this as an aspiration. It has to be kept in mind that the formulation of Hatshepsut's royal protocol occurred at the time of her assuming the full royal power. Her claims of inthronisation by her father are, indeed, a *post festum* attempt to justify her reach for power. The reference to "prosperous years" suggests that the *status quo* was quite different and that she tried to attract support by promising a prosperous future. This could possibly be an indication that Hatshepsut's *coup d'état* followed some adversity in the country. Its nature as well as the area affected by it cannot be determined by this indication alone. It would seem unlikely that the entire country was suffering, at least there are no indications, written or otherwise, that Upper Egypt was in any way affected; on the other hand, very little is known about conditions in the North. Any adverse events there would, however, have an impact on all of Egypt and might very well have led to a reaction by Thebes, as whose principal advocate Hatshepsut should be seen.

The Gold Horus name is *Nṯrt ḫʿw* which has been rendered "Divine of diadems" (Breasted), "Divine of Appearances" (Gardiner), "Göttlich an Erscheinungen" (A. Burkhardt), "Divine d'apparitions" (S. Ratié) "Der an Kronen Göttliche" (Barta) and Redford "with-divine-diadems." *Nṯr* obviously refers to Hatshepsut because of the feminine gender of the term and not to *ḫʿw* as Redford seems to suggest. It is not the rule that a living human is denoted as *nṯr* as the term conveys the nature of permanence, a quality principally attained by humans only in death. The name *nṯrt-ḫʿw* gives the impression of Hatshepsut's claiming the quality of being *nṯr* on account of *ḫʿw*, which could be understood here as alluding to the acts of authority or authorization, but also to the crowns as symbols worn at such occasions.[3] The two are different aspects of the same notion. In other words, the passing through "appearances" is considered the cause of becoming *nṯr*, a phenomenon usually reserved for the ritually buried dead. In line 8 of the text Hatshepsut uses the term "my divine heart" (*ib.i nṯry*) in reference to her concern for the future.[4] Why this aspect of kingship is expressed by the Gold Horus designation is unknown as is the significance of this designation in general.[5]

[3] Margit Schunck, *Untersuchungen zum Wortstamm* ḫʿ (1985), 95 ff.

[4] See below, pp. 43 f.

[5] Cf. also J. von Beckerath, *Handbuch der ägyptischen Königsnamen*, MÄS 49, 17-21.

Where traditionally the *nswt-bit* designation should follow, the text has instead 𓊹𓄤 𓎟𓇾𓇾 which Gardiner and Redford rendered "the Perfect Goddess, Lady of the [Two] Lands," A. Burkhardt as "vollkommener Gott, Herr der beiden Länder." In Davies copy of the text there is no indication of a feminine ending in either part of the designation, though erasures are indicated. As is to be discussed separately, the traditional rendering "good god" makes little sense,[6] as Stock has indicated almost half a century ago.[7] It would imply that there is the conceivable case of a bad god, which would seem a contradiction in terms. The designation, which had its beginning in the late Fourth Dynasty in the form *Nfr-Ḥr* for *Rʿ-ḏd.f* has a parallel in *Nfr-tm*.[8] The latter identifies the young in relation to Atum, which applies also to *Nfr-Ḥr*. As a result the designation 𓊹𓄤 should be read *Nfr(w)-nṯr* and understood as the "young one of a/the *nṯr*," i.e., a/the deceased king. In other words, *Nfr-nṯr* should be seen as focussing on the (dynastic[9]) succession. As far as Hatshepsut is concerned, the "title" could only be read *Nfrt-nṯr* and has to be seen as emphasizing her descent from Thutmosis I.[10]

It is unclear, if *nb-tꜣwy* or *nbt-tꜣwy* is to be read here. In the first case it would qualify the preceding *nṯr*, in the other *nfr*. Disregarding the distinct possibility of a scribal error or adaptation, the male *nb-tꜣwy* would seem to refer to the deceased predecessor. A problem not followed up in this context is the question if *nb-tꜣwy* is a self-contained designation or rather a specification.

As for the Pre-nomen 𓇳𓁦𓂓 Gardiner (op.cit. 48, note a) rejected Sethe's reading of the name as *Kꜣ-Mꜣʿt-Rʿ*[11] in favor of the previously accepted reading *Mꜣʿt-kꜣ-Rʿ*, which has been followed since by von Beckerath, Ratié and Redford. Sethe had interpreted the name to mean "The Ka (i.e., divine lord) of the Goddess of Truth is Re", to which Gardiner justly objected. Other renderings are "Maat ist der Ka des Re" by A. Burkhardt, "Maât est le ka de Rê" (S. Ratié) and "Die nach Art der Ka-Kraft des Re Wahrhafte" (Barta). However, the combination 𓇳𓁦 is not restricted to the occurrence in Hatshepsut's Pre-nomen but occurs also for Amenophis III in 𓇳𓁦𓎟 and Seti I 𓇳𓁦𓏠 . If we assume that all those names are construed in the same fashion, they make sense only as statements about "the truth (Maat) of Reʿ" of which Amenophis III claims to be "possessor", while Seti I expresses the wish that it shall last and Hatshepsut proclaims herself as "divine force," i.e., executor, of "Reʿ's truth." It should be kept in mind that the

[6]The same applies to the rendering "der vollkommene Gott" (Barta), as if the notion of an "imperfect god" was conceivable.

[7]Hanns Stock, Nṯr nfr = *der gute Gott?* (1951); J. von Beckerath, op. cit., 30, who considers Stock's interpretation extends it as originally applying to the god Horus from whom it was transfered to the king. The problem with this view is the fact that the designation applies principally to the monarch and not to a deity. As a result it should reflect a feature specific to the former, who, despite his playing a religious role, is primarily a political figure.

[8]Hans Wolfgang Müller, "Der Gute Gott Radjedef, Sohn des Rê," *ZÄS* 91 (1964), 129-133; Rudolf Anthes, "Zum Ursprung des Nefertem," *ZÄS* 80 (1955), 81-89; *ZÄS* 82 (1957), 6-8.

[9]"Dynastic" should be understood here in the widest sense, just as "dynasty" is not to be understood in the strictly loyalistic sense as far as ancient Egypt is concerned. As in Greek Δυναστια the coherence of the group is not the physical relationship but rather in the common nature of outlook, basis or background of a sequence of individuals.

[10]Thutmosis III, who also emphasizes the designation, uses it as a reflection of his descent from Thutmosis II.

[11]Kurt Sethe, *Das Hatschepsut-Problem, noch einmal untersucht*, AAWBerlin 1932/4, (1932), 22 f.; cf. also Edouard Naville, *Annales du Musée Guimet*, XXX (1906), 8.

rendering "truth" of Maʿat is only partially correct; "divine order" might be a better one.[12] Considering Hatshepsut's history as an usurper, the claim to execute Reʿ's divine order would better fit into the political situation than Gardiner' s rather esoteric rendering "Truth is the (essential) attribute of Reʿ." Why should an usurper adopt this meaningless truism at the time of ascending the throne of Egypt?

Of the nomen and its introduction by *sȝt-Rʿ* practically nothing is preserved, but the appropriateness of the restoration is beyond doubt. There was certainly a hortative epithet after the name, either *di.ti ʿnḫ* or *ʿnḫ.ti ḏt*.

c) Davies had suggested *ir.n.s m mnw.s mn*] *wȝḥ* [*r*] *smnt* which Gardiner, with some adaptations followed in his translation "[She made this (?)] lasting [monument (?)] for the establishment of her great name (firm) like the sky . . ." Redford accepted most of it in rendering "she made it as her monument (?) . . .] her great name is to be established like heaven . . ." S. Ratié, op. cit. 179 translated ". . . pour perpétuer son grand nom, comme dans le ciel" and A. Burkhardt, op. cit. 42, "sie machte es als dauerndes Denkmal und [ließ] es dauerhaft 'bestehen', damit ihr Name groß sei wie der Himmel." All these interpretations have epigraphic and semantic shortcomings. The most important flaw is the disregard for the available space. The full royal protocol should be closed with a hortative statement such as *ʿnḫ.ti ḏt*. This reduces the available space to ± 2 1/2–3 squares. The other aspect is the lack of any linkage between the inscription and the shrine on which it is inscribed. For these two reasons, I suggest shortening the restoration to *ir.n.s mnw pn wȝḥ* "she made this lasting monument." The proposed restoration can claim *Urk.* IV 303, 5; 358, 4; 359, 16 as parallels,[13] dating also to Hatshepsut and concerning a rock-cut shrine.

As Gardiner already indicated a preposition *r* would be needed here to introduce the purpose of the action.[14] However, if the statement is understood as explaining the reason for the monument the emendation of a genitival *n* would be appropriate leading to a literal rendering "of establishing her great name like heaven," followed by the two deeds which brought it about. For the construction of genitival *n* + infintive, to indicate a purpose, see Gardiner, *Egyptian Grammar*, § 305. The perpetuity of the name is also the closing point of the text.[15]

d) *Smnḫ.s gnwt qnn.s ḥr wdrt nt Tpt-ḏw r wbnw* has been considered as one integrated narrative statement.[16] Whoever has been to the Speos Artemidos would agree that it is hardly the starting point of

[12]Jan Assmann, *Maʿat: Gerechtigkeit und Unsterblichkeit im Alten Ägypten* (1990), 28-36.

[13]"One made for (me) . . . this asting monument." The formulation in this case is in the form of a direct speech, which cannot be the case here because of the subsequent use of the third person pronoun.

[14]Redford saw *smnt* as a passive *sḏm.f*, rendering it "her great name is to be established like heaven," which, however, lacks an agent. Burkhardt envisaged a causative meaning of *wȝḥ* which not only lacks a parallel but also leads to a redundancy.

[15]See below, pp. 87 ff.

[16]Breasted, *AR* II § 297 "She hath made excellent the 'records' of her might over the Red Land of the Goddess of the Mountain as far as the rising of . . ."; Gardiner "that she might deftly carve the annals of her supremacy over the region of Her that is upon the Mountain, (even) unto whatsoever [the Sun] above the desert illuminates"; A. Burkhardt "Sie zeichnete die Annalen ihres Sieges auf

some desert highway whose travellers needed to be informed of Hatshepsut's fame. Nor is there much cause for her to brag about a supremacy "as far as the sun shines", which would include the entire *terra cognita*. Two aspects deserve emphasizing: one is that the formulation is not retrospective, i.e., that it does not make reference to the past but that the matter is ungoing. The other, that any claim of control concerns a very specific region and is not global.

Smnḫ gnwt, lit., "to make excellent the annals," is difficult to grasp in its full significance, if for no other reason than the lack of comparative annals. The verb *smnḫ* is used for Thoth's codification of the royal name.[17] However, the verb is also used for the executing of laws.[18] If the term does not indicate the enhancing of records, but rather their execution, *gnwt* takes on a new dimension. While its use for the records of a past ruler is beyond doubt,[19] its association with an ongoing reign would either change the character of the verb from executing to embellishing, or *gnwt* denotes both, the political program of a king and its execution in retrospect.[20] As, as already indicated, the statement has no retrospective orientation, it would result that Hatshepsut's "name" was established by her carrying out the political program. Such a statement would, however, require some description of the nature of this political program.

Such a statement I am inclined to see in *qnn.s ḥr wdrt nt tpt-ḏw* "that she will (always) be dutiful/brave÷valiant about the region of the One-upon-the-gebel." *Qnn*, which has the appearance of a geminating *sḏm.f*, thus indicating continuity or intensity of action, might be tempting to understand as belligerent action. .Neither the text itself nor any other record of Hatshepsut's reign would point to any belligerance. In addition, what follows concerns religious sanctuaries rather than anything military. The association with *gnwt* lets one think of "being dutiful"[21] which might make better sense than Gardiner's "supremacy" of which the text indicates very little.

Wdrt occurs only here; Redford's rendering as "desert-tract" lacks tangible support especially as the basic term for it is *mṯnw*.[22] Despite its speculative nature, I like the idea of an error for *wʿrt* due to a confusion of *d* (𓂧) for *ʿ* (𓂝), as Sethe already mused.[23] *Wʿrt* is a well established term for the "desert plateau," attested since the late Old Kingdom.[24] *Tpt-ḏw* is strikingly similar to the epithet *tp-ḏw.f* of Anubis. Both terms have in common that a deity is given the oversight over an undefined deserted area, without holding legal title.[25] The nameless reference allows an association with more than one "goddess," although

---

dem Felsen 'Der Ersten des Berges' (= Pachet) auf, bis dorthin, wo [die Sonne ?] aufgeht [. . .] auf der Wüste"; Redford "and the annals of her fame published upon the desert-tract of She-who-is-upon-the Mountain as far as the [Sun-disc] shines at Will (?)."

[17]Cf. W. Helck, *ZÄS* 82 (1957), 133-140; D. B. Redford, *Pharaonic King-Lists, Annals and Day-Books* (1986), 81 understands *smnḫ* as "to publish" concerning Thoth's activity.

[18]*Wb.* IV 136, 13.

[19]It is used in this fashion by Hatshepsut in *Urk.* IV 500, 13 "since the annals of the forebearers" and Pierre Lacau, *Chapelle Rouge* I, 137 "it is not in the annals of the forebearers"; cf. D.B. Redford, op. cit. 83 f.

[20]Cf. also D.B. Redford, op. cit. 95 f.

[21]Faulkner, *Concise Dictionary* 279 lists "dutiful" of a son or a heir for *qnn*; cf. also *Urk.* VII 56, 5; Leyden V 88.

[22]*Wb.* II 176; its specific nature transpires from its derivate *mṯnw* denoting the bedouin sheikh; cf. also Sinuhe B 26.

[23]*Urk.* IV 383, note b.

[24]*Urk.* I 223, 18; Sinuhe B 40; cf. Alan H. Gardiner, *Notes on the Story of Sinuhe*, 30.

[25]For the juridical connotation of *tp* in regard to land and its holding, cf. Hans Goedicke, "Titles for titles," in Schafik Allam,

the particular text is presumably intended for the goddess Pakhet.

Despite the clear writing *r*  the words have been taken as *r* + *sḏm.f* and rendered "as far as the rising of" (Breasted), "(even) unto whatsoever [the Sun] above the desert illuminates" (Gardiner), "jusqu'au lieu où le soleil se lève chaque jour . . ." (S. Ratié), "bis dorthin, wo [die Sonne ?] aufgeht" (A. Burkhardt), and "as far as the [Sun-disc] shines" (Redford). Such a wording would require **nfryt r* or *šꜣꜥ r*, in addition to a different spelling of *wbn* and the mention of a subject. None of them is the case and the term should be recognized as the "adverbial" expression "eastward."[26] The recognition of an adverbial expresion also indicates that the sentence ends here.

Section One

"The Lord [of the glow] over the coast-line—(while) his flames were outside the Two Mountain-ranges (i.e. Upper Egypt),e) braziers were distributed, which enlarghed the (darkened) shrines [into] favorite places.f) Every god—each one away from the dwelling which he had loved—his Ka was satisfied about his (temporary) seats, which I had established for residence.g) [The heart] of [those in] their pillared halls were gladdened, as the hiding place inside the structure was reinforced up to the place of (the rite of) removing the footstep.h) Every [god] fashioned in his body from electrum of ꜥAmau, their permanent feasts in the cycle of the cult-year and the seasonal festive gifts were in observation of the regulation of my maker.i) The ritual in its arrangement which had been done for the predecessors of the (present) persons was reinforced."j)

e) The claim that a new sentence commences at this point is corroborated by the change of personal pronoun. The suffix *.f* after *nbiw* requires a preceding mention of a male noun to which it can refer. As a result it is necessary to envision here an anticipatorily stated syntactic element, which, as will be shown, amounts to a circumstantial clause.[27] The lacuna at the beginning is particularly regrettable, but a basic restoration seems nevertheless possible. The initial can only be the word for "lord, possessor" because of the lack of a preceding word. This reading is confirmed by the change in the personal suffix. It would seem certain that this word *nb* "lord" is followed by a determinative. The indicated space of the lacuna is more than one square, which, however, I would not consider too precise. If assuming * it might fill the gap, although the reference would seem rather vague. For this reason I conjecture a more specific designation in which *ḥr mrw* does not qualify *nb* but rather a phenomenon which the "lord" possesses. Gardiner considered the possibility of restoring *nb itn*, lit. "lord of the sun(-disc)," which not only has no parallel, but also is difficult to connect with the adjunct *ḥr mrw* "over the coast-line." As a conjecture, I

ed., *Grund und Boden* (1994), 227-234.

[26] *Urk.* IV 1978, 8; Faulkner, op. cit. 59.

[27] For this syntactic feature, cf. Gardiner, op. cit. §§ 146 f.

propose restoring either **nb sṯt*, "lord of the rays," **nb ꜣḫt*, "lord of fire," or **nb nsr* "lord of flames." Either one ought to be imagined as being visible "over the coast-line" (*ḥr mrw*).

This is a point of extreme importance for two reasons. Egypt has principally only one coast-line, namely at the Mediterranean Sea, which forms Egypt's northern border. The North, however, is not a natural location of light, i.e., the reference to the source of "his flames" cannot concern the sun. A source of "flames" aside of the sun ought to be imagined as volcanic, in which connection the explosion of Thera/Santorin has to be taken into consideration.[28] In other words, the reference to this natural event is used here to determine Hatshepsut's actions.[29] Grammatically there seems to be a double anticipation, first to emphasize the source of the "flames," i.e., the suffix *.f*, and second the entire circumstancial statement which concerns the distribution of braziers.

Nbiw.f ḥr-sꜣ spty was rendered by Breasted as "set his flames behind the two hill-countries," by Gardiner "his flames (falling) upon the back of the Two Ranges," by S. Ratié ". . . pour donner sa flamme au-delà des deux districts désertiques," by A. Burkhardt "seine (= des Denkmals) Flammen (sind) hinter den beiden (Seiten der) Wüste," and by Redford "who sheds his heat upon the desert." Unfortunately, none of them commented on the meaning of this statement and how it is to be linked with what follows. It has to be emphasized that there is no verb present in what has to be seen as describing the circumstance for the actions delineated in the following. *Nbiw* denotes "flames" of a fire rather than heat,[30] which points to a disastrous phenomenon rather than an appreciated one. The compound preposition *ḥr-sꜣ* does not mean here "upon the back" (Gardiner), because the dual *spty* indicates delineations in form of a mountain ridge. In connection with a defined line, *ḥr-sꜣ* is known to mean "outside."[31] The undisputable dual *spty* is attested as *spty-nṯr* denoting Egypt.[32] The geographical layout of Egypt is such that only the Nile valley south of modern Cairo is defined by a mountainous ridge. As "his flames were outside the two mountain borders" the statement indicates that the devastations from a northern source did not affect Upper Egypt proper.

f) The allusion to the prevailing circumstances, that namely the fiery impact of an event to be seen "over the coast-line" did not affect Upper Egypt serves as introduction for measures taken in Egypt at the time. The first one is given as *sš ꜥḫw*. It is clearly a verbal clause, but in passive mood; the verb *sš*, lit., "to spread out,"[33] can only denote the distribution of the objects *ꜥḫw*. The term denotes not only a "brazier" for

[28]The impact of the volcanic explosion of Thera/Santorin on the entire eastern Mediterranean basin is gradually being recognized. There is physical evidence in the form of volcanic ash in the northeastern Delta and also substantial amounts of thephra found at Tell ed-Dabꜥa. For the former, see Daniel J. Stanley and H. Sheng, "Volcanic shards from Santorini in the Nile Delta, Egypt," *Nature* 320 (1986), 733-735, for the latter Manfred Bietak, et al., "Neue Grabungsergebnisse aus Tell el-Dabꜥa," *Ä&L* IV (1994), 35, Tf. 10 B; cf. also Manfred Bietak, *Avaris. The Capital of the Hyksos* (1996), pl. 34 B.

[29]For the chronological consequences, see Hans Goedicke, "The Chronology of the Thera/Santorin Explosion," *Ä&L* III (1992), 57-62.

[30]*Wb*. II 244, 7; the only other early occurrences of the term are *Pyr*. 1779 b and *CT* II 18 a.

[31]Gardiner, *EG* § 178.

[32]*Wb*. IV 98, 14.; *Pyr*. 1120 b where *nhmhm spty nṯr* is parallel to *sdꜣ tꜣ* and *Pyr*. 1770 b.

[33]*Wb*. III 482; see also Gardiner, *JEA* 32 (1946), 49.

roasting something as it is traditionally rendered,[34] but it is also a source of light, i.e., a "lamp." The distribution of "lamps" makes sense only when darkness prevailed. This in turn corroborates the previously offered thesis that this section of the text describes the impact on Egypt of the volcanic explosion of Thera/Santorin.[35] One of the phenomena typical for a cataclysmatic volcanic explosion is darkness caused by ash clouds. The eruption of the Krakatao in 1883 as well as the one of Mount St. Helens in 1981 are thoroughly documented volcanic events during which extensive darkness prevailed.[36] That at least the edge of the Delta was affected by volcanic ash from the Santorin eruption has been demonstrated by the discovery of ash flakes in several places along the northeastern part of the Delta.[37]

The distributed "braziers" are described in their effect. *Swsẖ*, different from previous translations, should be recognized as participle; accordingly the text refers to the "braziers which enlarged the (dark) shrines into a favorite place." The text has previously been taken differently: "the sanctuaries are enlarged—the desire of all gods" (Breasted), "and there being extended the sanctuaries, the delight of all gods" (Gardiner), "das Heiligtum wurde vergrößert, der Lieblingsplatz aller Götter" (A. Burkhardt), "and fanes—the favourite haunt of all the gods - enlarged" (Redford). Apparently, *swsẖ* was taken as a passive *sḏm.f* parallel to the earlier *sš ʿḫw* "braziers were distributed." There would be no logical progression because any construction causing enlargement should precede the setting up of braziers. The previous translations imply a (major) building activity, in which case the mention of the agent who caused it, could be expected. The assumed apposition of *st-ib* either disregards the space between ⊏⊐ and *st-ib* or it has to be assumed that all "shrines" were enlarged, for which the indicated circumstances provide no convincing cause. *Ḫmw* denotes specifically the closed shrine of a deity,[38] i.e., the place where it rests but without extending blessings. These shrines by their very nature should be imagined as being dark. "Favorite abodes" of deities are instead places from which they exert their benevolence, and, like human dwellings, require light for the deity present there.[39] The notion of a "favorite place" denoted as *st-ib* has in the "sun-temple" of Nywoserreʿ its earliest attestation;[40] it is also attested specifically for the earlier Eighteenth Dynasty in *Urk.* IV 183, 11-13 about the sanctuary built by Thutmosis III whose name was *mn-mnw-Mn-ḫpr-Rʿ* and which is described as "it is the favorite place of the lord-of-the-gods and a good resting place for

[34]For unknown reasons Redford gave for it "offering stand."

[35]For the need of artificial illumination in the wake of a Santorin outbreak, see also Hans Goedicke, "Two Texts from Tell ed-Dabʿa," *Ä&L* forthcoming.

[36]For the description of a tsunamis which devasted the northwestern Delta in A.D. 365 see Ammianus Marcellinus, *Res gestae* XXVI 10. 15 ff.; for a description of the Krakatao explosion, see the eye-witness report by R.D.M. Verbeek, *Krakatau* (1886).

[37]Daniel J. Stanley and Harrison Sheng, "Volcanic shards from Santorini in the Nile Delta," *Nature* 320 (1986), 733-35. In addition to the ash substantial amounts of tephra, also from the cataclysmatic outbrake of Santorin have been found during the excavations at Tell ed-Dabʿa; see Manfred Bietak, *Avaris: The Capitol of the Hyksos* (1996), 78, pl. 34 B.

[38]Patricia Spencer, *The Egyptian Temple* (1984), 104-08 focuses on a connection with the Lower Egyptian architectural form (▥), which, however, by the New Kingdom, when the term becomes frequent, played hardly any role. As she points out, the term is used specifically for the sanctuary of a temple, i.e. the part which is inaccessible and unknown for the outsider.

[39]It is indicative that the opening phase of the daily ritual consists of the opening of a shrine, followed by its illumination and cleansing. Cf. also Winfried Barta, *LÄ* III 841-843.

[40]Cf. Werner Kaiser, *MDIAK* 14 (1956), 108 f.; Mark Lehner, *The Complete Pyramids* (1997), 151 rendered it "delight of Re'."

his ennead of gods."[41] As already pointed out before, it is necessary to take *swsḫ* as a participle qualifying *ꜥḫw* "braziers"; as a causative it requires an object, which can only be *ˈḫmw* "naos." As the (closed) shrines are obviously not the favorite place of the gods, in which case they would not need an improvement, I restore *swsḫ ḫmw [m] st-ib* "which enlarged the (closed) naos into a favorite place."

g) At first sight it is unclear if *nṯrw nbw* qualifies *st-ib* or if it belongs to the next syntactic unit. In the past, all translators have linked them. However, as *st-ib* is a compound term an indirect genitive could be expected in such a case. Semantically, the connection would imply that "all gods" and their shrines were affected by the adversity, which would seem highly improbable considering the expanse of Egypt. A more convincing meaning results from taking the entire stretch from *nṯrw nbw* to *kꜣ.f* as an extended anticipatory statement, which seems typical for this text and might very well be a reflection of the individual idiosyncracy of Hatshepsut.[42] In other words, *nṯrw nbw*[43] is an anticipatory emphasis to stress the total inclusiveness of the following *wꜥ nb*, "each one".

While the effect of the "braziers" in enlarging the closed shrines (*ḫmw*) makes good sense, it is to be considered if the lacuna is not to be restored into [*r*] *st-ib nṯrw nbw*, "[according] to the wish of every god"; for this use of *st-ib*, Falkner, *CD* 206, who cites *Urk*. IV 170, 13 *mi st-ib nt ḥm.f r.s*. As this text concerns also a building, a rendering "favorite place of his Majesty for it" cannot be excluded instead of the suggested reading.

Ỉwnn poses a problem as far as defining its precise application. *Wb*. I 55, 12 gives for it "Wohnung (o.ä.) eines Gottes"; Faulkner, *CD* 13 lists it as "sanctuary," P. Spencer, op, cit., 99-103 emphasizes the uncertainty of the term beyond denoting a religious edifice after an exhaustive discussion of the occurrences of the term. Such occurrences are *Urk*. IV 16, 1-2 *rdi rḫ nṯr iwnn.f ḥbyt nt nṯr nb*, "who causes the knowing of a god and his *iwnn* and the feast-ritual of every god"; *Urk*. IV 834, 1-2 *ꜣb.n ḥm.i irt mnw n it.i Ỉmn-Rꜥ m Ỉpt-swt sḥꜥ iwnn sḏsr ꜣḫt*, "my Majesty wished to make a monument for my father Amun-Reꜥ in Karnak, to erect a *iwnn*, to embellish the 'horizon' ..." Neither of these passages really clarifies the meaning of *iwnn* except that it is in some way connected with a god's place of presence. The fact that the relationship with the divine is expressed here by the preposition *ḥr* does not help either; in the case of a continuous dwelling the preposition *m could be expected. In view of the basic meaning "above" of the preposition *ḥr*, the literal translation "every god, every one above his *iwnn* " could be taken to suggest that the deities were no longer inside the *iwnn* but rather "above" spacially[44] or causally. Putting oneself into the indicated situation it can be concluded that a number of deities had lost their traditional abode. This congrues with the previous reference to a natural disaster whose main brunt, however, did not impact the

[41]Cf. also *Urk*. IV 834, 5 *st-ib it nt sp-tpy* "the father's favorite place of the first occasion."

[42]See further below, p. 93.

[43]The spelling  is somewhat surprising in its detail and one could wonder if not the plural noun *nbw* is intended here.

[44]The later reference to the past nature of this relationship gives *ḥr* almost the connotation of "away from," but with the additional aspect of vertical distance.

southern part of Egypt.

The relative-form *mr.n.f* makes it clear, that the relationship between the deity and the abode was a feature of the past. In other words, the passage concerns a previous abode of the deity, which, however, is no longer its present one.

Despite this removal from the previously favored abode, the deity is not prone to a negative reaction.[45] Instead, the deity's *kꜣ* is "satisfied about its (scil., the deity's) seats" (*nswt*).[46] The specific implication of *nst*, lit. "seat" in this connection is not entirely clear as it can refer to physical objects but also to abstract "circumstances." There seems to be an intended contrast to *ỉwnn* as "permanent abode." If this is correct, *nswt* should refer here to temporary placements in which the plural is to be emphasized.[47]

All previous translators ended the sentence with *nswt* and considered *nẖb.n.ỉ* to begin a new sentence. For the sake of the inner balance of the text, it would seem necessary that *nswt* is qualified in a similar fashion as the earlier mentioned *ỉwnn*. This requires taking *nẖb.n.ỉ* as a relative-form (despite the missing feminine ending). As for *nẖb*, Gardiner rendered it "I opened up," to which Redford[48] objected, translating it instead "I was officially designated . . ." First, the form is certainly not a passive, and second, *nẖb* is attested with the legal meaning "to assign property."[49] The assignment is here further specified, but the reading is rather uncertain. The traces indicated in Davies' copy ( ) look like *r ḫt* which makes limited sense when rendered "for property." Another possibility is "for residence" or . The epigraphic uncertainty forestalls a definite reading beyond this vague point.

h) While the text concerns so far only the measures taken for the gods, it is continued by describing their response. *Ḫntš* "to have enjoyment," "to delight in," see *Wb*. III 311 f. The verb's subject is lost in a lacuna. Certain is that it is a plural because of the following suffix *.sn*, which requires an antecedent. The narrow gap after , the determinative of *ḫntš*, and the isolated would seem ideally for restoring , which is frequently specified as the organ of joy.[50] In this case the preserved sign *n* would be a genitive connecting those who felt the delight. For the restoration of the word there are two indicators: first, it has to denote beings, because only they can feel joy; second, their number must be plural because of the following *.sn*. The word *ỉwnyt* "colonade"[51] must be connected with them. Considering these points, I wish to restore *ḫntš [ỉb] n [ỉmy]w ỉwnyt.sn*, "the heart of those in their colonade enjoyed." The proposed *ỉmyw* is, of course,

[45]Behind this statement is the dominating feature of the divine/human relationship. It is the obligation of man to keep the divine in good humor otherwise it might react in a negative fashion. The principle of *do ut des* is the most precise formula characterizing this relationship.

[46]For the *kꜣ* as source of satisfaction, cf. *Wb*. III 188, 3, 5.

[47]For the rare mention of *nst* of a deity, cf. Klaus P. Kuhlman, *Der Thron im Alten Ägypten*, ADAIK 10 (1977), 36 f.

[48]P. 31, note 186. A. Burkhardt followed Gardiner and saw here the beginning of a personal speech rendering it "Ich habe festgesetzt . . ."

[49]*Wb*. II 307, 12; Faulkner, op. cit. 138; *Urk*. IV 2120, 10 "he assigned to them fields and herds"; Amennemope I 17; cf. Irene Grumach, *Untersuchungen zur Lebenslehre des Amenope*, MÄS 23 (1972), 15 f.

[50]Alexandre Piankoff, *Le «coeur» dans les textes égyptiens* (1930), 26 ff.

[51]*Wb*. I 54, 2; P. Spencer, op. cit. 63-67; cf. also above, p. 38.

not absolutely certain, but no better word comes to mind.[52] The lack of plural strokes is odd, but epigraphic uncertainty is indicated.

The cause for the delight is described as *sꜥḥꜣ.n imnt* <m> *ḫnw pr r st int-rd*, which Gardiner rendered "I made the Hidden Chamber, the inner part of the House, to vie with the Place of Removing the Foot," while Redford gave "I erected the Hidden Chamber within the house at the place of 'Bringing-the-Foot.'"[53] There can be no doubt that the "bringing-the-foot" refers here to the closing phase of a ritual performance; its meaning would be more transparent when rendered "removal of the foot-print."[54] It is done when leaving the cult sphere and thus should be understood here as an indication of the outward limit of a cult-place. The latter is refered to as *imnt* <m> *ḫnw pr*, "the hiding place inside the building"; as for *imnt*, "hiding place" might be a better translation than "secret place,"[55] because of its setting inside[56] a structure (𓉐) which apparently refers back to the aforementioned "colonade" (*iwnyt*). The predicate has no subject so that it has to be recognized as an impersonal *sḏm.n*-form which has passive mood.[57] *Sꜥḥꜣ* is obviously a causative of *ꜥḥꜣ* "to fight," for which Gardiner gave "make to vie"[58] and Redford "to erect." Because of its literal sense "to make able to fight," I render it "to reinforce."

Summing up this part of the text it refers to emergency measures taken to consolidate affected structures so that "those in their colonade," i.e., the divine statues which were placed there for protection, were delighted. This reference to emergency measures in sanctuaries continues logically the preceding sentence about the relocation of deities caused by damage to their previous abode. Both statements make sense only when taken as describing measures taken in the wake of a major calamity that affected Egypt or at least parts of it.

i) After describing the measures taken to alleviate the damage affecting divine buildings, the text turns next to the divine images: [*nṯr*] *nb msw m ḏt.f m dꜥm n ꜥmꜣmw*, "every [god] which was fashioned in his body out of electrum of ꜥAmu." The opening is traditionally considered a pseudo-verbal clause which is also responsible for Sethe's unsupported reading **ms.tw*.[59] However, the envisaged construction i s unparalleled in what is known about Egyptian grammar. *Msw* is not an Old Perfective, but rather a passive

[52] **Ḫntyw* would indicate a permanence of residence which would not be appropriate here.

[53] A. Burkhardt abstained from restoring and thus gave "Ich habe [. . .] die verborgene Stätte im Innern des Tempels zu einem Platz, wo die Fußspur verwischt word."

[54] For this rite, cf. Alan H. Gardiner, *JEA* 24 (1938), 87 ff.; Hartwig Altenmüller, *JEA* 57 (1971), 146-153.

[55] *Wb.* I 84, 10; Faulkner, op. cit. 21.

[56] The reading *m ḫnw* "inside" can be considered certain. Either the sign 𓈖 was omitted in the text or in the copying. Otherwise *imnt* would be the subject after *sꜥḥꜣ.n*, which makes no sense.

[57] Gardiner, *Egyptian Grammar* § 486. Gardiner, A. Burkhardt and Redford emended here a first person suffix which would imply a remarkable modesty on the part of Hatshepsut not found elsewhere. In addition, it would suggest that Hatshepsut herself was involved in the building activity.

[58] Also quoted in Faulkner, *CD* 215; *Wb.* IV 53, 1 lists it as "belegt einmal Dyn. 18 mit Bezug auf ein Gebäude—ob richtig?"

[59] Gardiner rendered "every [god] being sculptured in his bodily form out of gold of ꜥAmu," followed by S. Ratié "chaque Dieu a été sculpté en sa forme corporelle, en or fin du pays de Amou," A. Burkhardt "Jeder [Gott] ist nachgebildet in seiner Gestalt aus Elektron von *ꜥ-mꜣ.w*" and Redford "each [god] being fashioned, i.e. his body, of electrum of ꜥAmau."

participle qualifying *nṯr nb*. The entire opening is, as repeatedly in this text,[60] an anticipatorily stated definition of the subsequently mentioned divine recipients of religious services. For the use of *ms* for the fashioning of divine images, see *Wb*. II 138, 12. Of the two prepositional expressions, the first, namely, *m ḏt.f*, qualifies *nṯr*, while the second, *m ḏꜥm*, belongs with *ms*. As for *ꜥmw* it appears to denote the gold-mining region of the Eastern Desert between the Second and Third Cataract.[61] The detailed specification might seem surprising until one realizes that it differentiates among "gods" (*nṯr*). The emphasis on the fashioning from electrum should be seen as narrowing it to the owners of a cult-statue, while other *nṯr* do not receive the treatment described in the following.[62]

Next follows the specification of the religious service for the deities identified by anticipation and what was done concerning them: *ḥb.sn ḏd m rꜣ-dmḏyt ḥbyt r tr.s m nḏrt tp rd n irw.i*, "their feast established in the cycle of the cult-year and the seasonal festive gifts were in observation of the regulation of my maker."[63] Turning to the grammar first, the pseudo-verbal clause has *m nḏrt* as its predicate. For its meaning "to observe regulations," cf. A.H. Gardiner, *Admonitions of an Egyptian Sage*, 77; *Wb*. II 383, 22; *Urk*. IV 489, 4. As for the subject, distinction is being made between two forms of cult activity, one established according to the calendrical date, the other defined seasonally.[64] The participial construction *ḏd m rꜣ-dmḏyt* specifies *ḥbw.sn* and is not a sentence as Redford took it. 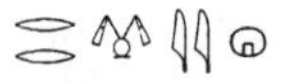 is a compound term with the 'abstract preformative *rꜣ*'[65] and denotes the entire calendrical cycle. For *ḥbyt* "festival offering" as distinguished from "feast," cf. Wb. III 61; Faulkner, *CD* 167.

j) *Tp-rd n*  cannot be translated "rule of my making" (Gardiner) or "instruction I laid down" (Redford). The first would require an infinitive *irt*, the second disregards the indirect genitive. Despite the lack of a determinative, I see no other way than taking it as nominally used participle "my maker."[66] This interpretation is also necesary in order to have an antecedent for the suffix *.f* in the next syntactic unit.

[60]For this feature, see further below, p.

[61]Karola Zibelius, *Afrikanische Orts- und Völkernamen in hieroglyphischen und hieratischen Texten*, TAVO B/1 (1972), 99.

[62]When realizing that *nṯr* applies also to ritually buried dead ones, the distinction becomes clear; see Hans Goedicke, "God", *JSSEA* XVI (1988), 57-62.

[63]Breasted: "Their feasts are permanent in the division of the time, the festival offering ['is made'] at its time by the 'authority' of the command of my maker"; Gardiner: "their festivals being (made) permanent in (men's) mouths, the entire festal cycle (occurring) at its (due) season, by holding fast to the rule of my making"; S. Ratié: "leurs fêtes étant assurés dès l'ouverture en toralité, en leur saison convenable, en s'en tenant fermement à la règle que j'établis"; A. Burkhardt: ""ihre (= der Götter) Feste bleiben im Gespräch der Menge [. . .], der Festbedarf ist zur rechten Zeit da, weil ich die Anweisung dessen, der (= Amun) mich geschaffen hat, befolgte"; Redford: "their festivals were fixed calendrically, (each) feast being at its season, in the observance of the instruction I laid down."

[64]The distinction still exists even in the modern calender with movable feasts, such as Easter and those depending on it and all other celebrations.

[65]Hermann Junker, *ZÄS* 77 (1941), 3-7; Elmar Edel, *Altägyptische Grammatik*, I, § 259.

[66]The way Hatshepsut alludes to her begetter is ambiguous and can be understood as reference to Amun or to Thutmosis I. As it is doubtful that she had already promulgated the political myth of her divine father at this point in her reign, a reference to Thutmosis I appears more likely.

Section Two

"When the stipulations of her being ruler were fulfilled, which he had made in the past to the chiefs:k) my divine heart was searching for the future,l) as the heart of the *bit* had thought of eternity upon the pronouncement of 'Him-who-splits-the-*ished*-tree':m) 'O Amun, Lord-of-Millions, I shall magnify the Maʿat, which is desired for him!,n) as one who lives on it knows: It is my bread! May I swallow its fragrance, when I am one flesh with him, who has caused me to exist in order to cause his fame to be powerful in this land!"o)

k) The insistance on the proper performance at the ritual occasions as instituted or held by Hatshepsut's father is the point of changing the subject from the service for deities to her own rulership: *srwḏ nt-ʿ nt ṯs.s ỉrt.n.f m pꜣw n tpyw*, "when the stipulations of her being ruler were fulfilled, which he had made in the past to the chiefs." As this rendering differs fundamentally from earlier ones,[67] a detailed discussion is required. The verb *srwḏ*, which has uniformly been recognized as passive *sḏm.f*,[68] is attested in connection with a contract in the meaning "to fulfil."[69] *Nt-ʿ*, lit., "that of the document" might best be taken as "stipulations," but rendering it "ritual, duty" makes also good sense.[70] It concerns a particular document as results from its specification *nt ṯs.s.*. The initial task is to identify what the suffix *.s* refers to; Gardiner considered the possibility of a reference to *dmḏyt* while rejecting a connection with Hatshepsut. Redford has an unsubstantiated "ritual of his service" which applies also to his interpretation of  as "made for him" which would lack an antecedent. As for the latter, *ỉr.ỉ*, "my maker" would be the only possible choice. Despite some qualms *ṯs.s* appears to be the correct reading of 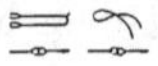 which serves here as specification of *nt-ʿ*. Taking it as direct quote of the original formulation, I render it "stipulations of her being ruler"; why the pronoun remained in this form is mysterious, but might be intended to add weight to its authenticity. *Wb.* V 402, 7-8 lists *ṯs* with the meaning "Herrscher sein" especially in connection with Hatshepsut.[71] When understood in this way, the statement makes reference to Hatshepsut's rulership as an intention of her father, as she claims repeatedly.[72]

The relative-form *ỉrt.n.f* makes it clear that it was performed in the past. This is corroborated by the

[67]Breasted: "the regulations of the commandant are perpetuated, which he made in his - - -"; Gardiner: "The rites of his ordering, (even) what He made in the primal by-gone (days ?), were made to flourish"; S. Ratié: "J'ai fait prospérer la tradition dans sa coutume comme il fit dans les temps primordiaux . . ."; A. Burkhardt: "Die Bestimmungen ihres Ausspruches, welche er in der ersten (?) Urzeit gemacht hat, bleiben bestehen"; Redford: "The ritual of his service (?), made for him in antiquity (?) was restored [. . .]"

[68]For its use in a circumstantial clause, cf. Wolfhart Westendorf, *Der Gebrauch des Passivs in der klassischen Literatur der Ägypter*, VIO 18 (1953), 53 ff. One could think that the passage concerns Hatshepsut's early years in competition with Thutmosis III. However, not only is there no suffix which could refer to her, but at the time the text was written Hatshepsut was king and the early years were no longer pertinent. It would require a narrative *sḏm.n.f*-form if reference would be made to this phase of her life.

[69]Neferhotep 35; Faulkner, *CD* 236; cf. also Alan H. Gardiner, *Admonitions of an Egyptian Sage* (1909), 102.

[70]Cf. John D. Schmidt, *Ramesses II* (1975), 124 f., who discussed its use in the treaty between Ramesses II and Hattusilis III.

[71]Occurrences are Mariette, *Karnak* 35; 54, 13; Faulkner, *CD* 307 follows Gardiner in rendering this occurrence "order, arrange rites."

[72]*Urk.* IV 254 ff.; 65; 288; cf. also S. Ratié, op. cit., 50-52.

word *pꜣw* following it. As Gardiner rightly remarked, no construction is known that could explain the **pꜣw n tpyw* of Davies' copy.[73] The hieroglyph  between *pꜣw* and *tpw* would seem to rule out the suggested similarity with **pꜣt tpyt* "primeval time" or *pꜣw tpw* (*Wb.* I 495, 12) "aboriginal form." This sign *n* is the main problem, because it is uncertain if it is a genitive or a dative. In the first case it would require a rendering "which he had made among the past ones of the people," in the second, "which he had made among the past ones for the people." In both cases I would consider *pꜣw* as an abbreviated spelling of a nominally used *pꜣwty*.[74] As for , I see no other possibility than to consider it a noun, because of the *n* introducing it. Without a determinative it is difficult to establish a rendering with any degree of certainty; the specific use of *tpy* in reference to a king's confidants[75] would make better sense than the inclusive use of the term.[76] At any rate, I have the impression that the text suggests that Hatshepsut's maker made the stipulations for her being ruler in the past and disclosed it only to a limited number of people. It would be a apologetic attempt to justify her later reach for power.

l) The allusion to her maker's intention to have her become ruler occurs as part of the execution of this plan which serves as setting for describing Hatshepsut's musings during the occasion when it was carried out. Her concerns are described in two sentences, which, however, are in temporal sequence. The pseudo-verbal clause states an ongoing concommitant activity,[77] while the *sḏm.n.f* construction following it concerns a relative past, i.e., a preceding activity. The search for the future,[78] possibly with the connotation of concern, is a topic of particular frequency in Hatshepsut's time.[79] The concern for the future is ascribed to Hatshpesut's "divine heart" (*ỉb nṯry*) which is juxtaposed with the *ḥꜣty bỉty* in the parallel clause. The time differential indicated by the two predicates makes it clear that *ỉb nṯry* is the present and *ḥꜣty bỉty* the past center of thinking. The difference is, I would say, due to the ascent to the throne that had happened. *Ỉb nṯry*, "divine heart"[80] should not be understood in a theistic sense, since Hatshepsut, despite her claim of a divine father, does not display tendencies towards divinization. The aspect expressed this way appears to reflect her permanence attained by becoming king.

m) *Ḫmt*, "to contemplate," as a constructive form of mental activity, cf. A.H. Gardiner, *Notes*, 86; H.

[73]On the basis of a poorer copy available to him, Sethe considered the restoration  which might have some appeal, except that it would turn over the apparent inner parallelism in the following.

[74]Cf. *Wb.* I 496 f. The choice of the term, if its interpretation is correct, would be remarkable, because it would combine the possibility of referring to the divine and the human procreator of Hatshepsut.

[75]*Wb.* V 280, II.

[76]*Wb.* V 268.

[77]For the construction, cf. Gardiner, *EG* § 319.

[78]For *m-ḫt* "future," cf. Faulkner, *CD* 198.

[79]*Wb.* V 540, 5; *Urk.* IV 57, 15; 6; E. Dziobek, *Das Grab des Ineni*, AVDAIK 68 (1992), 53; cf. also pAn IV 2, 8 where it is used in connection with navigation; also Jaroslav Černý, *Crum Studies*, 44 f. There might be an apologetic aspect to the statement, trying to excuse Hatshepsut's reach for power as having been motivated by her concern for the future.

[80]A. Piankoff, op. cit. does not cite the term. Although Hatshepsut claims "divine seed" (*mw nṯry*) the claim of a *ỉb nṯry* seems unique and might be restricted to a specific period in her reign.

Goedicke, *JNES* 19 (1960), 285;[81] the *sḏm.n.f* indicates a relative past to the temporal aspect contained in the preceding syntactic unit.[82] *Ḥḥ*, the object of contemplation, is interesting in its juxtaposition to *m-ḫt*, "future" as Hatshepsut's spiritual aim after becoming king. While the latter appears specific, *ḥḥ* would seem generic, i.e., a general concern about attaining permanence which she had accomplished by becoming king. Of particular interest is the difference in the source of the two different concerns. In both cases a term for "heart" is used,[83] once qualified by the adjectival *nṯry,* in the other as 𓆤. No such adjective is known, so that the word has to be recognized here as noun.[84] The opposite, namely *nṯry*, has no specific associations with the Upper Egyptian kingship, so that the common parallelism of the two parts of Egypt cannot be assumed to apply here. Furthermore, the grammar of the entire syntegma makes it clear that the contemplating of "eternity" occurred prior to attaining the quality of being *nṯr*. In other words, 𓆤 ought to denote the status of Hatshepsut prior to becoming king. It is difficult to come up with a social term from another culture to grasp this particular point. Because of its far-reaching ramifications I be allowed here to render it *ex cathedra* "patrician," i.e., the high social distinction Hatshepsut enjoyed without holding authority. It is in this social role that she "contemplated eternity," i.e., ways concerned to attain it. She obviously followed her thoughts through by becoming king.[85]

The circumstantial *ḥr tpt-rꜣ wpw-išd* "upon the pronouncement of the 'divider-of-the-*išd*-tree" is universally linked with what precedes.[86] It disregards the fact that the preceding syntactic unit has temporal character and that the main statement is the pseudo-verbal clause *ib.i nṯry ḥr ḏꜥr m-ḫt*. It is this statement which the circumstantial *ḥr tpt-rꜣ* continues; in other words, *ḥꜣty bit ḫmt.n.f ḥḥ* is a parenthetical clause injected into the sentence.[87] It specifies that Hatshepsut's contemplation about the future followed a specific pronouncement connected with becoming king. The sequence of events as portrayed earlier[88] finds here its full corroboration.

The "pronouncement"[89] is ascribed to *wpw išd,* after whose mention there is no determinative. Lit., "the divider of the *išd*-tree," it is a function frequently assigned to Thoth in conjunction with a king's

[81]Egyptian distinguishes at least three forms of mental activity, namely *ḏd*, *kꜣ* and *ḫmt*, each one with a particular dimension.

[82]The nature of the *sḏm.n.f* as an indicator of a relative past is insufficiently recognized, as the form is largely taken in isolation and not in its syntactic setting.

[83]The two terms are sometimes difficult to separate, but A. Piankoff, op. cit. 7-13 is to be followed in considering *ib* as denoting the heart in a moral sense, while *ḥꜣty* is predominatingly the physical organ. This differentiatiion can be seen here only in a faint way.

[84]Gardiner rendered "the heart of the King of Lower Egypt took thought of eternity" which A. Burkhardt and Redford followed closely, while S. Ratié gave for it "mon coeur-charnel de Roi anticipant sur l'éternité."

[85]See further below, H. Goedicke, "Thumosis III's early Years," p. 124 ff.

[86]Gardiner: "the heart of the King of Lower Egypt took thought for eternity at the utterance of Him who inaugurated the ished-tree, (namely) Amun . . ." S. Ratié: "mon coeur-charnel de Roi anticipant sur l'éternité, selon la parole de celui qui inaugura l'arbre iched, Amon «Seigneur des millions d'annés...»; A. Burkhardt: "das Herz des Königs von Unterägypten denkt an die Ewigkeit entsprechend dem Ausspruch, der den heiligen Baum öffnet, (den Ausspruch) des Amun . . ."; Redford: "the heart of the king of Lower Egypt takes thought for eternity, at the injunction of him that planted the *ished*-tree, Amun . . ."

[87]The role of the parenthetical clause is insufficiently recognized in the grammatical studies, but cannot be pursued here.

[88]See above, p. 44.

[89]For *tpt-rꜣ* "pronouncement," cf. *Wb.* V 287; *Urk.* IV 165, 13; 322, 10.

ascent.[90] In the mundane process leading to the ascent of a king certainly no deity was involved; at the same time the function ascertained in the mythical sphere ought to have had its corollary in political reality. In short, the statement refers to the specific moment of the pronouncement of a king's ascent to the throne.

It was following this pivotal moment that Hatshepsut's thoughts turned to the future. What motivated her "divine heart" consists of two concerns which are quoted in detail: "Amun, Lord of millions, I myself shall magnify the order which is wanted for him, as I know that he lives by it. It is/be my bread! May I swallow its fragrance when I am one flesh with him, after he has caused me to exist in order to strengthen his magnificence in this land!"

n) The reference to Amun opens the quote of Hatshepsut's thoughts when she mused upon her ascent about the future.[91] The mention of Amun has to be recognized as anticipatory emphasis, a syntactic phenomenon recurrent in Hatshepsut's text.[92] It has to be stressed that Amun has here no epithets which would identify him as the god of Thebes.[93] The mention is also without a determinative. Instead the only epithet is *nb-ḥḥw* "lord of millions"[94] which reflects his universality without any local attachment.[95] The reflected supremacy has the particulars of a monistic divine concept. Its nature as "hidden one" transpires quite clearly as does the universal recognition. This emphasis on a monistic religion[96] seems to have a peak

[90]See W. Helck, *ZÄS* 82 (1958), 130 f. It might be that the Germanic tradition of the splitting of the world-ash has influenced some of the notions connected with this term. It should be noted that splitting trees is not a particular ancient Egyptian practice, partly due to the general shortage of wood suitable for splitting, partly due to a lack of appropriate tools for it. In addition, there is no indication that the royal ascent was in any way associated with the splitting of wood in general and of an *išd*-tree in particular. As far as there are any illustrations to the mythical act, they depict Thoth inscribing the name of the newly ascended king on a tree-leaf.

Because of the lack of a physical basis for the term *wpw-išd* it should be recognized as a metaphor or a pun. The verb *wp* has not only the meaning "to open by dividing" but also "to inform" (German "eröffnen") particularly in the role of the "messenger" (see Michel Vallogia, *Recherche sur les "messagers"* (wpwtyw) *dans les sources égyptiennes profanes* (1976), 8 ff.). This is also the role of Thoth in the mythical realm as messenger between the domains of the divine and of the mortals (cf. Hans Goedicke, *Die Darstellung des Horus*, BWZKM 11 (1982), 140 f.).. The object of the announcement should be recognized as *šd*, which could, of course, not be a tree. I suspect that *išd* is a petrified passive participle of the verb *šd* "to take," i.e., "the one who was taken," namely in the process of becoming king.

[91]Gardiner and Redford did not recognize this division and rather considered "Amun, lord of millions" as apposition to *wpw išd*. Nowhere is Amun indicated in this role, which is principally the one ascribed to Thoth. Not clear is A. Burkhardt's "entsprechend dem Ausspruch, der den heiligen Baum öffnet, (den Ausspruch) des Amun, des Herrn von Millionen von Jahren." It gives the impression of a tree-splitting pronouncement possibly attributed to Amun.

[92]See below, p. 93.

[93]Epithets of this nature are *nb-nswt-tꜣwy* or *nb-ipt-swt*, etc., cf. Eberhard Otto, *Osiris und Amun* (1966), 117; Louis-Antoine Christophe, *Temple d'Amon à Karnak*, BdE XXI (1955), and Kurt Sethe, *Amun und die Acht Urgötter von Hermopolis*, AAWBerlin 1929, 4, 66 8 ff., p. 10 ff.

[94]As far as I am aware, this divine epithet is limited to this occurrence. In its nature it can be compared to Zeker-Baʿl's views expressed to Wenamun (2,19 ff.) that Amun takes care of all those belonging to the Two Lands.

[95]Siegfried Morenz, *Die Heraufkunft des transzendenten Gottes in Ägypten*, SBAW 109/2 (1964), 37 ff.; Erik Hornung, *Der Eine und die Vielen* (1971), 37 ff.

[96]Its main features can be summarized as having a single godhead at its center from which everything spiritual emanates. In a notion of descent this Absolute, by definition transcendental, is reflected in a multitude of individual forces who are the deities with whom man is in contact: cf. Hans Goedicke, "Unity and Diversity in the Oldest Religion of Ancient Egypt," (1974), 205 ff; E. Hornung, op. cit. 37; Jan Assmann, *Moses the Egyptian* (1997), 23 ff.; 206 ff.

in Hatshepsut's reign during which the Theban Amun-Reʿ is the dominant feature of her religious orientation.[97]

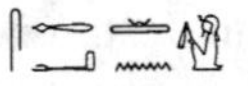 has been taken as a *sḏm.n.f*-form[98] which, however, leads to an illogical result. Hatshepsut has just made reference to her ascent as king, so that it would seem most inappropriate for her to speak of her magnifying the divine order in the past, which this verb-form would express[99] As she is describing her intentions at this occasion, the tenor has to be prospective. This makes it necessary to read the signs as *sʿꜣ.<i> n.i.*, i.e., "I shall for myself magnify the order." The verb-form should be recognized as a perfective *sḏm.f* with the suffix first person suppressed, followed by a *dativus ethicus*.[100]

While the reading *mꜣʿt* for  offers no problems, its meaningful translation is more difficult in this context.[101] Because the statement has a political overtone, I favor rendering it as "order" rather than "truth." It is qualified by  which has so far been taken as a *sḏmw.n.f*-relative-form.[102] Because of its elementary past meaning, this form would imply that the "order" which Hatshepsut is intending to carry out was invented only once in the past. As the order ought to prevail permanently, it has to be another verb form. There are two possible explanations: it is either to be read *mrt n.f*, i.e., a passive participle followed by a dative, or a perfective relative-form with the suffix first person suppressed. The assertion that the god lives by it would point to a change of subject. On the other hand, there are several cases in the text of omission of the suffix *.i*,[103] so that this could also seem a justifiable interpretation, requiring a translation"the order, which (I) wish for him." However, the god's demand is so superior to Hatshepsut's wish that the execution of maʿat has to be understood as an universal rule.

For the topic of the circumstantial clause, that the godhead lives from (the execution) of maʿat, see, J. Assmann, op. cit. 188 ff. For *ʿnḫ m*, "to live of something," see *Wb*. I 194, 5-6.

The notion of maʿat as sustenance is extended in the nominal *tꜣ.i pw* "it is my bread"; the fact that Hatshepsut claims that she lives on maʿat in the same way the godhead is sustained by it, corroborates that the earlier specification of maʿat has to be read *mrt n.f* "which is desired for him," i.e., that rightous behavior is what the godhead dwells on.

o) While maʿat is portrayed as the daily bread during lifetime, its full appreciation is anticipated when

[97]The only specific investigation of Hatshepsut's religious attitude is by S. Ratié, op. cit. 229-236, 318-322.

[98]Breasted: "I have made bright the truth which he loved"; Gardiner: "I magnified the Truth which he loved"; A. Burkhardt: "Ich habe die Maat, die er liebt, 'vergrößert'"; Redford: "I magnified *ma'at,* which he loves."

[99]There is no such a thing as a *sḏm.n.f*-form with present meaning.

[100]For the use of the *dativus ethicus* as a means to convey emphasis, see Gustave Lefebvre, *Grammaire de l'égyptien Classique*, BdE XII (1955), § 156; Adolf Erman, *Ägyptische Grammatik*3 (1928), § 437;

[101]There are, of course, numerous discussions about maʿat which is a central concept in the ancient Egyptian culture. It could suffice here to refer to Jan Assmann, *Ma'at* (1990).

[102]Gardiner, A. Burkhardt and Redford bypassed the indicated past by translating "which he loves," for which, however, there is no grammatical basis.

[103]It occurs in the preceding sentence and in the one following. It is an uninvestigated phenomenon, when the mention of the first person is omitted; cf. e.g., Hans Goedicke, *Pi(ankh)y in Egypt* (1998), 127.

Hatshepsut becomes one in being with the godhead. The pseudo-verbal clause *wn.kwỉ m ḥʿw wʿ ḥnʿ.f*, can only be circumstantial "when I am in one body with him" and not a main clause as Gardiner and Redford took it.[104] The passage does not refer to a physical divine paterinity, which appears to have been a later developed concepts, but rather to the prospect of emerging in the godhead after death.[105]

The prospect of bodily union with the divine has as its explanation the claim of a divine mission, namely, "to cause that his fame be strong in this land."[106] *Qft* "fame" appears to have here its earliest datable attestation. The etymological origin of the term, which replaces older *šfyt*, is a mystery. What it indicates is also unclear in the last analysis.

Section Three

"I am a [belonging] one of Atum [through knowing] Kheperi, who makes what is,p) one whom Reʿ intended at his designing that the lands be united under my supervision, and that Egypt and Desert (Black Land and Red Land) be under my dread!"q) My might be causing the foreigners to bow down, while the uraeus upon my brows making peaceful all the flat-landers for [me].r) El-Shawet and [*M*]*ỉww*—they do not hide from my Majesty. Punt shall overflow for me on fields whose trees bear fresh myrrh.s) The (desert) tracks which were closed because of the Two Ways shall be trodden again.t) My troops which had been neglected shall be supplied with excellent things.u)"

p) Against A. Burkhardt and Redford,[107] Gardiner's view that *ink* opens a new section would seem the only possible interpretation.[108] This point is of importance for the restoration of the small lacuna in the word following it. It defines Hatshepsut's relation to Atum[109] which has to be understood as unchangeable. This aspect was justly emphasized by Gardiner who ruled out a restoration [𓌸]𓇌. for which there is also not

[104]Gardiner: "I am one flesh with him"; Redford: "I was indeed of one flesh with him" which has the additional shortcoming of indicating it as a past reference. A. Burkhardt considered it a consecutive clause "Ich verschlucke ihren Tau, denn 'ich' bin doch eines Leibes mit ihm."

[105]The notion that the king as executor of the divine office mingles after death with the divine is first formulated in the opening of the Instructions of King Amenemher I; cf. Hans Goedicke, "The beginning of the Instructions of King Amenemhet", *JARCE* VII (1970), 15-21.

[106]Gardiner's "he bred me up to cause his fame to be powerful," A. Burkhardt's "Er schuf mich um zu veranlassen, daß sein Ansehen in diesem Land mächtig ist" and Redford's "he created me to magnify his renown in this land" insinuate aspects of Hatshepsut's later claim of a divine birth. The formulation with a subjective instead of a causative indicates that Hatshepsut was not to strengthen the divine fame, but rather to cause it to continue to be strong.

[107]A. Burkhardt had apparently problems with the text as she reduced it to 'Ich' bin [. . .] Atum [. . .] des Chepri, der tut, was ist," while Redford's "[as] master of Atum's [king]ship, in his name [of] Khopry who made what exists" cannot be reconciled with the Egyptian text.

[108]The independent pronoun cannot be part of a dependent clause. It rather has to be part of a statement of unalterable truth of permanent validity.

[109]It should be noted that Atum's mention is followed by a determinative while the previously refered to *Ỉmn* had none; cf. above p. 45.

enough space. Instead I propose restoring [𓈖]𓇌 "belonging one,"[110] i.e., "I am one of Atum." More difficult is the restoration of the second lacuna. Gardiner abstained from it, while Redford's "in his name Khopry" is epigraphically and theologically untenable. Khepery denotes Reᶜ in his mutable form in which he can be observed by man.[111] Epigraphically 𓅓 should be the preposition introducing a verb of which the initial 𓂋 is clear; it is followed by two thin vertical spaces, for which I propose 𓐍𓏛 as restoration. The resulting *m rḫ Ḫprỉ ỉrw ntt* requires the translation "through knowing/being aware of Kheperi who makes that what is."[112] The religiously oriented statement consists of Hatshepsut's claim, that she belongs to the godhead Atum through her knowledge of his visible form as Reᶜ.

q) The general reference to the creator "of what is" is the introduction of Hatshepsut's elaboration how her supreme decision is founded in the divine plan:[113] "(Inasfar as) Reᶜ had ordained (it) in his planning, all plot(-holders) altogether be under my supervision and the Black and Red Land be under my respect; my might be causing the foreign opponents to bow down and the uraeus on my brow be appeasing for <me> all (flat)-land(ers)."

Šꜣ.n Rᶜ has been taken either as a relative-form or as a narrative.[114] Both entail claims which have the character of sacrilegious blasphemy, because they would claim Hatshepsut's knowledge of divine decisions for which she could only hope but of which she could not be assured. In addition, the statement is clearly marked as past by the use of the *sḏm.n.f*-form, which also places it outside Hatshepsut's range. Instead of the assumption of knowledge of a divine decision, the reference to the divine plan makes sense when taken as a desired condition, i.e., assuming the divine had ordained so in his planning. In consequence, Hatshepsut insists that her intended rights be enacted.[115] For the notion of divine planning governing human

[110]For the nominal use of the nisbe-adjective, cf. Elmar Edel, *ZÄS* 84 (1959), 25. The same notion is expressed as *sꜣ-Rᶜ* "offspring of Reᶜ" since the Fourth Dynasty without implying any divine descent.

[111]For Khepery in his relation to Reᶜ, cf. Erik Hornung, *Die Nachtfahrt der Sonne* (1991), 185; idem, *Der Eine und die Vielen*, 88 f.

[112]Gardiner in contrast to Redford is correct in taking *ỉrw* as active participle and to render it "who makes what is" and not as retrospective, which would limit the creation to one point in the past.

[113]Other renderings are: "...whom Reᶜ predestined when he founded the lands, they being conjoined in my charge, the Black land and the Red land being subject to the dread of me, and my might causing the foreign countries to bow down, for the uraeus that is upon my brow tranquillizes for me all lands" (Gardiner); "... Rê assigna selon son plan les pays unis sous ma fonction; le Pays Noir et le Pays Rose me portent respect; ma puissance courbe (?) les contrées barbares; l'uraeus qui est à mon front protège tous pays" (S. Ratié); "Re hat bei seiner Schöpfung festgelegt, daß die Länder unter meiner Aufsicht zusammengefaßt sind, daß Ägypten und die 'Wüste' im 'Schrecken' vor mir sind, daß meine Macht die Fremdländer niederbeugt, denn die Schlange, die an meiner Stirn ist, 'beruhigt' für mich alle Länder" (A. Burkhardt); "Re, when he founded the lands, ordained that everything should be under my authority, that the Black Land and the Red [Land] should be in awe of me. My powers cow the foreign lands, the uraeus which is upon my brow terrorized all lands" (Redford).

[114]Gardiner: "I am ... whom Reᶜ had predestined when he founded the lands"; A. Burkhardt: "Re hat bei seiner Schöpfung festgelegt"; Redford: "Re, when he founded the lands ordained ..."

[115]For this kind of assumed condition, cf. *Urk.* IV 60, as discussed further in "Thutmosis III's early Years"; see pp. 122 f.

action, cf. Siegfried Morenz, *Untersuchungen zur Rolle des Schicksals in der ägyptischen Religion*, ASAW 52,1 (1960), passim.

Her claim of authority, in accord with divine planning, is expressed in two pairs of symmetrically built sentences. The first pair consists of two prepositional clauses, namely, *ỉdbw dmḏ ḥr ḥr.ỉ*, and *Kmt dšrt ḥr ḥryt.ỉ*, "the plot(-holder)s collectively be under my supervision" and "Black-land and Red-land be under my respect." Aside of the alliterative pun between *ḥr.ỉ* and *ḥryt.ỉ*, the two passages would seem to concern land. The association of *Kmt* and *Dšrt* "Black- and Red Land" would seem to include the entire world, but should be seen here primarily as the Egyptian realm comprising the Nile Valley proper and the adjoining desert as far as it was under political control.  traditionally read *ỉdbw*, "lands,"[116] makes sense only when understood as a reference to a specific type of land-holding and their holders. It has to refer to persons, because Hatshepsut's authority is over people rather than land plots. The Old Perfective *dmḏ* I consider solely as specification of **ỉdbw*.[117] These "plot-holders" are to be distinguished from the "land-owners" (*tꜣw*). While the latter appear to be "(permanent) land owners," *ỉdbw* appears to denote holders of riparian land, i.e., people who were assigned land on a temporary basis presumably in exchange for performing service.

r) The second pair of sentences are pseudo-verbal with *ḥr* + infinitive, thus indicating continuity. Both are formulated as expressions of Hatshepsut's authority, the first focusing on her "might" (*bꜣw*), the second on "the uraeus on her brow." In their indicated achievement they differ: the uraeus is the cause of contentment for her by all "landowners."[118] *Shryt* is clearly the infinitive of the causative three-radical verb.[119] The expressed notion is her acceptance as ruler, as symbolized by her wearing the uraeus. As only people can be made content, *tꜣw* should be recognized as denoting the owners of flat land, to be distinguished from the *ỉdbw* holders of riparian land. This positive attitude is juxtaposed to the application of "might" (*bꜣw*) which brings about the submission[120] (*sks*) by people identified as  . The first two

[116] *Wb.* I 153, 8-9 rendered it "Uferländereien, auch allgemein 'die Länder' im Gegensatz zu Ägypten." In Papyrus Wilbour it has been recognized as a kind of landholding; cf. Alan H. Gardiner, *The Wilbour Papyrus*, II (1948), 26; Sally L.D. Katary, *Land Tenure in the Ramesside Period* (1969), 73 understood *idb* to denote land that probably had the shape of the hieroglyphic sign in addition to have something to do with irrigation. It is not clear, if and how the term is related to *ỉdbw Ḥꜣw-nbw* occurring *Urk.* IV 21, 1 in the description of Ahhotep as "mistress of the shores of Hanebu" and *Urk.* IV 573, 1 "you shall rule the shores of Hanebu." For these two passages, cf. Jean Vercoutter, "Les Haou-Nebout", *BIFAO* 48 (1948), 136; 185; idem, "L'Égypte et le monde égéen préhellénique," *BdE* XXII, 1956, 27.

Gardiner by disregarding the parallelism joined the word with the preceding *snṯ.f* and rendered "Re predestined when he founded the lands, they being conjoined in my charge" in which he was followed by Redford as "Re, when he founded the lands, ordained that everything should be under my authority."

[117] Cf. Gardiner, *EG* § 317.

[118] Gardiner disregarded the prevailing parallelism and saw the second unit as explanation of the first: "for the uraeus that is upon my brow tranquilizes for me all lands." The implicit claim of universal recognition is indeed not supported by the historical facts. Redford's "the uraeus which is upon my brow trerrorrized all lands" is difficult to reconcile with the Egyptian text.

[119] Cf. *Urk.* IV 2156, 2

[120] For the causative *sks*, cf. *Wb.* IV 319, 3; the assumed use concerning "die besiegten Länder" is not born out by this occurrence.

signs have been taken as additional determinatives,[121] although hieroglyphic texts, different from hieratic ones, do not tend to use multiple determinatives. In addition, Hatshepsut has had no claim to "cow the foreign lands" (Redford). The signs are rather to be read *rq ḫꜣstyw* "the opposition of foreigners."[122] To sum up, Hatshepsut distinguishes two accomplishments in the domestic situation, one the suppression of foreign opponents in the country, the other, the satisfaction about her rule by the land owners.

s) After describing her domestic program, Hatshepsut turns to foreign topics. It is indicative that she does not approach them in belligerent terms, but that her concerns are basically commercial. As repeatedly in this text, the new thought is introduced by anticipatorily stated subjects, namely *Rꜣ-šꜣwt* and *<M>i͗ww*. They represent the two most important sources of raw material for the Egyptian society. The first, which should be read El-Shawet,[123] is attested since the Middle Kingdom as the name of a region which produces turquois in particular, but also antimony. It was inhabited by Semites who traded with Egypt.[124] All this suggests that el-Shawet should be recognized as the designation of the central and north-eastern part of the Sinai Peninsula. As a trading partner the region was significant for Egypt's economy in supplying turquois, antimony, and probably also copper. The other, which has been read *I͗ww* by Gardiner and Redford,[125] has also been assigned to the Sinai. It does not seem to have another attestation and it would be entirely unclear what raw material should have come from there. I rather wonder if this is not an error and the name should be identified with *Mi͗ww*.[126] This topographical term appears first under Kamose[127] and becomes frequently mentioned during the Eighteenth Dynasty. The area to which it applies is in the southern Nile Valley, where Thutmosis III hunted a rhinoceros.[128] A likely identification has been suggested by Karola Zibelius[129] as the Nile bent between the Third and Fourth Cataract. The area, which had Kerma as its center, came under Pharaonic control only during Thutmosis III's reign. Located to the south of the Pharaonic empire in Hatshepsut's time, it was the natural commercial bridge to Africa.

The verbal clause following the anticipatorily stated subjects, *n sdgꜣ.sn rn r ḥm.i*, has been taken as

[121] Faulkner, *CD* 252.

[122] For *rq*, cf. *Wb.* II 456. The indicated attitude should be recognized as internal oposition. It seems feasable that it is a compound term in which *ḫꜣstyw* serves as qualifier "foreign"; for this use of *ḫꜣst*, see as discussed by Paule Posener-Krieger, *Les archives du temple funéraire de Néferirkarê-Kakaï*, BdE LXV/1,(1976), 166 f.

[123] It was formerly read Roshawet (Gardiner and Redford); the first element, written , should be recognized as a transcription for the Semitic article *el*. This is corroborated by the occurrence of this topographical term as *Šꜣwt* (Henri Gauthier, *Dictionnaire géographique*, V (1928), 99; 130), i.e., without the article. For the term see further, Farouk Gomaà, *Die Besiedlung Ägyptens während des Mittleren Reiches*, II, TAVO B 66/2 (1987), 255; H. Gauthier, op. cit. III, 127; Jaroslav Černý, *The Inscriptions of Sinai*, II (1955), 3; J. R. Harris, *Lexicographical Studies in Ancient Egyptian Minerals*, VIO 54 (1961), 108.

[124] Wolfgang Helck, *Materialien zur Wirtschaftsgeschichte des Neuen Reiches* (1969), 995.

[125] The term occurs in this spelling in *CT* IV 46 j as source of gold, which would seem to eliminate any connection with Sinai and rather point to the Eastern Desert, as F. Gomaà, op, cit. 279 suggested..

[126] It should be noted that both terms are written with the hieroglyph , which is not a common phonetic indicator.

[127] Hans Goedicke, *Studies about Kamose and Ahmose* (1995), 20.

[128] *Urk.* IV 1246, 3-4.

[129] K. Zibelius, op. cit. 118 f.; cf. also William Y. Adams, *Nubia: Corrodor to Africa* (1977), 220 ff.

past.[130] Such a rendering injects a reference to the past into the reiteration of Hatshepsut's thoughts about the future at the time of her becoming king. In other words, it has to be realized that the sentence is prospective "not shall they be hidden from my Majesty" and not retrospective.[131]

Initially puzzling is Hatshepsut's next statement about Punt when met in its traditional rendering: "Pwenet overflows for me on the fields, its trees bearing fresh myrrh" (Gardiner).[132] Again, it is essential to keep in mind that the text describes Hatshepsut's thoughts at the time of her ascent to kingship. At that paramount moment she had no idea what was going on in Punt, nor was it of any consequence what fruits were there. A grammatical analysis shows that here again the subject, namely Punt, is anticipated. Different, however, from the preceding sentence, the predicate is an Old Perfective which is largely destroyed. Sethe[133] conjectured restoring , is an otherwise unattested spelling, especially for its lack of a determinative, but appears to be an ideographic writing with a phonetic complement. The ending reveals an Old Perfective, used optatively.[134] Because of the orthographic peculiarities, I propose restoring in the lacuna and to read the entire sentence *Pwnt [wn].ti n.i ḥr ꜣḥwt nhwt.s ḥr ꜥntyw wꜣḏ*, "May (a) Punt belong to me on fields whose trees are under green/fresh myrrh." When understood this way it emerges that Hatshepsut already at her ascent conceived of plans to produce myrrh in Egypt, a plan which she carried out in year nine.[135]

t) The final statements about Hatshepsut's projections at the time of her ascent are not directly associated with a topographical area. Only indirectly it emerges that they concern the region adjoining Egypt's northeast. Syntactically the passage is a pseudo-verbal clause like the preceding one and should thus be understood as having a hortative connotation. It has always been understood as concerning interrupted trade-routes which Hatshepsut opened again.[136] It is not only the lack of a geographical specification about the envisioned commercial contacts that has to be resolved, but also the specifics of the words used in this sentence. *Mṯnw* denotes specifically the desert track on which especially the bedouin

[130] Gardiner: "Roshawet and Iuu have not remained hidden from my august person"; S. Ratié: "Rochaout et Iouou ne se cachent plus de Ma Majesté"; A. Burkhardt: "*R'--šꜣw-t* und *'Iw-w* blieben vor Meiner Majestät nicht verborgen"; Redford: "Ro-shawet and Iww, they have not been hidden from my Majesty."

[131] It is difficult to render the verb *sdgꜣ* in a meaningful fashion. As areas do not hide themselves the meaning is more likely to be in the vein of being inaccessible. The connotation is without doubt in a commercial vein, i.e., to refrain from participation in commerce.

[132] S. Ratié "Pount (resplendit) pour moi sur les champs et les arbres portant l'oliban frais"; A. Burkhardt: "Punt ist 'erglänzt' für mich auf den Feldern, seine Myrrhenbäume tragen frische Myrrhen"; Redford: "Pwenet overflows for me with fields of trees bearing fresh myrrh."

[133] *Urk.* IV 385, note b. His emendation is listed *Wb.* I 294, 12 with the meaning "überquellen."

[134] For this use, see Gardiner, *EG* § 313.

[135] For the Punt expedition sponsored and memorialized by Hatshepsut, cf. S. Ratié, op. cit. 139-161.

[136] Gardiner rendered it factitive "the roads that were blocked on both sides are (now) trodden"; similarly S. Ratié "les chemins qui étaient fermés de chaque côté sont foulés"; A. Burkhardt "Die Wege, die auf beiden Seiten vesperrt waren, sind nun zu betreten"; Redford "The roads that were (formaerly) blocked on all sides, are (now) trodden."

moves.[137] When realizing the specific nature of the paths, it becomes clear that they are not to be seen within Egypt, but rather outside of it. These "tracks" are the arteries for over-land commerce, which in the case of Egypt is basically to the northeast. Their condition is described as *wnw šri*, "which had been blocked." For *šri*, which has the specific connotation of the barring of passages by obstacles,[138] cf. *Wb.* IV 527, 12-13; H. F. Lutz, *Egyptian Tomb Steles*, (1927), pl. 34; *JEA* 35 (1949), pl, IV, 16. As for *wꜣty*, its previous rendering as "both sides" (Gardiner) and "all sides" (Redford) makes no sense, especially after the above improvements in the understanding of *šri*. Meaning literally "the two ways" it apparently refers to two very specific routes, which commenced at Tell ed-Dabʿa to judge from its name *Rꜣ-wꜣty*;[139] from there they run northeastwards to the actual frontier point at *Ṯl*, i.e., Tell el-Anwar.[140] The mention of these "two roads" is introduced by the preposition *ḥr*, which specifies the reason for the interruption of the commerce. In other words, it is "because of the Two Roads" or "the (commercial) tracks which had been blocked on the Two Roads" that no goods had moved to the northeast. This detail helps understand Hatshepsut's statement. The commercial routes were disrupted in a particular section, namely at the easternmost fringe of the Egyptian realm, a disruption that cannot be due to human cause. The later specifications make it clear that it was this area which was impacted by a natural desaster.[141]

The predicate is the Old Perfective , which, as in previous sentences, is most likely to be understood hortatively.[142] In connection with *mṯnw*, "paths," *ḥwi* should be recognized as "to tread," but with the specific connotation of "forcing a way" which otherwise is difficult to use.[143] This particular meaning suits especially in the indicated case, because it refers to the traditional commercial paths which will be "forced open (again)" after they had been barred because of what happened to the "Two-ways."

[137] This meaning transpires from *mṯnw* as the word for the bedouin sheikh; cf. *Wb.* II 176, 10. The metaphorical use of *mṯn* for the life's path should be understood on this basis, that it is not a clearly laid out road, but that it is rather a pursuit through alien terrain.

[138] The choice of *šri* seems significant, because it implies that the commercial routes were impassible because of the presence of physical obstacles. Obviously they had not existed always, but appeared only recently to the detriment of commerce. To have physical obstacles that made trade-routes unpassible requires a cause which cannot be man, thus requiring an impact of nature to create the problem.

[139] For *Rꜣ-wꜣty* as name and the two roads which commenced there, see Hans Goedicke, "Two Inscriptions from Tell ed-Dabʿa., *BACE* 13 (2002), 1 ff.; idem, ""The Building Inscription from Tell ed-Dabʿa of the Time of Sesostris III," *Ä&L* XII (2002),

[140] For the location of Egypt's eastern frontier at the time of Hatshepsut the passing of *Ṯl* at the start of Thutmosis III's first campaign provides a definite indication; cf., Hans Goedicke, *The Battle of Megiddo* (2000), 9 f.

[141] See further below, pp. 99 ff.

[142] The alternative would be taking it as an accomplishment, i.e., "the paths, which had been blocked because of the Two Roads were trodden (again)," which would remove the passage away from Hatshepsut's reflections at the time of her ascent and would rather make it part of Hatshepsut's review of her achievements since she had become king. There is no clear indication were such thoughts would begin here, especially since a link with her person would seem lacking. A possibility would seem to commence the reporting section with *iw ʿrr tpt ḥꜣt.i ḥr sryt n.(i) tꜣw nbw* "as the uraeus which is upon my brow is pleasing all (flat)land(ers), El-Shaut and <M>iuu can no longer hide themselves from my Majesty,"

It would seem curious that Hatshepsut places such importance on her international commercial contacts that they would be the first item of her achievements.

[143] *JEA* 22 (1956), 38; *Wb.* III 47, 23-24.

u) By realizing that the previous statement does not concern the past reopening of commercial links, as has been generally assumed,[144] but rather Hatshepsut's intentions at the moment of her ascent, the overall syntactic composition gains greatly in clarity. The listing of her anticipations should not be seen as two isolated statements, but rather as an integrated pair in parallel to the rest of her account. As this final sentence concerns people in Hatshepsut's military employ, it would seem a justified assumption that the people in the complementary clause were of the same occupation.

As simple as the passage would seem, it requires some fundamental reflections. The entire section of the text recounts Hatshepsut's intentions at the time of her ascent. This excludes any mention of her coronation as an event of the past. It also rules out any comparison between past and present attitudes as is generally assumed. In other words, what begins with *ḏr ḫꜥt.i m nswt* is not part of this sentence but belongs to what follows as an adverbial adjunct anticipatorily stated for reasons of emphasis.[145] Furthermore, the sentence follows the same general pattern found also in those preceding it, i.e., it is basically a pseudo-verbal clause with an extended subject at the opening. 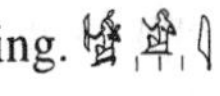 might thus best be rendered as "my soldiers" rather than "my army."[146]

The hortative predicate of this sentence is clearly *ꜥpr.w ḥr špss(.i)*, "(they) shall be supplied with (my) excellent things."[147] The contrast to the aspired support of the military is indicated by 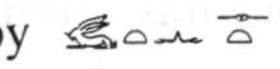 which has been generally taken as the particle *wnt* followed by a negative **n n.st*. As is well known, the enclitic use of the particle *wnt* is almost exclusively restricted to cases after the independent pronoun first person.[148] Its occurrence in the given context would be as much a grammatical novelty as the presumed negative statement **n n.st*, dependent on an anticipatorily stated subject. The grammatical and also the semantic incongruities vanish by reading the sentence *mnfyt.i wnt.n(.i) śt ꜥpr ḥr špss*, "my army, which I have neglected, shall be equipped with excellent things." The crucial word  I take as a relative-form of the verb *wn* "to neglect"[149] with a determinative not attested elsewhere, but certainly commensurate. The resulting statement congrues with the preceding one. Both express Hatshepsut's change of mind concerning the military or some of it. After rejecting them earlier, she decides to come to terms with them, domestically by improving their income and by allowing some that had been expelled to return to service.

[144] Former renderings are "my troops which (formerly) had nothing, are (now) equipped with the finest things since my accession as king" (Gardiner and Redford); "Mon armée qui n'avait pas d'équipement, elle est chargée de richesse depuis que je me suis levée en Roi" (S. Ratiée); "Mein Heer, das nicht ausgerüstet war, besitzt nun Herrlichkeiten, seit ich als König erschienen bin" (A. Burkhardt).

[145] See below, p. 93.

[146] Because of the following pronoun  Gardiner considered a reading *mnfyt* possible. However, the Old Perfective *ꜥpr* has no feminine ending, so that *st* might better be taken as a collective.

[147] It is not clear what is to be understood under the term *špss*, especially because it has no determinative. I have qualms about rendering it as "riches," because soldiers are hardly supplied in this fashion. To keep it as indifferent as possible the rendering "excellent things" is offered here.

[148] Gardiner, *EG* § 249.

[149] See *Wb.* I 214, 1.

Section Four

"Since my appearance as king, the temple of the Lady of Qusae which had fallen into oblivion, the earth had swallowed its noble sanctuary.[v] A/the child could dance on its roof as there was no tradition, which would cause respect.[w] As crooks were accounting the 'damage' dishonestly, there were indeed not its date of appearances.[x] I consecrated it, when it was built anew. I made her guiding serpent statue of gold in order to protect her city out of the ark for land-procession."[y]

v) After delineating her thoughts or intentions at the time of her ascent, in an entirely new section Hatshepsut lists her accomplishments since becoming king. A certain apologetic overtone is difficult to overlook and might be due to some discrepancy between her intentions and their realization. As a marker of the change of topic, the text uses the rare syntactic measure of placing the adverbial phrase at the beginning of the sentence in order to achieve maximum emphasis.[150] In short, *ḏr ḫꜥt.ỉm nswt* "since my appearance as king" is, different from earlier translations, to be recognized as the opener of a new section. For *ḫꜥ m nswt* "to appear as king," cf. Margit Schunck, *Untersuchungen zum Wortstamm* ḫꜥ (1985), 73.[151]

Despite this introduction, the text continues in the vein of anticipation; the insistance on its use is more than a literary device and is most likely a reflection of Hatshepsut's diction.[152] Her review of pious acts commences with "the temple of the mistress of Qusae." The goddess associated traditionally with Qusae is Hathor,[153] although her name is not mentioned at all. The mention of the town, which lies approximately 450 kilometers north of Thebes on the other side of the Nile, is interesting. At the time of Kamose it marked the limit of the realm of the Hyksos ruler Apophis.[154] Since then almost 80 years had past and it would be difficult to ascribe the delapidated state of the snactuary to the Hyksos. Why Hatshepsut displays interest in this place, as well as the Speos Artemidos 45 kilometers further south on the eastern side[155] and the Hare-nome with Hermopolis as its center on the western side is not really disclosed. It could be that this report about religious activity had been taken out from a larger document dealing with the entire country and that its display at the Speos included also the two adjoining places of attention, namely Qusae to the south and Hermopolis to the north. The detailed description of the state of the Qusae sanctuary makes it

[150]For this construction, cf. Gardiner, *EG* § 148.

If *ḏr ḫꜥt* does not belong to the preceding as *"my military, which I had neglected is equipped with excellent things since my appearance as king," the division between the past inattention and the present improved conditions becomes isolated from their specific cause.

[151]It can not be emphasized enough that the "official" terminology for the royal ascent is *ḫꜥ m nswt* which makes it clear that the royal designation is *nswt* and that it has basically nothing to do with a partial rulership limited to Upper Egypt.

[152]Cf. further below, p. 93.

[153]Cf. Schafik Allam, *Beiträge zum Hathorkult (bis zum Ende des Mittleren Reiches)*, MÄS 4 (1963), 23-41.

[154]H. Goedicke, *Studies about Kamose and Ahmose*, 44.

[155]Dieter Kessler, *Historische Topographie der Region zwischen Mallawi und Samalut*, RAVO B/30 (1981), 245 ff.; Farouk Gomaà, *Die Besiedlung Ägyptens während des Mittleren Reiches*, TAVO B/66, 281 ff.

clear that the decay occurred over a long period of time and that none of her predecessors was interested in repairing it.[156]

w) The description of the physical conditions introduces its consequences; the conclusion states the remedial measures of Hatshepsut. It is generally assumed that the section is narrative,[157] i.e., the decay was complete. The idiom *wꜣ r* also indicates an ongoing tendency[158] as well as its completion. As *fḫ* means lit. "to dissolve," the situation appears to be more in the direction of disfunctioning than of physical disintegration.[159] What really happened is stated in two bipartite clauses, one dealing with the purely physical conditions, the other with the moral collapse. The statement "after the earth has swallowed its august sanctum" describes the material precondition, which, however, is not necessarily fulfilled; for the second part it says, "a/the child can always jump around on its roof." The latter is an anticipated vision, which not necessarily had taken place. Even more unclear is the exact nature of this vision. It would seem difficult to imagine how an ancient Egyptian temple would be swallowed up by the earth. Taking one of the smaller sanctuaries as a model, it would require an accumulation of 3-4 meters of dirt to achieve this. While such an accumulation is, indeed, possible over centuries, the possible time range in this case would in all likelihood have been considerable shorter. No natural desaster could be envisioned in Middle Egypt causing it and there is no indication that human destruction was responsible for it either. As a result, the image of the earth swallowing the temple of the Lady of Qus should best be seen as a worst case scenario and not as a fact. Part of this disturbing vision is the misuse of the sanctury as playground for a child. A number of details in this statement deserve attention. First, the verb *ḫb*, "to jump around" is an imperfective *sḏm.f*, i.e., it does not express a past but a continuous ongoing activity. Second, the term *ḥꜥꜣw* is rather unusual and denotes, as far as can be determined, a child of approximately 10 years.[160] Third, the text makes reference to only a single child and not a plural. The envisioned place of exercise, namely the "roof" of the shrine,[161] might have a special significance, which is not known. However, before this situation could have come about Hatshepsut acted.

Two features might be of, so far undeterminable, significance: One is that Qusae, specifically the Hathor temple, was again the border between the North and the South, i.e. Thebes, as it had been in the Seventeenth Dynasty. The other, Hatshepsut's political antagonist Thutmosis III was at the time of youthful age. If and what this means in this context is obscure. In short, Hatshepsut's effort might have been

[156] Although there is no tangible information available, the sudden interest of Hatshepsut in Qusai might have something to do with the role of this place as demarkation between the Theban rulers of the Seventeenth Dynasty and the Hyksos in Avaris. Considering the fact that there are practically no known monuments of Hatshepsut in the North, one could wonder if she focussed on Qusae as the northern limit of the ideal Theban realm.

[157] Gardiner: "The temple . . . which was fallen into dissolution"; A. Burkhardt: "Der Tempel . . . war zerfallen"; Redord: "The temple . . .which had fallen into ruin."

[158] *Wb*. I 246, 5-7; cf. also Alan H. Gardiner, *Admonitions of an Egyptian Sage* (1909), 52 f.

[159] The latter would rather be expressed by the verb *wꜣs*, as in *Urk*. IV 102, 3; 169, 11.

[160] *Wb*. III 42, 1 which indicates that it denotes a child older than a *nḏs*; cf. also *CT* V 258 f.; Turin 1447.

[161] For *tp-ḥwt*, Alan H. Gardiner, *Ancient Egyptian Onomastica*, II, 216*.

concerned with the deliniation between her and Thutmosis III's realm, possibly in anticipation of the eventual reconcilliation which occurred in Year 15.

The second argument brought forth by Hatshepsut is equally intriguing: "without a *qrḥt*, that she causes respect, crooks are accounting storm-devastations inaccurately:, not even the days of *sḫʿw*. After I consecrated it, when it is built anew, I will fashion its guiding serpent-statue of gold [. . . ?] in order to protect her town out of the ark of land-procession."[162]

x) As in the other clause about the consequences of the disconcern for the sanctuary at Qusae, this statement is not a narrative describing past happanings, but it is rather a projection of possible developments. The envisioned problem is described as *ḥwrw ḥr ḏʿḏʿ m nwd n-ms sww sḫʿw*, a sentence with several lexicographical problems. The subject of the envisioned objectionable activity is the plural *ḥwrw* which should be noted in contrast to the singular *ḥʿ3w* of the parallel clause. The term *ḥwrw* does not primarily indicate social inferiority,[163] but rather a moral one.[164] Neither the background nor the ambition of these *ḥwrw* is indicated. What they are accused of is indicated as *ip* "to count." While this is a material process, the objection concerns the performance *m nwdw* "inaccurately."[165] The crux is, of course, the meaning of the word *ḏʿḏʿ* which is the object of the counting (*ip*). In this form it is a *hapax*, which, however, appears to be a reduplication, presumably to indicate intensity. Although it can hardly be more than an educated guess, I am inclined to link it with the noun *ḏʿ*, "storm"[166] and the verb *ḏʿ* "to be devastated."[167] The result would be a term for "storm devastation" without being able to define it in any way, such as extent, cause and severity. It is obvious that it refers to something specific and that the consequences in view of the pseudo-verbal construction with *ḥr* + infinitive were still being felt.

The complaint about inaccurate accounting is extended in one particular aspect, indicated by *n-ms sww.s ḫʿw*. The introductory *n-ms* I take as negative counterpart to the affirmative *iw-ms* "surely";[168] the implicit emphasis leads to the rendering "not even." As for *sww.s ḫʿw* it has caused problems: Breasted rendered it "no processions marched," Gardiner as "its appointed festivals not being celebrated" and

[162] Other renderings are: "The tutelary serpent-goddess affrighted not, and men of low station accounted . . . as crockedness (?), it appointed festivals not being celebrated. I hallowed it, built anew, and I sculptured her sacred image of gold to protct her city in a bark of land-procession" (Gardiner); "Nicht gab es die Urschlange, die Schrecken verbreitet hätte. Die Armen zählten Lockeres beim Wanken (der Mauern), und seine (= des Tempels) (Fest-)Zeiten wurden nicht mehr gefeiert. Ich aber heiligte ihn, indem er von neuem erbaut wurde, ich bildete sein Kultbild aus Gold, damit sie seine Stadt schütze in der Barke für die Prozession" (A. Burkhardt); "the 'cavern-serpent' produced no respect and common folk evilly (?) reckoned . . . and there were not even festival-appearance days!—I (re)-consecrated it and it was built anew; I fashioned her cult image of gold to protect her city in the cult-boat of the land."

[163] Gardiner rendered it as "men of low station" and Redford as "common folk."

[164] Cf. *Urk.* IV 122, 15; also Hans Goedicke, *The Protocol of Neferyt* (1977), 123; Sinuhe B 227.

[165] *Wb.* II 225, 8-9; cf. also Peasant B 1, 92; 262. The prepositional expression should be recognized as an adverb; cf. Gardiner, *EG* § 205, 3.

[166] *Wb.* V 533 f.; cf. also Hans Goedicke, *Die Geschichte des Schiffbrüchigen*, ÄA 30 (1974),

[167] *Wb* V 534, 12; Kitchen, *Ramesside Inscriptions* IV 3, 7 (= Mariette, *Karnak*, 52, 8).

[168] Gardiner, *EG* § 251.

Redford as "and there were not even festival-appearance days." While *sww* "(time = days)"[169] would seem clear, the selective emphasis resulting from *n-ms* establishes an inner connex between *sww.s ḫʿw* and *ḏʿḏʿ* with the latter constituting the more inclusive term. The "inaccurate accounting" by dishonest people (*ḥwrw*) might be related with the absence of "her days of appearance," i.e., days of procession by the deity.

Upon second thought, the parallelism is between *ꜣbb ḫʿꜣw ḥr tp ḥwt.s* closed by *n qrḥt di.s nrw* and *ḥwrw ḥr ip ḏʿḏʿ m nwd* closed by *n-ms sww.s ˙ḫʿw*, but I am not clear what this means, especially in regard to the sanctuary of the Lady of Qus. Equally puzzling are the two kinds of evil-doers, with the difference that one is singular, the other plural. As speculation, one could think concerning the single boy of Thutmosis III and the *ḥwrw* as his followers. During the final reviewing of the text it occurred to me that *ip* might not be used here for an enumerating process but rather in the sense of "to account for," i.e., to recognize the impact of something in a reaction. In this case the people evaluated as *ḥwrw* did not take the consequences of the event described as *ḏʿḏʿ* into account in their attitude to Hatshepsut. But what this has to do with Qus escapes me, except that Qus might have been reinstated as division point between north and south, a possibility that could draw support from the worship of Hathor there.[170]

y)The measures intended by Hatshepsut in the face of the envisioned problems are equally unclear in their significance. It would appear that Hatshepsut consecrated the "sanctuary of the Lady of Qus" after it had been built anew, which does match exactly the ealier claim that it had fallen in disuse. Her intention to have made a "guiding serpent"[171] of gold might be more than just a pious decoration for the divine ark. If the blank end of the line[172] can be disregarded, the purpose of the snake statuette was "to protect her town from the ark for land travel" could give the impression of a military standard[173] or should rather be recognized as a religious emblem mounted on the conveyance of the deity. The particular conveyance, namely a divine ark "for ( ) the travel of the land" is curious and indicates a distinction from one used on the water, i.e., Nile travel. The "ark" (s) as conveyance of divine images has not only a long history in Egypt,[174] but has in the "ark of conveyance" of Israel its parallel which has also some social as well as

[169]Despite Gardiner's criticism, the word is listed in *Wb.* IV 57. He considered after it as suffix, which, however, would entail problems. The last feminine noun preceding it is *qrḥt*, which would not be a likely term associated with "time." In such a case an inidirect genitive could be expected between the two nouns, such as **sww.s n ḫʿw*.

[170]Of particular interest in this connection is the mention of "Hathor, mistress of Qusae" in an inscription of *Ḏḥwty* dating to the reign of Hatshepsut (*Urk.* IV 432, 9) in conjunction with Bastis residing in Bubastis.

[171]For *sšm(t)*, cf. *Urk.* IV 267, 9 *swḏ.n.f n.f sšmt.f* "he dedicated to him his *sšmt*-snake" praising Thutmosis I's deed for Amun.

[172]There are three blank endings of columns in this text which seem to have no impact on the continuity of the text; this could be due to simultaneous inscribing of the text on the stone, i.e., that several masons were working at the same time and that their alligment did not match correctly.

[173]R.O. Faulkner, "Egyptian Military Standards," *JEA* 27 (1941), 12-18.

[174]The written documentation commences in the Archaic Period, but the most detailed information dates to the New Kingdom and later; see *LÄ* I 619-625

military function. For uraei as part of a processional ark, see e.g., P.:Lacau–H. Chevrier, *Une chapelle d'Hatchepsout à Karnak*, pl. 226.[175]

Section Five

"Pakhet, the Great, who roams the wadis in the midst of the East, [she opened] the roads for the water-torrent without drenching me, in order to catch the water.z) I made her a shrine by dig[ging a rock-chapel] for the Ennead of her gods. The doors were of acacia-wood inlaid with copper, in order that [it be closed, except for the performance of the] seasonal [offering] as the priest had learned its time."aa)

z) There is a distinct difference between the first and the second pious project of Hatshepsut. The first one concentrates on a sanctuary without identifying its deity by name, the second focusses first on a specific goddess and secondarily on Hatshepsut's deed. There is no apparent reason for the difference, except that in the latter case the sanctuary erected by Hatshepsut had not existed before, while the one in Qus is described as a restoration. The goddess *P(ꜣ)ḫt* is first mentioned at Beni Hasan[176] which is, of course, close to the Speos Artemidos. The name seems to be a derivate of the verb *pꜣḫ*, "to scratch".[177] In her terriomorph representation as lioness she reflects her violent nature, which would agree with the militant background of the people whose graves are at Beni Hasan.[178] The extent of her recognition is dubious and was apparently not universal.

The qualities focussed upon are twofold: one is her "roaming the wadis, that are in the midst of the East."[179] Why Pakhet was eventually worshipped at the Speos Artemidos is most probably connected with the Batn el-Baqara which formed an access towards the East.[180] It is not certain if her role there is to be understood as being protective, or if she is rather to be envisioned as representing the natural forces prevailing there.

The second attribute, though marred by a lacuna, is of particular interest. Gardiner, A. Burkhardt and

[175]The Ark of Covenant has been considered an Israelite creation closely associated with Moses' Egyptian aspects; cf. Jan Assmann, *Moses the Egyptian* (1997), 73.

[176]*Beni Hasan* I 25, 18; 24 (indicating a shrine); *Urk.* IV 286, 10; cf. A.H. Gardiner, *Ancient Egyptian Onomastica*, II, 89 f.*

[177]*Wb.* I 498, 13; *Pyr.* 440 d; cf. also Hermann Kees, *MIO* 6 (1958), 162.

[178]Cf, Hans Goedicke, "Abi-Sha(i)'s Representation in Beni Hasan," *JARCE* XXI (1984), 203-6.

[179]*Ḫnst inwt ḥry-ibt Ꜣbtt* ndicates her lack of a firm center. She is specifically associated with the "East" without a clear geographical delineation. This applies especially to the northern and southern limits, i.e., if *Ꜣbtt* denotes a defined area. On the other hand, the mention of *ḥry-ibt* might be of significance. If *Ꜣbtt* is understood as the entire east known to the Egyptians, the term could comprise the Levant as well as the Eastern Desert; the central part would then be the northern Sinai coast, i.e. , the area east of Pelusium.

[180]Cf. Hans Goedicke, *JARCE* XXI (1984), 204, note 11.

Redford envisioned her beneficial activity concerning "rain-swept roads,"[181] which is difficult to reconcile with her practice of "roaming the wadis." In the regretable lacuna at the beginning ought to be a participle parallel to the one in the other clause. Sethe restored it as  which is the basis for Redford's rendering. Despite some qualms about the assumed orthography of *wpt*, I cannot think of a more suitable restoration. *Wp wꜣt*, "to open roads," in the sense of making them accessible, is a recurrent attribute of deities.[182] The roads Pakhet is credited to have opened are specified as *snmw*. The term occurs only once more as a figure of speech describing the carnage Thutmosis I generated in his campaign of year 2 at the Third Cataract:[183] "their gore was like flowing torrents." Gardiner's notion of "rain-swept roads" does not take the geographical facts into account. It might be nice to talk of rain-swept roads in England, but any form of torrent in the desert washes away anything that might resemble a road. The term conveys the violence and destructiveness of a torrent without reflecting the hydrological specifics of its cause. Either epigraphically or factually the two words *wꜣwt* and *snmw* should be seperated by a dative *n* "for" or the preposition *r*. The latter is less likely because of the following *r ẖnp mw*, which continues the sentence after the parenthetical *nn ỉbḥw.ỉ*.[184]

Different from previous translations[185] I insist on taking as a writing of the suffix first person.[186] As for *ỉbḥ*, it is attested with two meanings which are diametrically opposed: it expresses the pouring of liquid but also the resulting condition of being excessively wet.[187] It is the latter which I see here used as passive *sḏm.f* "without my being suffused."[188] In other words, Hatshepsut claims that Pakhet "opened the roads <for> the torrent" without her being impacted by the flood.

When realizing *nn ỉbḥw.ỉ* as a parenthesis, the significance of *r ẖnp mw* becomes instantly clear.[189] The

[181] Gardiner: "[and who] . . the rain-swept roads"; A. Burkhardt: "und regenüberflutete Wege [gangbar macht]"; Redford: "who opens the rain-swept roads."

[182] See *Wb*. I 300 IV; the activity is primarily associated with Wepwawet and Neith, both in some ways belligerent of nature.

[183] *Urk*. IV 84, 9; cf. *Wb*. IV 165, 11-12 translates it as "Regenflut, Regenströme" which would hardly suit the hydrographic situation in southern Nubia.

Considering the setting, *ḥwyt* makes little sense as "rain" except when imagined as a cloud-burst. It might be good to remember that the first intrusion of the Mediterranean Sea into the eastern Delta was at the time not yet 50 years past, a span that might very well be remembered.

[184] Parenthesis as well as anticipation are a recurrent phenomenon of the text and appear to reflect Hatshepsut's personal diction; cf. below p. 93.

[185] Gardiner: "there being no libationer who came (?) to pour water (?)"; A. Burkhardt: "Es gab keinen Priester, um (ihr?) Wasser zu spenden"; Redford: "(for whom ?) there was no libationer to pour water."

[186] Gardiner considered a possible emendation of to for which there is no justification. If it would refer to an officiating person the determinative could be expected.

[187] *Wb*. I 64, 6-9; Faulkner, *CD* 16; Neferyt 52 (cf. H. Goedicke, *The Protocol of Neferyt*, 116).

[188] For the construction, cf. Gardiner, *EG* § 307, 11 Helmut Satzinger, *Die negativen Konstruktionen im Alt- und Mitteläg yptischen*, MÄS 12 (1968), § 51.

[189] Previous translators did not recognize the parenthetical nature and thus attached *r ẖnp mw* to the preceding. The result was, as Gardiner put it,"very obscure" entertaining the question "was it meant that the place was half inundated by the rains, so that no libationer was required in the temple to pour water?". It is only afterwards that the text speaks of the building of a shrine, which rules out the notion of a regular libation service. The situation at the Speos Artemidos is such, that any degree of inundation would seem physically impossible.

verb *ʿẖnp* is well attested with the meaning "to snatch, to catch,"[190] which applies here as well. Object of the catching is "the water" which refers back to the "torrent" mentioned earlier in the sentence. In other words, Pakhet is credited not only with opening the roads, i.e., guiding the torrent, but also with the intent to catch the water for the benefit of Hatshepsut, so that she, i.e., her realm, was not affected by the torrent.

aa) In recognition, or probably better out of gratitude, Hatshepsut built a shrine for the goddess who until then had no permanent abode, at least not in the place. It deserves noticing, that Hatshepsut made a *ḥwt*, i.e., an encampment, and not a *ḥwt-nṯr*, "sanctuary."[191] The description of the sanctuary contains several gaps, but they do not present unsurmountable obstacles.[192] Sethe's old restoration [ ]T *n psḏt.s* is principally convincing. Gardiner's conjecture "worthy" would seem to lack any support, while Redford's "from the ground up" in reference to "readying foundations, sacred lake, etc." disagrees with the physical facts of the Pakhet sanctuary at the Speos Artemidos, to which the passage unquestionably refers. As a description of the Speos any "digging" ought to concern the rock-cut nature of the shrine.[193] It should also be kept in mind that the sanctuary was built for Pakhet (*ḥwt.s*) and not for her ennead. The latter refers rather to the extent of the goddess' spiritual power, i.e., the eastern gebel.[194] The extant 𓈖 is probably datival, requiring a restoration *m šꜣ[d ḏw] n psḏt nṯrw.s*, "by dig[ging the gebel] for the ennead of her gods."

"Doors of acacia-wood," are mentioned first in the First Intermediate Period in Dendera; cf. Henry G. Fischer, *Dendera in the Third Millennium* (1968), 158. Those doors were sheethed with copper, a way to enhance their durability.[195] The ensuing lacuna of almost 8 squares has been partially translated by Gardiner "in order (?) to be . . . at the due season," by A. Burkhardt as ". . .] bis zur rechten Zeit," while Redford has "with the scenes [thereof being of . . .] at the (proper) season." The context does not accord with a special mention of any decoration of the rock-shrine's doors. The emphasis on "proper time" (*tr*)[196] points to a restricted use of the sanctuary, a notion supported by the sentence about "its time" (*nw.s*) following it. As a

[190] *Wb.* III 290, 5-13; Faulkner, *CD* 192. The meaning "to pour water" is solely based on the passage under discussion which should be understood in the same way as the verb's other occurrences.

[191] Cf. P. Spencer, op. cit. 21 ff.; 42 ff.

[192] Breasted, *AR* § 301: "I made her temple with that which was due to her ennead of gods. The doors were of acacia wood, fitted with bronze . . ."; Gardiner: "I made her temple worthy (?) . . . for her Ennead, the doors of acacia inlaid with copper in order (?) to be . . ."; A. Borchardt: "Ich aber machte ihren Tempel 'als Höhle' [. . .] für ihre Götterneunheit, die Türen aus Akazienholz, überzogen mit Kupfer [. . .? . . .]"; Redford: "I made her temple from the gr[ound up . . .] for her ennead, the doors being of acacia with bronze bands, with the scenes [thereof being of . . .]."

[193] For *šꜣd* for digging a shrine out of the natural rock, cf. *Wb.* IV 415, 1-2; especially Kitchen, *RI* II 765, 14 , concerning the hallowing of the Abu Simbel temple.

[194] W. Barta, *Untersuchungen zum Götterkreis der Neunheit*, 59 f. It deserves noticing that the notion of an ennead, one associated with Thebes, the other with Abydos occurs in the reign of Thutmosis I (*Urk.* IV 86, 13; 99, 3).

[195] *Wb.* II 247, 1 correctly renders it "beschlagen sein mit Kupfer," while Faulkner, *CD* 143 gives for it "band door with metal" leading to Redford's "doors . . . with bronze bands.:" The use of metal sheething for wooden doors is used especially as enhancing the protection, cf. Otto Königsberger, *Die Konstruktion der ägyptischen Tür*, ÄF 2, (1936), 24.

[196] *Wb.* V 314, 15.

suggestion, I propose restoring *m mryt wn.[sn ḫtmw wp-r i͗rt ḥbyt] r-tr i͗w wꜥbw ḥr rḫ nw.s*, "in order that they be closed except the performing of the seasonal offering as the priests know its time." Accordingly, the doors of the shrine of Pakhet, located in a deserted area, were to be kept closed except for the performance of a specific seasonal feast. The latter I would surmise to be the anniversary of the intrusive torrent from which Hatshepsut and her country had been saved by the grace of the goddess. The qualifying sentence *i͗w wꜥbw ḥr rḫ nw.s* is curious, because the verb *rḫ* does not really lend itself to this kind of pseudo-verbal construction. I wonder, if it should not be understood as "as long as the priests know its time," with the implicit aspiration that this would be permanently. This closes the section on the Speos Artemidos and Hatshepsut's activity there.

Section Six

"Hor-wer, Wenu and Sha-[ꜥaa—all the people there were satisfied] after I gave provisions and I consecrated the shrines (again).ab) Their towns were settled with unwelcomed ones from [. . . They went to] the storeroom while begging 'Give!'"ac)

ab) After describing her act of gratitude for saving her and her domain from a "water-torrent," the text commences with the mention of three place-names: *Ḥr-wr*, *Wnw* and *Š-ꜥꜣ*.[197] They were all located on the left bank, approximately vis-à-vis of the Speos Artemidos. The distance to Qus is approximately 150 kilometers. The places are all located in the 15th Upper Egyptian district, whose dominating deity was Thoth with his principle cult-center at Hermopolis. The interrelation between these four places is not entirely clear, which concerns also the reason of their mention in the text.

There are gaps in this section which have not been tackled in the past. Several indicators can be used in an attempt to grasp the drift of the passage. At the end of the first lacuna can be read *(r)di.n<.i> ḏfꜣw*, "(after I) gave food."[198] There is no indication of any recipient(s) included, which necessitates their mention in the lacuna. Food is principally given to people in need; the relative past indicated by *(r)di.n.<i>* implies that the giving of food led to a change in the situation. On the basis of these considerations, I propose restoring *[rmṯ.sn ḥtpw r]di.n<.i> ḏfꜣw*, "their people were satisfied after I gave food," following an anticipatory mention of the three places. In other words, the three towns profitted from Hatshepsut's efforts to alleviate an adverse situation. The second beneficial act is described as *snṯr.n.i rꜣw-prw*, "I (re)-consecrated the shrines."[199]

[197]For these towns, see Sir Alan Gardiner, *Ancient Egyptian Onomastica*, II, 81-87*; D. Kessler, *Historische Topographie der Region zwischen Mallawi und Samalut*, TAVO B/30 (1981), 83 ff.; 120 ff.; Farouk Gomaà, *Die Besiedlung Ägyptens während des Mittleren Reiches*, I, TAVO B/66,1 (1986), 288 ff.; 312 ff.

[198]The emendation of the suffix first person is not certain; there could be a *sḏm.ny*-form which would require a rendering "after food was given."

[199]So also Gardiner; A. Burkhardt's "Ich habe ihre (= der Götter) Tempel geweiht" links the *rꜣw-prw* with deities, which,

ac) There is something of a syntactic problem. The initial syntactical unit was a pseudo-verbal clause followed by a *sḏm.n.f.* The next is a *sḏm.n.f*-clause after which follows a pseudo-verbal clause. It would be a good case of syntactic chiasm if the two units are considered interconnected. Consequently *nἰwt.sn grgw m pr-hꜣ.f*, should be connected with the preceding as a conditional clause and rendered "I re-consecrated the shrines, as their 'towns'[200] were settled with (northern ?) refugees." For *grg m*, "to be settled with," cf. *Wb.* V 187, 16.[201] As for *prw hꜣ.f*, it is a sentence used as a noun.[202] Lit. "the one who came up may he go down," it appears to describe an unwelcome refugee from the north, who went upriver south.[203] The implicit wish for a departure indicates in this case the undesirable nature of such a person.

The ensuing lacuna offers problems. The traces reported by Sethe suit best a reading *, while Davies' copy gives , so that Gardiner rendered "those who were in . . . ." However, the whereabouts of the people was already indicated, which speaks against the proposed reading. In view of the closing sentence of the previous section (line 22),[204] I am inclined to envision here a similarly construed pseudo-verbal clause which I would restore *. One square remains undecided as an indicated trace in it is ambiguous. Feasible words are  (*rwt*) "gate" or  (*šnwt*) "granary." The projected mention of people is confirmed by the indication of their aim *m dbḥ*, ""while begging."[205] The word of the supplication, the imperative *ἰm*, "give!" closes the description of the conditions in the three towns prior to Hatshepsut's relief.[206]

Section Seven

"Thoth, the Great, who came forth from Reᶜ—may he instruct [me about finding the things of] his

---

however, are not mentioned in the preceding. Redford's "I made their temples godly" misses the aspect of renewal. It should be noted that *rꜣw-prw* is without a suffix, i.e., it is not specifically linked with the three places mentioned at the beginning of the section. As *rꜣ-pr* denotes principally a place of worship (cf. P. Spencer, op. cit. 55), a rendering "temple" might better be avoided because of its connotations. The term is particularly associated with tombs and I wonder if it should not be understood here in this vein, i.e., that the tombs had been desecrated by people using them as emergency shelter, as it happened only recently in Cairo.

200 The writing  is not the usual one for *nἰwt* "towns" and I wonder if it has here a somewhat different meaning. It might make sense if the term is understood here to denote the "living-quarters" rather than concerning the legal natue of the social unit.

201 Gardiner: "they being furnished with thronging (crowds)"; A. Burkhardt: "ausgestattet mit vollen (Haufen)", interpreting the literal meaning "es geht heraus und kommt (wieder)"of *pr-hꜣ.f* as "mit ständigem Kommen und Gehen, vielleicht im Sinne von Überfluß." Redford's "founded (each) with its enceinte (?)" with the alternative "its surroundings (?)" has neither a basis in the text nor does it conform with the context.

202 For similar compounds, cf. Gardiner, *EG* § 194; also Admonitions 6, 12 *iw-ms ᶜḥntsr m pr-ha.f* "Indeed, the judge's hall belongs to coming and going."

203 For *prἰ* "to go up (the river)," cf. *Wb.* I 521, 1; cf. also *Wb.* I 520, B IV "to escape a danger," which could also apply here.

204 See above p. 61,

205 For *dbḥ*, "to beg," cf. *Wb.* V 439,9; Cairo 20543, 15; Dendera pl. XI C (= H.G. Fischer, op. cit. 181); Neferyt 40 (= H. Goedicke, *The Protocol of Neferyt*, 101); Suicidal 80 (= H. Goedicke, *The Dispute of a Man with his* Ba, 139); Admonitions 7, 11.

206 This meaning was already alluded to by Gardiner's rendering ". . . the magazine is begging 'Give' (?)"; similarly A. Burkhardt "die sind [. . .] (kein?) Lagerhaus bittet 'Gib!'," while Redford gave an unintelligible ". . . storehouse, as something requisitioned therefrom (?)."

[house:] the altar of silver and gold, the chests of linen, all kinds of chattels which are to remain in its place.[ad]) (Even) the one who enters eye-to-eye with the leader of the Ennead of gods was ignorant of it. Of all the gods, there was none familiar with his house.[ae]) The god's-fathers were in distress without recognizing the arm of (my ?) father over my Majesty. May he give alertness to the supporters of the god,[af]) (after) I built his main temple from limestone of Tura, its gates from alabaster of Hatnub, the doors of Asiatic cooper, the inlays therein in fine gold.[ag]) (As) one sanctified by 'the-one-high-of-plumes' (scil. Amun)—I [conducted] the statue of this god during the two festivals, namely the *nḥb-kꜣw*-feast and the Thoth feast, which I established for him anew, that they are in the calender and not as seasonal ones.[ah]) Since the feast celebration be one, I doubled for him the divine offerings beyond what had been done before,[ai]) as my acting for the Ogdoad, for Khnum in his forms, for Heqat, Renenet and Meskhenet, who had joined together to form my body and [to] Nehmet-ʿaway, my Nekhbet-ka, who said: 'Hers is heaven and earth!'"[aj])

ad) After describing her relief-efforts for three communities in the 15th Upper Egyptian district plagued by refugees from the North, Hatshepsut's text turns next to her deeds for Thoth. His role is not associated here with a specific place but the proximity with three settlements in his principal district make it likely that Hermopolis should be envisioned as the place of concern. The description is divided into two sections, one dealing with the god himself and the impoverished state of his cult, the other with the measures taken by Hatshepsut to improve this situation. Because of the extent and the details, it is obvious that Hatshepsut considered it a very important act, which leads, after establishing the text as firmly as possible, to the question what motivated her.

The deity is identified as "Thoth, the Great, who came forth from Reʿ." The qualification of the deity as *wr* "great" is not merely euphemistic, but identifies it as the main representative with this name to be distinguished from other deities occupying a lesser role.[207] While the emanation from Reʿ is a recurrent theme,[208] the origin of Thoth in this fashion is unusual.[209] The syntax, namely anticipatorily stated subject followed by a *sḏm.f*, is a clear indication of the hortative character of the statement.[210] Accordingly, *swhꜣ.f*

[207]The epithet *wr* or *wrt* occurs with a number of deities, especially Mut and Isis. The theological significance of it has not been fully recognized. It could be compared with that of saints with a local role to be distinguished from those of a universal one.

[208]Cf. *Wb.* I 522, 2.

[209]While the notion of Thoth as "son of Reʿ" is attested once at the transition from the Eighteenth to the Nineteenth Dynasty (see Jan Assmann, *Ägyptische Hymnen und Gebete* (1975), 463), the emergence of Thoth from Reʿ is paralleled only once at Dendera (= Patrick Boylan, *Thoth, The Hermes of Egypt* (1922), 118).

The orthography of the word *rʿ* is curious without any divine determinative as could be expected for the god Reʿ. It resembles more the spelling for "sun." While this adds to the misgivings about a rendering "Thoth the great, who came forth from Reʿ" it still does not produce a meaningful rendering. A translation "Thoth, the great, who comes forth during daylight" is unfortunately not more than a guess. It could be taken as refering to the moon appearing in daytime, invoked here as an additional help in the pursuit of missing things.

[210]See Gardiner, *EG* 450. 5 e). Gardiner's rendering of the passage as "Thoth . . . instructed me" disregarded this grammatical

ḥr.i,[211] should be rendered "may he instruct me," which is usually construed with the preposition *r* "concerning." The problem is, what kind of instruction Hatshepsut desires. As she later reports about building a new temple for the god, it would seem unlikely that she first desired instructions how some of the religious furnishings are to be made. This notion is further supported by the later statement that the priestly personnel was destitute. Especially the latter and the adjoined plea to take care of the god's supporters points to a desparate situation regarding the temple of Thoth. Although the cause is not revealed *expressis verbis*, it seems quite transparent that it was the impact of destitute refugees that beset the area. All symptoms point to a stripping of the god's temple of its valuables, leaving it in a state of misery. On the basis of this reading of the prevailing situation, I understand Hatshepsut's plea for divine guidance to concern the recovery of things missing. This leads me to suggest as restoration 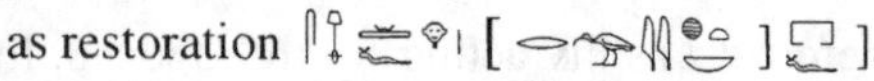, "May he open my face concerning my finding all things of his house."[212] What follows is an enumeration of ritual objects, which, as already indicated, I suspect of being missing. The list begins with  *hnw nyw mnḫt hnw nb mn ḥr st.f*, "the altar of silver and gold, cases of clothing, every kind of chattels, which are to remain on its place." The items which Hatshepsut is concerned with as being missing are almost exclusively of a kind which could be used in everyday life, with the exception of the altar made of precious metal.[213] By its uniqueness it can only be the main offering place for oblations.[214] Its removal cannot have any practical reasons, but should be a case of grave larceny with the aim to make it to money. The disappearance of cases with fabric[215] suggests their use by the earlier mentioned refugees. The same can be surmised for the "chattels"[216] which have the specification that they not be removed, i.e., "which are to remain in their place."[217] It is probably a general reference to inventory belonging to the sanctuary[218] which appears to have been pilfered to meet the dire needs of the people that had flocked to Middle Egypt.

---

aspect, which also applies to A. Burkhardt's "Thoth . . . er leitete [mich]." Redford made it into a dependent clause "Thoth the Great who came forth from Re, that he might open (?) . . ." which also disregards the particular construction occurring here.

[211] The traces are not a perfect match for this reading, but, as Gardiner has pointed out, it is the most appealing possibility.

[212] The proposed restoration does not claim to be accurate in all details but hopes to reflect the basic tenor of the passage.

[213] The text clearly indicates a single table and not a plural as Redford renders it.

[214] It appears that there was a main offering table, distinguished by the precious material of which it was made; examples of other cults are *Urk.* IV 629; 867, 11-12. The precedence of silver over gold would fit the evaluation of the two metals in the early Eighteenth Dynasty before its eventual reversal; cf. J.R. Harris, *Lexicographical Studies in Ancient Egyptian Minerals*, 41; W. Helck, *Wirtschaftsgeschichte des Alten Ägypten*, 270 f.

[215] It is open to individual interpretation to take *mnḫt* as finished or unfinished pieces of fabric. It would be unlikely to concern the clothing of the divine statue, so that it seems more likely to concern sheets of cloth from which clothing could be made if necessary.

[216] Gardiner, following a suggestion by Gunn, rendered it "furniture," which, however, might inspire the notion of wooden meubles. When taken in the generic sense of chattels it would include a wide range of goods; for the term, cf. *Wb.* III 107; Faulkner, *CD* 172; but cf. also *Urk.* IV 870, 16 denoting vessels endowed by Thutmosis III.

[217] Gardiner: "being established in its place"; A. Burkhardt: "jedes Ausstattungsstück fest an [seinem] Platz (gestellt)"; Redford: "each vessel set in its (proper) place" did not recognize the juridical nature of the expression as reflecting irremovability. For *mn ḥr st*, cf. *Wb.* II 61, 8-9.

[218] The inventories of the temple cult of Neferirkareʿ give a good idea of a cult's belongings; cf. Paule Posener-Krieger, *Les archives du temple funéraire de Nʿferirkarê-Kakai*, BdE LXV/2 (1976), 125 ff.; cf. also *Urk.* IV 98; 173 etc.

ae) The seriousness of the situation,[219] why Hatshepsut pleads for the god's help in recovering the things, is exemplified by the fact that not even the cult-leader knew an answer. The entry "eye to eye," which equals "vis-à-vis," with a deity is restricted to the chief priest of a cult or a king.[220] The collective ignorance expressed by *st* refers back to the entireness of missing items of the cult.

Difficulties have been experienced in the interpretation of the ensuing  . Gardiner rendered it "the leader of the divine Ennead," while A. Burkhardt and Redford gave for it "the celebrant (for) the entire(?) ennead" incorporating parts of the next sentence into it.[221] There is a blank space at the end of the line following *sšmw*, which might be irrelevant but might also contain a determinative of *sšmw*. There is no need to take *sšmw* as a participle qualifying **ʿq ỉr/ỉrt*, but rather as a noun "the leader of the ennead of gods" and to understand it as a descriptive reference to Thoth and his role in relation to the other gods worshiped in the same place.[222]

Psḏt nṯrw is followed in the text by  which has caused problems for previous translators. A. Burkhardt and Redford basically ignored it by adjoining it to the preceding as "the celebrant (for) the entire ennead," while Gardiner, after rejecting the notion of an "Ennead of six gods," considered the possibility of an erroneous reference to male and female deities making up the ennead. He also confessed having difficulties with the word  which he eventually took as the name Atum. The envisioned problems dissolve easily, when recognizing that the two plurals *nṯrw* are separate words. The first, as already discussed, belongs to *psḏt* as *psḏt nṯrw* "ennead of gods" of which Thoth is "leader" (*sšmw*). The second plural *nṯrw* with the qualifying *tm*(*w*) "complete, total"[223] following it, stands in anticipatory emphasis.[224] As for the suffix *.f*, it refers to Thoth as "leader of the gods" whose temple is in disarray. Consequently, the sentence *nṯrw tm(w) n wnt šsꜣ m pr.f*, is to be rendered "(of) the total gods, not was there one familiar with his house."[225]

af) In connection with the accounting of the physical devastation of Thoth's cult-place and the neglect of all deities connected with it, Hatshepsut's text also dwells on the misery of the religious personnel

[219]Other translations are: "He who enters face to face, the leader of the divine Ennead, (even) Atum (?), was ignorant of it, and there was none well-acquainted with his house" (Gardiner); "Der, den man nicht kennt (?), der durch die Augen eintritt (in den Menschen) der Leiter der gesamten Götterneunheit, nicht einmal in seinem Hause gab es einen Kundigen" (A. Burkhardt); "'He-who-directs-his-gaze,' the celebrant (for) the entire (?) ennead, was ignorant—there was none skilled in his house" (Redford).

[220]The metaphor was unravelled first by Gardiner, *PSBA* 35 (1913), 169 f.; for this form of direct confrontation with the divine, cf. also Kamose II 33 f.(cf. H. Goedicke, *Studies about Kamose and Ahmose*, 96 f.) Why Redford wants to consider it a priestly title escapes me.

[221]See below.

[222]For *sšmw* "leader," cf. Wb. IV 288 f. This particular epithet of Thoth does not seem paralleled elsewhere, but it is within the theological role of the god, especially as dominating the cult. As for the role of Thoth in relation to the assembly, i.e. the "ennead of gods," cf. W. Barta, op. cit. 59 f.; P. Boylan, op. cit. 197.

[223]For this use of *tm*, cf. Gardiner, *EG* § 317.

[224]Cf. Gardiner, *EG* § 148; see also below, p. 93.

[225]It is impossible to decide the exact connotation of *pr.f*; it can denote the temple proper, but also the entire religious estate under the god's sway.

identified as *ỉtw-nṯr*, "god's fathers." For their role in the divine cult of the New Kingdom, see Hermann Kees, "'Gottesväter' als Priesterklasse," *ZÄS* 86 (1961), 115-125.[226] The understanding of their mention is somewhat hampered by a lacuna whose restoration offers problems, but also by a seemingly ambiguous syntax. *Ỉtw-nṯr m tp-sw* has been taken as an adverbial clause without a transparent connection with what follows.[227]

Gardiner's restoration [ ] is listed Wb. IV 427, 15-17 as indicating a distraught condition of people or buildings.[228] The ensuing lacuna of ± 1 1/2 squares is the crux for understanding the passage. Gardiner thought of restoring a preserved trace into [ ], by considering it "intelligible to understand this clause to mean something like 'the god's fathers (i.e. the leading priests) starting anew bereft [of teaching] from (their) father(s)'." How this is to fit into the context is not clear to me.

As an adverbial clause *ỉtw-nṯr m tp-sw* . . . is parallel to the previous statement about the difficulties faced by the gods, with a similar structure; *ỉtw-nṯr* thus corresponds to *nṯrw tmw* in the parallel clause. I am not sure if *tp-šw* is followed by a suffix *.sn* or not. The cause of the priests dispair is to be envisioned in the lacuna for which I propose the restoration [ ] *ḥr ḥm.i*. The proposed negation is in parallel to the one in the preceding clause. For *mꜣꜣ m* "to be cognizant of," cf. *Wb.* II 8, 19. Although recorded without a diacritical stroke, I see no other way than considering as the word ꜥ "arm."[229] Its being "over" a person is taken as a metaphor for protection. Somewhat ambiguous is the term . which is more likely to refer to a divine father than a human one, i.e. Thutmosis I. One could consider it an allusion to Amun, but the context, exclusively concerned with Thoth, speaks against it. It is either to be taken as the god's dominating role in the cult or Hatshepsut considers herself under Thoth's divine paternal patronage. It is curious that the word is without determinative, while Hatshepsut is denoted here as *ḥm.i.* This palatable emphasis on her role as king points very much to a date soon after her assumption of kingship.[230]

af) The oblivion about Hatshepsut's divine protection is followed by a wish *dỉ.f spd-ḥr n rmnw nṯr*. The antecedent of the suffix *.f* can only be *ỉt.(i)*"father," whose action is formulated by a hortative *sḏm.f.*[231]

[226] A. H. Gardiner, *Ancient Egyptian Onomstica*, I, 51 f.*; Hermann Kees, *Das Priestertum im ägyptischen Staat*, Probleme der Ägyptologie, 1 (1953), 56 f.

[227] Other renderings are: Gardiner, "the god's fathers being in destitution (?) . . . seeing (?) with (?) his father. The insight (?) of my august person gave discernment to the bearers of the god"; A. Burkhardt, "die Gottesvärer waren unwissend [. . .], die <mein?> Vater gemacht hat. Aber das Antlitz Meiner Majestät gab den Gottesträgern Aufmerksamkeit"; Redford, ". . ., and the god's fathers were incompetent [. . .] made through my father's agency for My Majesty, that it(?) might make the god's bearers alert."

[228] Kitchen, *Ramesside Inscriptions* II, 325, 14 *mꜥḥꜥw.sn ỉmyw ꜣbḏw wꜣww r ḫpr m tpšw* "their cenotaphs, which are in Abydos, beginning to be in ruins." Why Redford rendered it as "ignorant" is ununderstandable.

[229] Although the orthography would suggest a reading **m-ꜥ* "by" such a preposition does not suit the context.

[230] This topic plays a varying role in Hatshepsut's reign, with its peak between Year 7 and Year 15, when some form of political compromise was achieved between Hatshepsut and Thutmosis III. This does, however, not exclude the fact that Hatshepsut stressed this point in the form of claiming divine descent in her Deir el Bahari memorial temple. For Hathsepsut's political apologesis, cf. S. Ratié, op. cit. 108-118.

[231] Gardiner divided the sentences differently and rendered "The insight (?) of my august person gave discernment to the bearers

Spd-ḥr has to be a noun because of the *n* following it. It has been considered a dative, which, however, leads to an undefined reference of alertness without specifying what it is about. A more meaningful statement results from a genitival interpretation as "when he cause(d) the alertness of the god's supporters." "Alertness" as a desirable quality is mentioned together with "praise, love and experience about any secret."[232] A physical interpretation of *rmnw nṯr*, as "bearers of the god," which Gardiner took as "a pretty clear periphrasis for *wꜥbw* 'the lower priests'" might be too narrow an interpretation, because any limitation to the lower or lowest members of the cult would not be of any significance. Although the "god" is not identified, *nṯr* allows only an identification with the cult served by the previously mentioned *ἰtw-nṯr* "god's-fathers." The pronominal subject of the clause can only be *it* "father" whom I see as the beneficiary of Hatshepsut's deed, i.e. as Thoth.

This lengthy introduction should be understood as an explanation of Hatshepsut's interest in Thoth and his cult. Although not detailed further, its cause was already indicated earlier in the text by alluding to the *wp ἰšd*, i.e., the role of Thoth as announcer in the royal succession.[233] Because practically nothing is known about this process, it is impossible to evaluate it to any significant degree. In the undoubtedly complex political manoeuvering, which presumably accompanied Hatshepsut's ascent as king, it might be that her aspirations were supported not only by Amun but also by Thoth, i.e., by the cult of both gods.

The wish for "alertness" by its very nature can only be prospective and has no logical basis in the description of the destitute condition of the cult of Thoth. In the composition of the text the hortative *sḏm.f*-clause is disjunct until it is connected with the *sḏm.n.f*-clause following it. The latter was by all trqanslators separated from its preceding and considered as opening an unconnected topic dealing with Hatshepsut's building of a temple for Thoth.

As the inscription on the Speos was formulated and executed not later than year 8, i.e., less than two years after Hatshepsut became king, there was no time for her to complete planning and executing a major building project as a *ḥwt-nṯr wrt* would have been. It results that the clause *qd.n.ἰ ḥwt-nṯr.f wrt* is not an independent narrative, but rather states the circumstance when the desired "alertness" of the "god's supporters" is to take place, i.e., after Hatshepsut has built a temple for Thoth. At the time of writing the text this was still in the future, if it ever occurred.

ag) While earlier there was mention only of the disappearance of the cult-inventory, Hatshepsut's projection to "build his main sanctuary out of Tura limestone, its gateways of alabaster of Hatnub, the doors of Asiatic copper, its inlays in fine gold" are impressive The details about the intended construction emphasize the use of precious materials. The building is labeled *ḥwt-nṯr wrt* which should not be taken as the physical quality "great," but rather as an indication that it was the god's "main" temple, which does not

---

of the god"; A. Burkhardt gave for it "Aber das Antlitz Meiner Majestät gab den Gottesträgern (= Priestertitel) Aufmerksamkeit", while Redford translated it "that it (?) might make the god's bearers alert."

232 *Urk.* IV 134, 8; cf. also *Wb.* IV 109, 16.

233 See above, pp. 44 .

exclude the existence of other places of worship.[234] It would seem that the ideographically written word for "to build" (𓃀) does rather suggest a mud construction than one using blocks of stone. For "Asiatic copper," cf. W. Helck, *Materialien zur Wirtschaftsgeschichte des Neuen Reiches*, 978; for Tura limestine as building material, see D. Arnold, *Building in Egypt*, 28 f.[235] *Ḫpw* denoting the decoration of the copper doors should be understood as "inlays" rather than "reliefs."[236] The word is identical with that for "naval-string"[237] and owes its use from the application of metal wire for inlays.[238]

ah) *Ḏsr ḥr Qꜣ-šwty* has been understood as specifying the inlay in the door.[239] This notion leads to some odd consequences. It would imply that the temple for Thoth built by Hatshepsut had its doors decorated with an image of Min or Amun-Min and that it brought about its sanctification. Neither one is likely. First, it would seem rather insulting to project the image of a deity, which was not worshiped there on the sanctuary's doors. Second, the consecration of a sanctuary is a ritual act and is not due to a design affixed to its doors. As a further objection to the quoted notions, there is no discernable reasons for placing the image of Min or Amun-Min at the doors of Thoth's sanctuary.

Qꜣ-šwty "the One with the high Plumes" is not only a descriptive name of Min, but through his association with Amun as Amun-Min it applies also to the Theban god.[240] The mention of the "One-high-of-plumes," i.e., Amun-Min, and Thoth's sanctuary can be reconciled only through the action of Hatshepsut deliniated in the following. The verb describing it is partially destroyed; Sethe's restoration [*sḫ*]ꜥ*.n.ỉ*] was specifically rejected by Fairman as quoted by Gardiner[241] who considered reading *sꜥꜣ.n.ỉ* as "I [extolled ?] this august god in two festivals." The object of Hatshepsut's action is specified as *ḥm n nṯr pn* which denotes specifically the "body," scil. the statue of the god.[242] It results that the passage describes a ritual and not a religious act, as the two suggested restorations would have to be taken. Instead, a restoration [*mꜣ*]ꜥ*.n.ỉ*

[234]For this use of *wr*, i.e. "important," "central," cf. *Wb.* I 327 b).

[235]The text emphasizes the geographical source of the limestone, a sign that Hatshepsut hoped for access to it at the time.

[236]So Gardiner "the reliefs thereof in gold" and Redford "with their reliefs in electron," while A. Burkhardt gave for it "die dazugehörigen Ornamente aus Elektron."

[237]*Wb.* III 365; Hildegard von Deines–Wolfhart Westendorf, *Wörterbuch der Medizinischen Texte*, Grundriss der Medizin der Alten Ägypter, V/2 (1962), 682.

[238]The technique of metal inlays is well known from three-dimensional art, but existed for twodimensional just as well. In the similar case described by Inana (*Urk.* IV 53, 10) the making of the divine figure in gold on the copper door is given as *msi* "to fashion." Despite the difference in wording it should also be imagined as an inlay.

[239]Gardiner:". . . and (made ?) holy with him high of plumes," considering it a reference to Min; A. Burkhardt: "heilig unter dem (Gott) mit hohem Federpaar" following Gardiner's identification as reference to Min; likewise Redford: "sanctified with (an image of) 'Him-with-Lofty-Plumes'" and also considering it as a reference to the "ithyphallic god Min."

[240]For Amun-Min in the reign of Hatshepsut, S. Ratié, op. cit. 318-322; P. Lacau–H. Chevrier, *La Chapelle Rouge*, 213 ff. She continues a tradition prevalent under her father as particularly demonstrated by the santuary built by Inana (*Urk.* IV 56, 8-10) where the image of Amun-Min was displayed in gold on the bronze doors; cf. E. Dziobek, *Das Grab des Ineni*, 53.

[241]Loc. cit. 47, note 8. It did not stop Redford to translate the passage "I caused the Majesty of this god [to appear] at [his] festivals.

[242]For *ḥm* denoting the statue of a god, see Joachim Spiegel, "Die Grundbedeutung des Stammes 𓄑 *ḥm*," *ZÄS* 75 (1939), 112 fF.

() "I presented the statue of this god," possibly with the connotation of ritual introduction, suits the context flawlessly.[243]

The motive or inspiration for this ritual performance is not inate in Hatshepsut, but she pays tribute to her divine guidance, namely Amun-Min. Syntactically, *ḏsr ḫr Qꜣ-šwty* can only be taken as an anticipatorily stated qualification of Hatshepsut and her deed, and is thus to be rendered "One sanctified by the One-high-of-Plumes."[244] For *ḏsr ḫr* "to sanctify with a divine image," cf. *Wb.* V 614, 1, although listed only for the Ptolemaic Period; I am not entirely clear if Hatshepsut was physically accompanied at the consecration by the figure of Amun or if it should be understood metaphorically.

The event concerned two festivals, namely the *nḥb-kꜣw* and the Thoth-festival, which are assumed to have been established anew by her.[245] This rendering is apparently based on the assumption that  is a relative form. The importance of the *sḏm.n.f* form in this text makes such a notion highly unlikely. Instead, *wꜣḥ.n.i* should be taken as a main clause, on which *iw.w m rꜣ<-dmḏyt>* depends. It is curious, that it contains what appears to be a late-Egyptian plural *w*.[246] The  I take as an abbreviation of *rꜣ-dmḏyt*, "the calender year," as used before.[247] *Tp-trw* as term for seasonal feasts, cf. Sir Alan Gardiner, *JEA* 38 (1952), 21. The innovation introduced by Hatshepsut that "they be in the calender and not on top of its season" is difficult to evaluate in full because little is known of the significance of either feast. Basically it is an indication that the two feasts are to be celebrated in accordance with the civil calender and not as a seasonal feast; for this distinction, cf. S. Schott, *Altägyptische Festdaten*, 36 ff. As for the *nḥb-kꜣw*- feast and the Thoth-feast, see below, p. 71.

ai) The words *ḏr wꜥ sšm ḥb* have formerly been considered as an explanation for the combining of the two feasts. Previous translators had major difficulties with this statement imagining an otherwise unmentioned "festival-leader."[248] The solution is quite simple once it is realized that it is not a continuation of the previous sentence, but, as recurrent in the text, an anticipatorily stated adverbial clause.[249] *Ḏr*

[243] As there is no mention of Thoth in this context, *nṯr pn* "this god" can only refer to the *Qꜣ-šwty* mentioned just before. It results, that Hatshepsut was accompanied by the statue of Amun-Min when she consecrated the sanctuary she had built.

[244] It is another instance of the resurrent phenomenon in this text to use anticipatory arrangements to achieve a maximal emphasis; see further below, p. 93.

[245] So Gardiner "which I appointed for him anew"; A. Burkhardt, "die ich 'von neuem' für ihn gestiftet habe" and Redford "which I had re-instituted for him."

[246] For it, see Burkhardt Kröber, *Die Neuägyptizismen vor der Amarnazeit* (1970), 35 ff.

[247] See above, p. 41. Neither Gardiner's "they being (only) in (men's) mouths" nor A. Burkhardt's "die wohl in (jedermanns) Munde waren" nor Redford's "since they had been (only) in word of mouth" makes any sense.

[248] Gardiner: "since the festival-leader was alone (??)"; A. Burkhardt: "seit der Einzige (= Urgott) ein Fest feierte"; Redford: "since the festival-director was only a single person." Gardiner commented "Davies's desperate guess, which at least translates the words, though the sense is enigmatic."

[249] See further below, p. 93.

introduces consecutive facts, either in time or in logical development.[250] The obvious predicate of the clause is the verb *wꜥ* "to be one."[251] Its subject is the nominally used infinitive *sšm*, "to conduct (scil. perform) a feast."[252] The resulting "since the feast-performing was one" serves as emphasized explanation for Hatshepsut's doubling of the "divine offering upon what existed before."[253] The term *ḥtp-nṯr* denotes the regular offerings, i.e., the income of a cult.[254]

The increase in the income resulted from endowments by Hatshepsut for a number of deities. Although not specified in detail, those deities are to be envisioned as worshiped in the sanctuary for Thoth in the form of a cult residence as expressed by *ḥry-ib*.[255] Their inclusion was a reflection of Hatshepsut's personal piety which had a rather egocentric motif. The way Hatshepsut's donation for various deities is formulated as *m ỉrr.ỉ n* might look strange at first sight because an infinitive could be expected, but appears to be idiomatic with forerunners in the Middle Kingdom.[256]

aj) The list of deities to whom Hatshepsut is dedicating opens with the Ogdoad as a collective of its eight members.[257] Their mention as the first recipients might seem logical for a sanctuary at Hermopolis. As the deities following them are associated with the forming of Hatshepsut, their inclusion might here be in recognition of their role as representing the physical world. The next is "Khnum in his forms" which apparently refers to different iconographic renderings of the deity.[258] His mention together with three goddesses reminds of Pap. Westcar.[259] They are Heqat, Renenet and Meskhenet. Each one represents a specific aspect of her creation: Heqat appears to be credited with the initial conception, Renenet with her

[250] See Rudolf Anthes, "Zur Übersetzung der Präpositionen und Konjunktionen *m* und *ḏr*," *Studies in Honor of John A. Wilson*, SAOC 35 (1969), 1-13.

[251] *Wb*. I 277, 1, which lists only *Pyr*. 232 c, but the attestations listed in *Wb*. I 275, 1-3 have the same nature.

[252] See *Wb*. IV 286, 21-22; *Urk*. VII 56, 14.

[253] Gardiner's "I doubled for him the offerings in excess of what there has been before," A. Burkhardt "Ich verdoppelte für ihn die Gottesopfer zusätzlich zu dem, was früher gewesen war" and Redfprd's "I more than doubled the god's income for him compared with what had been formerly" might give the impression that the increase was extravagantly large. It is rather a matching of the amount that had existed before. This form of increase is a recurrent expression of a king's generosity; see, e.g. *Urk*. I 99; 146.

[254] Although much has been said about the spiritual significance of the "divine offering" (*ḥtp-nṯr*), its economic aspects are less thoroughly investigated. *Ḥtp-nṯr* does not only denote the material for the sacrificial act, but also the income and the endowment of a cult. These three usages are different in their economic nature, varying from the specific to the continuous.

[255] For the associated presence of a deity in a cult in contrast to a central role (*ḫnt*), see *Wb*. III 138, 16. As a help for envisioning the situation, it could be compared with a catholic church dedicated to one saint, in which, however, other saints might also be served.

[256] See *Wb*. I 111, 8; Berlin 2292.

[257] *Wb*. III 283, 3; K. Sethe, *Amun und die acht Urgötter*, §§ 81 ff.

[258] Aside of his terriomorphic representation, Khnum has hardly any other rendering than in human form. In Hatshepsut's reign Khnum occupies the conspicuous role of shaping her and her *Ka* on the potters wheel without being part of a myth of divine birth; cf. H. Brunner, op. cit. 68 ff.

[259] 9, 23; 10, 21; cf. Hans Goedicke, "Rudjedet's Delivery," *VA* 1 (1985), 19-26; idem, "Anthropoligcal questions and gynecological problems," *Mélanges offerts à Edith Varga* (2001), 117 f.

growth,[260] and Meskhenet with the actual delivery.[261] Since the Old Perfective *dmḏy* is masculine, Khnum is to be included in this grouping which is responsible for her "creation." The term *qd* used for it is derived from the shaping on the potters wheel as depicted in the description of her divine birth at Deir el Bahari.[262]

The enumeration of deities to whom Hatshepsut feels special gratitude ends with *Nḥmt-ʿwꜣy*, who is identified as *nḥbt-kꜣ.i*. The section contains some major uncertainties, largely due to epigraphic problems. Gardiner had assumed here a sequence of four deities,[263] a notion which can be discarded for there is only once an appropriate determinate, namely after *Nḥmt-ʿwꜣy*. The latter is attested elsewhere since the time of Thutmosis III as a goddess connected with Thoth in Hermopolis.[264] Her name "who saves the robbed one,"[265] might have political aspects as well, namely that Hatshepsut considered herself unduly deprived of kingship by Thutmosis III supporters.[266] The fact that *Nḥmt-ʿwꜣy* has the epithet, or is identified as *nḥbt-kꜣ.i* supports this notion. The latter is here not a separate goddess, but rather a reference to her role as "who tied on (scil. assigned) my ka." Different from Redford,[267] I consider *ḏdt* an active participle introducing the goddess's saying, which is *iw n.s pt tꜣ* "Her's are heaven and earth."[268] This statement is of such a nature that it cannot have a continuation, i.e., it should be the end of a syntactic unit. There is an unfortunate lacuna following it. However, as there is no discernable reference to a religious activity it would seem safe to assume here the beginning of another topic unrelated with Hatshepsut's religious building activity.[269]

Section Eight

"The 'followers-of-Horus' in *Ḥbnw*—their settlements were festive after I ascerted that 'I don't know temporary shelters in my design!'"ak) After I establish it and after I adorn it, I shall give houses to their

[260] For Renenet, cf. Dr. J. Broekhuis, *De godin Renenwetet* (1971), 7 f.; 89 f.

[261] She is a personification of the contraption used in the delivery; cf. F. Weindler, *Geburts- und Wochenbettsdarstellungen auf altägyptischen Tempelreliefs* (1915), 33 f.

[262] Edouard Naville, *The Temple of Deir el Bahari*, II (1896), pl. 48; H. Brunner, op. cit. 68-74, Tf. 6.

[263] His translation was "(to) Naḥmet-ʿway, Naḥbet-ka(u), Idjet-iu-nas-pe-to and Imi-utyw in Ḥe[b]nu" while Redford rendered it "Neḥmet-ʿawy, my (own) Neḥbet-kau (of whom?) it is said 'Heaven and earth are hers'." A. Burkhardt translated "Nehmet-awai, die meine Kas vereinigte, die man nennt 'Ihr gehören Himmel und Erde'."

[264] *Urk*. IV 10014, 11; Jacques Parlebas, *Die Göttin Nehmet-awaj*, (Diss. Tübingen) 1984, 8-21. The mention in Hatshepsut's text is her earliest one.

[265] *Wb*. II 297, 7; A.H. Gardiner, *Notes on the Story of Sinuhe*, 42; J. Parlebas, op. cit. 22-25.

[266] As there are no earlier mentions of *Nḥmt-ʿwꜣy* it might very well be the arrangement by Hatshepsut at Hermopolis that fostered the emergence of this cult figure. The only problem associating it directly with Hatshepsut is the male gender of the beneficiary of *nḥbt*.

[267] See above note 263.

[268] For this kind of global attribution, see also *Urk*. IV 216, 16.

[269] Previous translators did not envision here a change of subject, but continued. Gardiner had assumed here a sequence of names, ending in "Idjdet-iu-nas-pe-to and Imi-utyu in Ḥe[b]nu, the towns thereof being in festival . . ."; A. Burkhardt: "[. . . ?}. Die dazugehörigen 'Städte' sind froh . . ."; Redford: and [. . .] . . . in [. . .] their cities are in festival."

owners,al) (namely) everyone who does say on his own (i.e., voluntarily): 'One who shall act eternally is the one whom Amun had let appear as permanent king on the throne of Horus!'"am)

ak) Despite some uncertainty in the opening, the basic drift of the text can nevertheless be established. As recurrent in the text there is a anticipatory statement.[270] The principal statement follows as *niwt iry m ḥb*, "its towns were festive," followed by a relative past *mtr.n.i* As for the anticipatorily stated words, the Davies' copy would allow a reading  which is basically Gardiner's reading but not his translation.[271] The mention of *niwt iry*, "its dwellings," points to a preceding mention of some kind of geographical indication and its people, a notion further supported by the festivity there, which would require people. Their mention I surmise ; different from Gardiner, I suggest reading these signs as *imyw ḥsb Ḥr* "the one(s) in (paid) service of Horus."[272] *Ḥsb* () as a term for "workmen" occurs since the Middle Kingdom.[273] The specific social status conveyed by it is not fully determined, but can be surmised to be related to the basic meaning of the word *ḥsb*, "to reckon," either as people paid or acquired by payment. The construction with *imy* suggests a rendering "those who are in reckoning" without a possibility to determine their status in detail. The hieroglyph of the bird, which Sethe gave as 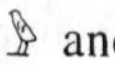 and Gardiner as  might posibly be .[274] The reading  would make sense only as plural of a nisbe from a feminine word; however, in this case plural strokes could be expected.

Although not indicated directly there can be no doubt that the word concerns people; the omission of a determinative might best be attributed to the social standing of the people. They are associated by the preposition *m* with a place called ,[275] which Gardiner identified as the center of the 16th Upper Egyptian district at Kom el-ahmar south of Zawiyet el-amwat.[276] That it is followed by *niwt iry* "its towns" speaks against such an identification because a defined settlement could not include a plurality of "towns."[277] A further problem is the identification of the place *Ḥbnw* because the actions indicated as cause

[270]See further below, p. 93.

[271]Gardiner translated "Imi-utyw in Ḥe[b]nu, the towns thereof being in festival" taking it as a rather unusual name of an otherwise unknown deity. A. Burkhardt avoided the opening words, which she attached to the preceding, commencing her translation as "Die zugehörigen 'Städte' sind froh." A similar view was presented by Redford.

[272]The expression might also occur in Griffith, *Siut*, pl. 17, l. 37, where it had been read as *imy wt(yw)* "he who is among the embalmers" by Gardiner.

[273]*Wb.* III 168, 1-2; *Beni Hasan* I, 8, 14; Georges Goyon, *Nouvelles inscriptions rupestres du Wadi Hammamat* (1957), 83; *Urk.* IV 1669, 1; p.Kah. 31, 4-25; William K. Simpson, *Papyrus Reisner I* (1963), 34; idem, *Papyrus Reisner III* (1969), 18; O. D. Berlev, *BiOr* 22 (1965), 266. Prof. U. Luft provided also pBerl 10016 rt r; p.Berl. 10111 Aa II rt 3-5; pBerl. 10095 rt 5 for which I cm grateful to him.

[274]Considering the epigraphic uncertainties this cannot be more than a guess, which could possibly lead to a meaningful sentence.

[275]Sethe in *Urk.* IV 389, 9 had read *m ḥb*; this reading is improbable because of the presumed double prepositional adjunct.

[276]A. H. Gardiner, *Ancient Egyptian Onomastica*, II, 382*; W. Helck, *Die ägyptischen Gaue*, 111; D. Kessler, *Historische Topographie*, 209 ff.; Farouk Gomaà, op. cit. 310 f.

[277]A possibility would be that *niwt iry* refers to "its towns-folk"; for *niwtyw* "city-dwellers," cf. *Wb.* II 213, 1-3; *Siut* IV 18; Merikareʿ E 105.

for delight do not apply to a town in Middle Egypt. Another place *Ḥbnw* is mentioned in the Instructions for King Merikareʿ E 88 in "the mooring-post is staked in the district I made in the East from Hebenu to the Horus-way."[278] Despite Kees' insistance[279] that this passage refers to Middle Egypt, the indicated defense of the eastern Delta requires that *Ḥbnw* be located at a point of possible intrusion from the East, i.e., at Egypt's northeastern frontier. A definite identification is lacking, but the general location seems certain.[280] To be *m ḥb* is a figurative idiom for being "happy" obviously derived from the emotional reaction typical for Egyptians.[281]

This happiness is the result of a promise made by Hatshepsut.[282] As  is beyond doubt a *sḏm.n.f*, it can only be the verb *mtr*, "to instruct, to announce."[283]  introduces the direct quote of the saying as in *Urk.* IV 365, 10-11 *sꜣw ḏd.ṯn m n rḫ.ỉ sp 2 ỉr.n.tw nn ḥr m-ʿ*, "Guard your saying 'I don't know, wherefore this was done'." The curious construction resembles the use of *m* introducing the text of a document[284] or else is an abbreviation derived from *m ḏd* similar to the use of *ḥr* for *ḥr ḏd*. For reasons unknown, the suffix *.ỉ* is omitted after *r'*.[285] *Sp-2* has here the character of an exclamation mark.[286] Hatshepsut's disclaimer  *m snṯt* is indeed puzzling in the former translations. Gardiner and Redford had divided the text and attached *n rḫ<.ỉ> sp-2* to the preceding.[287] First, the verb *rḫ* as a transitive requires an object; second, there is no discernible cause for "their settlements being festive." The remainder of the text the two translators took as anticipatorily stated object of the next two clauses.[288] The flawedness of their

[278] Miriam Lichtheim, *Ancient Egyptian Literature*, I (1973), 103; 108; Joachim Friedrich Quack, *Studien zur Lehre für Merikare*, Göttinger Orientforschungen IV/23 (1992), 53 who accepted the reading *Bnw* and its identification with the 14th Lower Egyptian nome.

[279] *MDIAK* 18 (1962), 6; already objected to by Alexander Scharff, *Der historische Abschnitt der Lehre für König Merikarê* SBAW 8 (1936), 30; idem, *MDIAK* 12 (1943), 150-152. See further Farouk Gomaà, *Die Besiedlung Ägyptens während des Mittleren Reiches*, II, *Unterägypten*, TAVO 66/2 (1987), 219-222.

[280] Pierre Montet, *Géographie de l'Egypte ancienne*, I (1957), 188 ff. identified it with *Bnw*, the center of the 14th Lower Egyptian nome, followed by Adelheid Schlott-Schwab, *Die Ausmaße Ägyptens nach altäyptischen Texten*, ÄAT 3, 1981, 93 and F. Gomaà, op. cit. 220 ff.

[281] For *m ḥb*, cf. *Wb.* III 58, 13 ff.

[282] Previous translations assumed here the mention of an affidavit which is in awry with the context. Gardiner rendered ". . . in festival, which bears witness to me all unbeknown (?)"; A. Burkhardt gave for it "Die zugehörigen 'Städte' sind froh, denn ich habe das, was unbekannt war, bezeugt," while Redford has "I give attestation in all innocence (?)."

[283] Faulkner, *CD* 121; *Urk.* IV 2156, 8. The actual meaning is probably more in the way of a veritable pronouncement.

[284] See Hans Goedicke, "Zur Einleitungsformel didaktischer Texte," *ZÄS* 86 (1961), 147-149. *Wb.* II 444, 6 quotes *m n rḫ* with a meaning "im Geheimen," which would imply that Hatshepsut's secret instruction inspired the settlements to be festive, an obvious illogism.

[285] It does not seem a case of polite omission of the first person, but rather one of political design to avoid responsibility.

Redford's "I give attestation in all innocence (?)" is grammatically incomprehensible. Any statement of such nature could only be **m tm rḫ* or *m ʿḥm*. In addition, why should an innocent attestation make "the settlements festive"?

[286] See Wilhelm Wessetzky, "Über die Verwendung des Schriftzeichens sp 2," *OrAn* 1945, 147-151; Siegfried Schott, "'Zweimal' als Ausrufungszeichen," *ZÄS* 79 (1954), 54-65.

[287] See the quotes in note 283.

[288] Gardiner: "Battlements (as yet only) in plan, I provided them and I made them festal"; Redford: "corniced walls (?) in foundations I emplaced, I made them festive." Rather unrelated is A. Burkhardt's "Die Dächer, die (erst) im Grundriß bestanden, habe ich ausgeführt, ich habe sie prächtig gemacht"

view becomes especially apparent by the resulting contradicition that "their settlements being festive" after "I made them festive."

The key for unravelling the conundrum lies in . This group contains either a superfluous second feminine ending, or two different words are wrongly put together. It is certain that the next sentence contains an anticipatory emphasis, as will be shown shortly. At the same time the verb *rḫ* requires an object, so that the first possibility appears to be the correct one because otherwise the word *wrmwt* would be without determinative.. The word *wrmt* occurs once in the Pyramid Texts denoting some kind of temporary shelter.[289] A similar meaning applies here as well with  as its determinative and an excess feminine ending. The description of Hatshepsut's intentions is completed by *m snṯt.(i)*, "in (my) planning." The supplying of the suffix first person seems necessary to identify the planner and corresponds to the same omission after *n rḫ*. For *snṯt* , in its extended use as "design," cf. *Wb*. IV 179, 14.[290] The implicit aversion to temporary shelter implies the favoring of permanent dwellings, at least on her part. When seen in this way, Hatshepsut's statement amounts to a policy of settling people instead of allowing them a kind of peregrinating lifestyle. Her pronouncement is the first effort by an Egyptian king in this direction which has its emulators in the Ramesside Period.[291] How far this policy met the kind of joyous acceptance Hatshepsut claims is another question.

al) Her plans are described in detail. As in other instances in this text it has a peculiar syntactic balance. This plan of settlement depends on two acts which are placed at the beginning. Formulated as *sḏm.n.f* clauses, they describe the conditions to be completed before her intended deed will take place. The two parallel clauses are *grg.n.i st* and *sḥb.n.i st.* Both use the neutral *st* as object, which is to some degree a reference to her plan (*snṯt*). As for *grg*, it concerns the physical process of designing and setting up a structure.[292]

The parallel *[s]ḥb.n.i st* is also a temporal clause which is followed by the stating of consequential intention.[293] Two important details can be deduced from this statement. First, at the time the text was formulated, Hatshepsut had not only plans for some major settlement project, but that the work was actually started. Second, the work was not yet completed, but was still in progress. Only after its completion Hatshepsut had designs for using the projected buildings. As a detail it should be noted that the completion of the project was to be celebrated in festive form, without necessarily implying religious ceremonies.

[289] Pyr. 2100 b *pšš.n Stš wwrmwt.k. Wb*. I 33,2 gives for it "Laube," while R.O. Faulkner, *The Ancient Egyptian Pyramid Texts* (1969), 299 rendered the passage "Seth has spread out your awnings." The word does not seem to be related to *wmt* "thick wall" attested only in the Ramesside Period; cf. P. Spencer, op. cit. 266.

[290] Faulkner, op. cit. 234 gave for it "plan." The term is taken from construction techniques, for which cf. Alexander Badawy, *ASAE* 54 (1956), 54 ff.

[291] Cf. Hans Goedicke, "Comments on the 'Israel-Stela,'" *Orientalia* , 2003,

[292] The word *grg* is used for a wide range of activities, from settling people to establishing their domicile (*Wb*. V 186 f.). The context suggests here a rather sweeping application, i.e. that various steps in the execution of Hatshepsut's plan are meant.

[293] For this construction, cf. Gardiner, op. cit. § 212.

What Hatshepsut offers to do after the consecration is to "give houses to [their] owners."[294] What might, however, appear a simple statement, includes an important juridical aspect. To "give the houses to their owners" implies a transfer of property rights, i.e., the recipient of a house becomes its owner without having had a prior legal claim to it. What Hatshepsut is promising is a settlement program for people living under temporary conditions.

am) As most generosity contains frequently a hitch, the promised gift of a house has a condition attached to it. It is in the form of an apposition qualifying the "owners" who might get a house. The word, apparently written with a small hieroglyph is lost. Sethe restored it  , while Gardiner seems to assume [*nṯr*] *nb*.[295] As there is no involvement of any deities in the indicated deed, but rather a strictly mundane legal process involved, I favor  , which is the most neutral of all general terms for people.[296] The anticipatory position of [*ḥr*] *nb* makes it clear that the ensuing *ḏd.f n.f* has to be realized as being a prerequisite for the receiving of a grant.[297] The *dativus ethicus* "to say for himself" has the connotation of describing the act as being voluntary.[298] At this point the text is somewhat damaged; it caused Sethe to restore *ḏd.f* [*r*].*i*, while Gardiner on the basis of the improved copy opted for emending *ḏd.f n.f* <r>*.ỉ* because the *sḏm.ty.fy* -form is not attested with an initial 𓇋. While there is no question about the latter, the proposed emendation is not convincing. First, it is a rather crucial point in Hatshepsut's claim to kingship that an omission would seem strange. Second, while Hatshepsut might use the suffix first person concerning her own acts,[299] the issue is less a personal than a majestic one so that a wording **r ḥm.ỉ* could be expected. This leads me to consider 𓇋 as the affirmative interjection "Indeed!"[300]

The statement required from anyone aspiring to become owner of a house donated by Hatshepsut is a declaration of loyalty. Grammatically, it is a nominal clause of identification.[301] The principal equation is between *ỉr.ty.fy nḥḥ* and *sḫʿ.n ỉmn*. Both are nominally used verb-forms, the one a *sḏm.ty.fy*, the other a

[294]While Gardiner gave for it "whilst, lo, I was giving houses to [their] owners," A. Burckhardt changed it into "Ich gab die Tempel [ihren] Eigentümern" although there is no indication that the "houses" had religious use. In either case the political contents of the deed is disregarded.

[295]A. Burckhardt did not follow Gardiner and rendered "'jeder' sagt [über] mich."

[296]*Wb* III 130, 4. An investigation of the implicit nuances in the different collective terms for people is lacking. However, it would seem that the narrowing of the term to the face denies any recognition of personality.

[297]For the construction, cf. Gardiner, *EG* § 148. The required statement is not in the future, but rather expressed as a requirement for being eligible to receive a house.

[298]The significance of the *dativus ethicus* is alluded to by A. Erman, *Neuägyptische Grammatik*² (1933), § 600, but not fully defined in most grammatical studies.

[299]See above, p. 73.

[300]*Wb*. I 25, 7-9.

[301]Gardiner translated "One who shall spend eternity, whom Amun has caused to appear as king of eternity on the throne of Horus"; A. Burkhardt, "Er (= Hatschepsut) ist einer, der ewig sein wird, einer, den Amun als König der 'Ewigkeit' auf dem Horusthron erscheinen ließ"; Redford, "The One who makes eternity, one whom Amun has caused to appear as king himself, on the Horus throne."

These translations propose two unconnected statements without a link between them, in addition to disregarding the implication of the different verb forms.

sḏm.n.f relative-form. The first has a prospective, the second a retrospective character. As for the first, *iri nḥḥ* is listed *Wb.* II 300, 11 as "die Ewigkeit verbringen," which makes limited sense for Hatshepsut, who was at the time king, but nevertheless mortal. A better meaning is attained by rendering it "to make eternity" in the sense of attaining it.[302] This prospect is assigned to *sḫʿ.n ỉmn m nswt*, i.e., "the one whom Amun had made appear as king." Obviously, this makes reference to the elevation of Hatshepsut to be king during the great festival of Amun, when she staged a coup d'état in cahoots with the Amun priesthood.

The inthronisation by Amun[303] has an unusually detailed specification, namely *m nswt ḏt ḥr st-Ḥr*, "as eternal king on the Horus-throne."[304] The term *nswt ḏt*, as is undoubtedly to be read, is not unique.[305] The curious designation "eternal king" should be understood as reflecting her insistance to hold the position as *nswt* for her life-time, i.e., that her elevation to this role was not a temporary one. This concern for the permanence of her kingship is not restricted to this instance, but is also reflected in a statement attributed to Weret-hekau:[306] "I reared thee as one upon his (scil. Amun's) throne as king lasting for eternity (*ḏt*)" and in the text of her partisan *Snmiʿḥ* [307] "happy times during an enduring kingship, after she took the throne of the one who made her." As will be discussed later[308] the emphasis on her takeover of kingship helps placing the inscription in her reign.

Section Nine

"Listen to him, you, namely all patricians and common folk in its multitude![an)] I did these things by the design of my heart and the forgotten one shall not sleep for me![ao)] While I restored what had decayed, I levied the mayor's draft since Asiatics were in the region of Avaris of Lower Egypt.[ap)] Resident aliens among them were disregarding the tasks (after) (I) ruled them,[aq)] while thinking that Reʿ would not be blind when the god (scil. Amun) assigned the steering rope to my Majesty.[ar)] When I was established over

[302] One could see it as being related to the wish *ʿnḫ ḏt r nḥḥ* (*Wb.* II302, 1), which, of course, could only be a wish and not a fact. It seem related with the eschatological prospect for the king in a Hereafter associated with Reʿ.

[303] Amun is also credited with the coronation of Hatshepsut on her northern obelisk in Karnak (*Urk.* IV 357, 13) reflecting the unusual circumstances of her ascent.

[304] Gardiner's rendering as "king of eternity" is misleading, because *ḏt* is used here adverbially; for this use, cf. Gardiner, op. cit. §§ 88; 205,6. This is corroborated by the similar statement *ḫʿ nśwt-bit Mꜣʿt-kꜣ-Rʿ ḥr st-Ḥr ḏt* (*Urk.* IV 254, 13).

Redford's "one whom Amun has caused to appear as king himself" not only maintains Sethe's former reading, but produces an illogical contradiction as the king appears erither by himself or is caused to appear by the god.

[305] Not only Hatshepsut emphasizes the permanence of her kingship, but Thutmosis III as well as *nswt wꜣḥ* "lasting king." It is worthy to note that Hatshepsut apparently had gathered Thutmosis III consent to her holding the position and designation of *nswt-bit* for the durastion of her life (*ḏt*). While it is basically unknown what the constitutional ramification of being *nswt-bit* are, it is quite transparent that there were some political accords between the two contestants. It appears that they reached their final form in the year 15 and were the cause of the "jubilee" of this year.

[306] *Urk.* IV 285, 17.

[307] *Urk.* IV 501, 11-12.

[308] See below, p. 97.

the thrones of Reʿ, I became known through a period of years as a born conquerer.as) And when I came as Horus, my uraeus threw fire against my opponents.at) And after I expelled the abomination of the gods, the earth removed their foot-prints!au) This was the governance of the *tf tfw*, who came at his time on one day.!av)"

an) The prospect of her benevolence to anyone promising loyalty to her is followed by an account of what happened to a group of people who did oppose her. Only by combining the final section with what precedes it, does it become understandable in its function.[309] While nothing in the previous text is addressed to anyone specifically, the closing part is in the form of a populistic address. This kind of global address has parallels in the reign of Thutmosis I and III.[310] It commences with an imperative and the invoking of both stratas of the Egyptian society. The plural imperative  is followed by  traditionally considered a reinforcement.[311] However, a reinforcing *ỉr.f* requires a coordination which is not the case here. Instead, it should be understood as the plural imperative *sḏmw* followed by the prepositional *ỉr.f*, after which the dependent pronoun *ṯn* summarizes the social distinction following it. This leads to translating it as "listen to him! you, namely all nobility and common folk in its multitude." The antecedent of *ỉr.f* is, of course "the one whom Amun had made appear as permanent king on the Horus-throne."[312] Although the social differenciation is nothing unusual, it is nevertheless significant that Hatshepsut addresses herself not only to the common folk, but that in this case she includes the "nobility" as well. Who was considered members of it in her reign is unfortunately obscure.

ao) It is generally assumed that Hatshepsut commences her address with the assurance that the enumerated deeds were her own doings, i.e., that she had no external instigator. The aim of this assertion is puzzling, because of the juxtaposition with *n ʿʿwy n.ỉ mhy* which was considered as her denial of

[309] By removing it from its context, thee section has received inappropriate attention because of the mention of "Asiatics in the region of Avaris" which has been equated with the Hyksos of the Fifteenth Dynasty (Donald B. Redford, "The Hyksos Invasion in History and Tradition," *Orientalia* 30 (1970), 1-51; A.H. Gardiner, *JEA* 32 (1946), 45; idem, *Egypt of the Pharaohs* (1961), 170 saw it as the result of a "process of falsification." In similar fashion postulated W. Helck, *Geschichte Ägyptens* (1968), 154, a concerted aversity of Hatshepsut against the Hyksos as dominating her political course. As a adherence to the political ideology, that the king establishes order after chaos, S. Ratié, op. cit. 181 rejects any historical value in the reference to the "Asiatics at Avaris" and rather credits Hatshepsut with the role of "pharaon abstrait."

[310] An address of this type occurs first for Ahmose (*Urk.* IV 20, 9-10). One ascribed to Thutmosis I (*Urk.* IV 256,9-13 and 257, 11) dates to Hatshepsut, but has in the encompassing invocation of the entire priesthood of the Osiris temple at Abydos by Thutmosis I (*Urk.* IV 100, 10-1) a forerunner. Thutmosis III's use of the global adressing (*Urk.* IV 1234, 6) is in all probability a match for Hatshepsut; cf. also *Urk.* IV 508, 12.

[311] Gardiner, *EG* § 337.3.

[312] See above, p. 76.

forgetfulness.[313] For *kt-ib*, "personal thought," cf. *Wb*. V 84, 3.[314] The problems in rendering the passage begin with the fact that there is no clear antecedent for a demonstrative *nn*. The last point in her text was the promise that she would give a house to anyone promising her unwavering loyalty. This is certainly not an accomplishment but rather the opposite of it. In other words, *nn* cannot refer back to the various deeds Hatshepsut enumerates in her text. It rather should be taken as concerning "those in my design," i.e., things she is still planning and which have not yet materialized. When realizing this point of reference, the nature of the sentence as temporal clause emerges; the ensuing *n ʿʿwy n.i mhy* forms the main clause with prospective outlook: "not shall sleep for me the forgotten one" or "a forgettful one." I take the negation 𓈖 as an incorrect writing for *nn*.[315] The ending 𓇌 in the nominally used participle *mhy* points to a perfective passive one; as it would seem rather irrelevant if a forgotten one sleeps or not, I surmise that the term refers here to a specific person.[316]

ap) While the previous syntactic unit is made up of two non-verbal clauses, the next one consists of two *sḏm.n.f* forms of which the second is introduced by the particle *iw* to emphasize its actuality. Due to its identity in time, the first takes on the character of a circumstantial clause for the modern mind.[317] "While I restored what had been devastated, I (actually) levied the foremost (or mayor's) draft since Asiatics have been in the region of Avaris in Lower Egypt."[318] Major historical conclusion have been drawn from this passage.[319] Traditionally one envisions here two parallel narrative statements, disregarding their syntactic relationship as indicated by *iw*. The latter should have been taken as a signal that the two clauses are not parallel but are in an interrelationship.[320] For *wnt wȝs*, cf. *Wb*. I 260, 10; it is not clear if the word denotes

[313]Gardiner rendered it "I have done these things by the device of my heart. I never slumbered as one forgetful"; S. Ratié, "J'ai accompli cela en l'humilité de mon coeur; je n'ai pas sommeillé comme un négligent"; A. Burkhardt, "ich habe dies getan aus enem Einfall meines Herzens heraus. Nicht [. . .] von dem, was ich getan habe, ist vergessen"; and Redford, "I have done this in my heart's design; I was not [negligent?] in what I did as an absent-minded one."

[314]The expresion *kt-ib* seem a favourite of the time; Senenmut uses it (*Urk*. IV 406, 10) "designs which (I) had made from my thought"; Thutmosis III (*Urk*. IV 637, 12) "jewel which his Majesty had made from his own thought"; *Mn-ḫpr-rʿsnb* (*Urk*. IV 932, 6) "(previous materials) which his Majesty had made from his thought."

[315]Cf. H. Satzinger, *Die negativen Konstruktionen*, §§ 2-4.

[316]The rendering as nominally used passive participle "forgotten one" requires a definite application because the opposite makes little sense. In the prevailing political situation following Hatshepsut's *coup d'état* the most likely candidate for this evaluation is Thutmosis III of whom there is no record between year 7 and year 13. What happened to him during these years is a mystery.

Redford's "I was not [negligent?] in what I did as an absent-minded one" is rather puzzling.

[317]Previous translations have separated the two connected clauses: Gardiner: ". . . but have made strong what was decayed. I have raised up what was dismembered, (even) from the first time when the Asiatics were in Avaris of the North Land"; S. Ratié: "j'ai fait refleurir ce qui était en décréptitude, j'ai redressé ce qui était en ruine depuis le temps où les Asiatiques étaient au milieu du Delta, à Avaris"; A. Burkhardt: "Ich habe restauriert, was zerfallen war, ich habe aufgerichtet, was anfangs zerlegt war, seit die Asiaten in der Gegend von Avaris im Nordland waren"; Redfprd: "I have restored what was destroyed, I raised up what had formerly been shattered, since Asiatics were in the midst of the Delta (at) Avaris."

[318]For the problems stemming from the uncertain reading *stpt* or , see below, p. 79 f.

[319]They either postulate the existence of devastation by the Fifteenth Dynasty Hyksos, whose rule at Avaris had ended some 80 years earlier, or a kind of political myth of the Egyptian king battling and overcoming evil; cf. further below, p. 101.

[320]Traditionally (cf. Gardiner, *EG* § 461) it is considered "the copula" possibly related to the verb *iw* "come" restricted in its use

here natural decay over time or if it applies to devastation of a specific nature. *Srwḏ* , lit. "to strengthen" has a wide range of application from maintaining order to restoring buildings,[321] so that no conclusion can be made about the kind of work done under Hatshepsut. As said before, this clause provides the circumstance for the deed especially emphasized as indicated by the introductory *iw*.

This focal point in Hatshepsut's review offers major difficulties. Gardiner has spear-headed the notion that Hatshepsut claims the restoration of decay which had prevailed over a long time, specifically "since Asiatics were in the region of Avaris in Lower Egypt."[322] Asiatics in the Avaris region are now established archaeologically since the Thirteenth Dynasty which chronologically amounts to approximately 300 years prior to Hatshepsut's reign.[323] This enormous time-span of envisioned neglected decay would also include the early Eighteenth Dynasty with the reigns of Ahmose, Amenophis I and Thutmosis I. The idea that Hatshepsut would imply neglect on the part of her otherwise highly adored father should seem surprising. There is no doubt that Hatshepsut refers to the presence of Asiatics in the Avaris region. It serves to emphasize what is described as 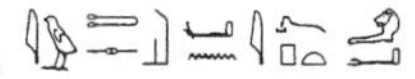 . It contains three problems, namely the meaning of *ṯs*, of *stpt* and *ḥꜣty-ꜥ*. As for the first, *ṯs* does not only occur for the raising of walls,[324] but, especially in the New Kingdom, for the levying of duties.[325] *Stpt* was declared identical with 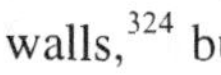 by Gardiner,[326] but the basic meaning of *stp* is rather "to pick out, to choose."[327] The application to food, especially meat, does not emphasize the dissolution, but rather the choiceness of the indicated deed. This aspect of choosing applies also to the selection of people especially for involuntary service.[328] A noun or nominally used verbal form would thus be "that what chooses." For 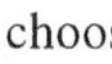 [329] Gardiner[330] suggested a literal meaning "(at the)

---

to sentences with adverbial predicate or with *sḏm.f* and *sḏm.n.f.* Without going here into a detailed discussion, I consider *iw* as a particle which indicates actuality. As such it is the affirmative equivalent to  indicating non-actuality.

[321] *Wb*. IV 194, 11-13.

[322] Cf. also above note 317.

[323] Manfred Bietak, *Avaris* (1996), 10 ff.

[324] *Wb*. V 405, 11; already in *Urk*. VII 56. 7.

[325] *Wb*. V 404, 7-8. The conflation of two verbs *ṯs* commences already in the late Old Kingdom; cf. Hans Goedicke, *Königliche Dokumente aus dem Alten Reich*, ÄA 14 (1967), 207.

[326] While the extention from "to select" to "to dismember", is beyond doubt in particular in connection with the slaughtering of animals (cf. Arne Eggebrecht, *Schlachtungsbräuche im Alten Ägypten*, Diss. München 1973, 160) there seems little justification to equate the word written with and without the determinative. In *Urk*. IV 1541, 16 it seem difficult to see *s stpt Ḥr-m-ꜣḫt* as "near the ruins of Harmachis" despite the later statement by the Sphinx *m.k sḫr.i mi wnn mšnw ḥꜥw.i nb stpw* "Lo, my condition is like all my disjunct limbs being encumbered." W. Helck, *Urkunden der 18. Dynastie, deutsch* (1961), 141 rendered the former "bei der Sehenswürdigkeit des Horus-im-Horizont" which might inject a modern touristic idea into the text. Although much of the body and especially the paws of the Sphinz were probably covered by sand, the Sphinx was never a "ruin." The king's resting place at the Sphinx is described in great detail, but, according to the text, Thutmosis IV got there without his followers. This difference seems to be expressed at this point, thus a rendering "in order to select Harmakhis" seems appropriate, i.e. the king choose the Sphinx for himself, while his followers were somewhat left behind. The writing  might best be seen as containing a metathesis of the two small signs.

[327] *Wb*. IV 337 f.

[328] *Stp* is used for the drafting of recruits since the Middle Kingdom; see *Wb*. IV 337, 10; cf. also *Wb*. IV 338, 1 in regard to material selection by the "lord of the Two Lands."

[329] The reading of  is not entirely certain according to the Davies copy.

[330] *JEA* 32 (1946), 47, note 13 stressing that "The adverbial use of *ḥꜣt-ꜥ*, for which Gunn and I could find no parallel." His

beginning since" although  is not attested for the beginning of units of time. Aside of marking the beginning of a text,[331] 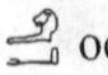 occurs only as the social designation *ḥ3ty-ʿ* commonly rendered "count, mayor."[332] As a result of these considerations, *stpt ḥ3ty-ʿ* can be rendered "that what the mayor selects," a term for a locally executed levy for corvée.[333]

We come back once more to the qualification "since the Asiatics were in the area of Lower Egypt's Avaris."[334] It does not concern any envisioned destruction by those Asiatics, but rather serves to define the long period of time that the local corvée had not been called up. As a result, the people living there were not accustomed to this levy.

aq) While Hatshepsut was taking emergency measures to cope with devastations afflicting some parts of the country by invoking a corvée that had not been used for centuries, her measures did not meet an universal positive reaction. Those objecting to the orders are identified as *šm3w m q3b.sn*, which indicates that they were part of "the Asiatics in the area of Lower Egypt's Avaris."[335] Those people indicated as *šm3w* have been considered "roving hordes" (Gardiner) or "nomads" (Redford).[336] The term is obviously derived from the verb *šm3* generally translated "to wander."[337] The exact rendering is essential for the proper evaluation of the socio-ethnic nature of the people concerned. The very fact that the term *šm3* occurs repeatedly in the late Old Kingdom as a personal name casts doubt on this rendering, because those person did neither wander nor are they away from Egypt but are rather resident there in important positions.[338] The same applies to the various application of the word which do not point to an emphasis on "wandering" as a movement, but rather as a means to reach a goal and to remain there.[339] Applying this to people, they should be seen as "Zugewanderte," i.e., as "resident aliens." For the understanding of the passage under discussion, this identification is of paramount importance. The *šm3w* should not be seen as "roving hordes" of "nomads" but rather as people of foreign extraction living in Egypt. The term defines only their social standing in Egypt but does not reflect any specific ethnic origin.[340]

---

reference to Mond & Myers, *Temples of Armant*, pl. 103, 1.2 = *Urk.* IV 1244, 16 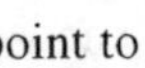 *ḫt tpyt* which he considers as "(at the) beginning under the first generation," might be better taken with Helck (op. cit. 13) as "der Fürst unter der ersten Generation."

[331] As opener of a text  should be recognized as "beginning of a document"; cf. Hans Goedicke, "Zur Einleitungsformel didaktischer Texte," *ZÄS* 86 (1961), 147-149.

[332] The designation identifies the "foremost" (*ḥ3ty*) of the register (ʿ) of a social unit, either incorporated, i.e., a "mayor," or non incorporated, i.e., a "count."

[333] We know more about the drafting of people for public work projects in the Old Kingdom than in the New Kingdom; cf. H. Goedicke, *Königliche Dokumente*, 244-247.

[334] See above, p. 79.

[335] It is not clear if the specification *t3-mḥw ḥwt-wʿrt* is only a reflection of administrative exactitude, i.e., that the place is listed with the region in which it is located, or if there is an effort to idistinguish Avaris of the North from another Avaris, about which nothing is known.

[336] These interpretations seem unjustly influenced by Manetho's derogatory description of the invading Hyksos.

[337] *Wb.* IV 470, 2.

[338] Cf. H. Goedicke, *Königliche Dokumente*, 181 ff.

[339] The title *ḥry-šm3w* (*Wb.* IV 470, 10) makes it quite clear that those foreign people were in Egyptian service.

[340] In its nature the term can be compared with *š3sw* which seems to replace it. Again, it is a descriptive term derived from the

These resident aliens living among the Asiatics in the Avaris district are accused of continuously "overthrowing" (*sḫn*).[341] The object of their continuous "overthrowing" is given as . Gardiner and Redford rendered it "what had been made."[342] Without any qualification a global reference to "what had been made" produces very little sense as object of a continuous destructive attitude. Instead *iryt* should be recognized here as "that what is to be done," i.e., the assigned tasks.[343]

ar) What follows has found rather bewildering renderings and interpretations.   Gardiner rendered "they ruled without Reᶜ, and he acted not by divine command (?) down to my august self," which later translators closely followed.[344] These words are puzzling for grammatical and semantic reasons. *Ḥqꜣ* "to rule" is principally a transitive verb and thus requires an object. There is no indication that the resident aliens (*šmꜣw*) had ever ruled in Egypt. As for the assumed identification with the "Hyksos"[345] there is nothing that shows them as having been hostile to the Egyptian religious institutions. Reᶜ is recurrent in the"Hyksos" royal names[346] in addition to their consistent use of the designation *sꜣ-Rᶜ*, "son of Reᶜ. The notion of Reᶜ acting by "divine decree" lacks textual corroboration. Furthermore,  is not an orthography for the noun "decree" nor is the assumed **wḏ nṯr* a likely spelling for it. Furthermore, the idiom "down to" in a sequence of time is *nfryt r* and not **nfryt ḥr* as the text has it.[347] Assuming the passage would actually refer to the "Hyksos," why should Hatshepsut some 70 years after the establishing of the Theban hegemony in Egypt be concerned with them? Finally, it would seem a remarkable case of self-esteem if Hatshepsut, who certainly did not suffer from excessive modesty, would proclaim herself the first rightful ruler. All these points would seem valid reasons for a fresh investigation of the passage.

To begin with, resident aliens were continuously "overthrowing duties." The essential qualification of those neglected duties, namely how they are related to those people, is missing in this statement. It is the

habit of roving around in which these people were engaged, but should not be understood as reflecting any ethnicity, as Raphael Giveon, *Les Bédouins Shosou des Documents Égyptiens*, 219 ff., prefers to see them.

341 In Sethe's edition the reading is left uncertain, while the Davies' copy indicates some breakage but leaves no doubt about a reading *sḫn* for older *sḫnn*; cf. *Wb.* IV 293, 19-20. The pseudo-verbal construction is an indicator of the continuity of the activity.

342 Gardiner: "(with) roving hordes in the midst of them overthrowing what had been made"; S. Ratié: "avec des nomades parmi eux, détruisant tout ce qui avait été fait"; A. Burkhardt: "und die Nomaden unter ihnen 'zerstörten', was geschaffen worden war"; Redford: "when the nomads in their midst were destroying what had been made."

343 *Wb.* I 113, 6-7 lists it as "das Gemachte, die Tat." In Tutankhamun's restauration stela the word occurs twice: *Urk.* IV 2026, 20 "they (i.e. the gods) abandoned what was to be done" and *Urk.* IV 2028, 13 "he gave an increase upon what was to be done before." In p.Westcar 4, 11 and 6, 17 the miracles performed are due to "what was to be done" (*iryt*).

344 S. Ratié: "ils gouvernaient sans Rê; on n'agissait plus selon l'ordre divin jusqu'à ce que vint Ma Majesté"; A. Burkhardt: "Sie herrschten ohne Re, er gab keinen Befehl bis zur (Herrschaft) Meiner Majestät"; Redford: "They ruled without Re, nor did he act by divine decree right down to my majesty('s time)!."

345 See above, pp. 78 f.

346 E.g., *Sḫᶜ-n-Rᶜ*; *Mꜣᶜ-ib-Rᶜ*; *Mr-wsr-Rᶜ*; *Swsr-n-Rᶜ*; *ᶜꜣ-wsr-Rᶜ*; *ᶜꜣ-qnn-Rᶜ*; *Nb-ḫpš-Rᶜ*.

347 *Wb.* II 262, 14; Gardiner, *Grammar* § 179. It seem that  after *nfryt* was erroneously taken as a determinative, which, however, is incorrect.

attached *ḥq3.n.(.i) sn* "(after I) ruled them" which provides it.[348] In this way the objectionable activity of the "aliens" would be meaningfully defined.

is not the compound preposition, but rather the verb *ḫmt*, "to expect, to anticipate."[349] Depending on it is a *sḏm.f* with an anticipatorily stated nominal subject[350] indicating the nature of the expectation: Rᶜ is curious because the hieroglyph has no pupil.[351] Obviously it cannot be the verb **iri*, "to do," but should be recognized as an ideographic writing for *šp*, "to be blind."[352] Depending on it is the verbal clause introduced by *m* stressing the particularity of the action.[353] In this clause, *m wḏ nṯr nfryt ḥr.i*, *wḏ* is the predicate, *nṯr* is the subject, *nfryt* is the object and *ḥr.i* prepositional adjunct. As for *wḏ* , "to command someting to somebody", cf. *Wb*. I 395, B.[354] The use of *ḥr* instead of *n* is due to the kind of person involved, in addition to reflecting or suggesting the personal presence of Hatshepsut at the act.[355] As for *nṯr*, here, as before,[356] it refers to Amun and his timely intervention for her. *Nfryt*, written without a determinative, is not the word for "end" as has been generally assumed and which would make no sense in the given context;[357] it rather should be recognized as the word for "tiller rope," *Wb* II 262, 9-10, which is used metaphorically as the instrument for supreme guidance.[358] Summing up the details, the passage explaining the continuous "overthrowing of the duties after (I) ruled them" requires rendering "while thinking, that Reᶜ will not be blind when the *nṯr* assigns the tiller-rope to my Majesty." To put it in other words, the aliens did not expect that Hatshepsut's reach for power would be successful. No further details

[348]For *ḥq3* "to rule people," cf. Wb. III 170, 14. The somewhat unusual formulation seems to reflect Hatshepsut's ascent to kingship which made her ruler over those people. The suffix *.i* appears to be omitted here, while shortly thereafter Hatshepsut refers to herself as .

[349]For the orthography see *Wb*. III 285.

The common rendering "without" of *m ḫm* is not rooted in the Egyptian, but rather a reflection of modern idiomatics. Sinuhe B 44 = R 68 *wnn ir.f t3 pf mi-m-ᶜ m ḫm.f nṯr pf mnḫ* "How will that land be when it does not know that excellent god?"; Admonitions 10,4 *iw pr-nswt . . . r-ḏr.f m ḫm b3kw.f* "while the entire palace (scil. royal administration) is ignorant of its dues"; Amenemhet VII f *nn ḫpr šp mᶜr m ḫm mkw* "Success never occurs in ignorance of a protector."

[350]For other cases of this construction, cf. below, p. 93.

[351]It is specially marked in the Davies' copy, while Sethe had ignored it. The suffix *.f* can only refer to the mention of Reᶜ preceding it, as Gardiner also concluded. This not only confirms the syntactic structure as submittd here, but also the fact that Reᶜ belongs to this and not the previous sentence.

[352]*Wb*. IV 443. Despite the spelling Gardiner read it *irt m* "act by means of."

[353]Cf. Gardiner, *Grammar*, § 444. 3.

[354]If it is the noun, *wḏ* is written with the determinative which can be omitted for the verb.

Gunn had considered *wḏ nṯr* "by god's command" to mean "by oracle," but Gardiner extended it to divine inspiration by dream, although Reᶜ is not known to interfere in human affairs in this fashion. If it were **wḏ-nṯr* "divine decree" is should be written in analogy to *wḏ-nswt* or with an indirect genitive.

[355]Cf. Alexandre Varille, "Un emploi particulier de la préposition *Kher*," *Kêmi* 4 (1931), 119-125.

[356]See above , p. 76.

[357]Previous translators did not comment on the word. Gardiner seems to associate it with *nfryt r* which ineicates the limit of a period of time or space. There is no case where *nfryt* has a determinative. A. Burkhardt solved the conundrum by injecting the word "Herrschaft" while Redford added "time."

[358]*Wb*. II 262, 10; *Med. Habu* VI 432 B. Ship's ropes as metapher for the means of exercising authority by Hashepsut is also used by Inana; see *Urk*. IV 60, 6-8.

for this expectation are disclosed; if the reference to Reʿ in this connection has any particular religious significance is impossible to decide.

as) The disregard for the duties assigned by Hatshepsut by a group of aliens of Asiatic extraction living in the area of Avaris is followed by a review of her political career. Again, the text has offered serious problems to earlier translators.[359] Grammatically, the opening pseudo-verbal clause *mn.kwi* has to be taken as a sentence of circumstance, however, not of the present but of the past.[360] It introduces the main clause *sr.n.tw.i*. Although Gardiner pointed to a seeming parallel in the Rosetta stone (Urk. II 192, 1), *r ḥnty rnpwt* refers here to a defined period of time and thus has to be recognized as being principally past.[361] The plural *nswt* is otherwise attested with Geb and especially with Amun but not with Reʿ;[362] as Reʿ is principally not envisioned as sedentary, the mention of *nswt-Rʿ* cannot refer to any real or imaginary "thrones."[363] As in the case of Amun, the term *nswt* appears to apply rather to those holding a "seat," i.e., full-righted citizen.[364] Hatshepsut's situation described as *mn ḥr nswt-Rʿ* should thus be envisioned not as a physical but as a legal one, i.e., that she "was established over" people as a result of her authority.[365] The

[359]Gardiner: "I being firmly established on the thrones of Rʿ. I was foretold for a (future) period of years as a born conqueror"; S. Ratié, "Je fus établie sur le trône de Rê; on m'a prédit une éternité comme devant être efficace en actions"; A. Burkhardt, "denn ich bin fest auf den Thronen des Re, ich wurde angekündigt für eine Periode 'von Jahren' als eine 'Sie entsteht und erobert (= geborener Eroberer)'"; Redford, "I am ensconced upon the thrones of Re, I have been foretold aeons ago as a natural conqueror."

[360]Gardiner, *Grammar*, § 314.. For placing the pseudo-vebal clause at the beginning, cf. e.g., Sinuhe R 7-9.

[361]In *Urk*. IV 1154, 8 *ḥnty rnpwt* unquestionably denotes an unlimited period of time, but in its association with a part of Hatshepsut's life it has to be of defined duration. This contradictory situation might be resolved by supplying a suffix *.i* after *rnpwt*, i.e. "during a (or the) period of (my) years."

[362]As for Geb, see *Wb*. II 322, 9; cf. also K.P. Kuhlmann, *Der Thron im Alten Ägypten*, 48 f.

[363]What appears as "thrones of Reʿ" makes no sense, because there are no specific *nswt* associated with this god. In addition, the passage concerns clearly a period when Hatshepsut had not yet become king, which makes any association with Reʿ rather unlikely. During the years prior to her reach for power, she was firmly in control of matters in Thebes and the rest of the South. The dominating deity for her during this time and later as well was, of course, Amun, Any references to Reʿ in the Speos text refer to him not as deity worshipped in Heliopolis, but rather in his cosmic aspect as world ruler. While being established in Thebes she certainly had no influence in Heliopolis. These reflections make it rather unlikely that *nswt* should be directly connected with Reʿ.

Syntactically, it is beyond doubt that *sr.n.tw.i* "I was pronounced" opens a new sentence. At the same time Reʿ might be part of the preceding sentence. This seemingly isolated mention of Reʿ becomes, however, meaningful, when taken as an assertion of the validity of the ensuing statement. The pseudo-verbal clause *mn.kwi ḥr nswt(.i)*, like afterwards *ii.kwi m Ḥr*, serves as circumstancial/temporal specification of the ensuing main statement. As a result of these considerations, It seems best to render "While I was established over (my) seats, o Reʿ, I was reported as a do-getter. When I had come as Horus, (my) uraeus is spitting fire against my opponents." For invocations of deities as an assertion, cf. Hermann Grapow, *Wie die alten Ägypter sich anredeten*, II, AAWB 1940, 12, 73 ff.

[364] See Hans Goedicke, "*Imn nb nswt tꜣwy*," *The Intellectual Heritage of Egypt, Studies Kakosy* (1992), 197 ff.

[365]The legal implication of the statement "I was established on/over the thrones of Reʿ" are not clear to me, especially since it concerns the years before Hatshepsut became king. During those years her influence was concentrated in Thebes and no apparent link with "thrones of Reʿ comes to mind.

verb *sr* is well attested in the sense of "to make known" without prophetic implications.[366] For the word-pair *ḫpr.s iṯi(.s)*, cf. Gardiner, op. cit., 55, note v and Berlin Leather Roll I, 12.[367]

The passage, which is parallel to a similarly composed one concerning the prevailing situation following next, describes Hatshepsut's success during the time she acted semi-indepedently in the South, while Thutmosis III, still fairly young, was mostly restricted to the North.[368] What her constitutional position was during this time is not clear in all detail because there are no dated records of Hatshepsut for it. At any rate, this situation lasted for a defined "period of years" (*ḥnty rnpwt*), in chronological term somewhat more than six years.

at) The change in Hatshepsut's legal status is expressed as *ii.kwi m Ḥr* "(when) I had come as Horus."[369] The Old Perfective not only implies the completion of the move, but also the continuity of its consequences;[370] for *ii m* "to come as someone," cf. *Wb.* I 37, 20;[371] the attaining of the role as "Horus" is the advance to sole rulership.[372] The designation of the uraeus as *wꜥtt* occurs also for Thutmosis III.[373] For the metaphor of the uraeus spitting fire against enemies, see H. Grapow, *Die Bildlichen Ausdrücke*, 49; *Wb.* II 335, 8. It is important to note the use of the pseudo-verbal construction with *ḥr* indicating continuity, i.e., her attitude towards her enemies was a continuous one. The targets of Hatshepsut's continued forceful action are indicated as *ḫft(yw).i* "my opponents," which reflects only their attitude but not their background.[374]

au) The next syntactic unit, like most before it, consists of two clauses, one a *sḏm.n.f*, the other a *sḏm.f*. This sequence of verbal forms indicates the first as a relative past to the second, a feature not recognized in previous translations.[375] Without it a non-sequitur results. For *sḥri*, "to drive away foes," cf. *Urk.* IV 209,

[366] *Wb.* 190 IV.

[367] Hans Goedicke, "The Berlin Leather Roll (P. Berlin 3029)," *Festschrift zum 150jährigen Bestehen des Berliner Ägyptischen Museums* (1974), 95.

[368] For the political situation at this time, see below, "Thutmosis III's early Years," pp. 121 ff,

[369] Gardiner: "(And now) I am come as the Sole one of Horus darting fire against my enemies"; S. Ratié: "Je suis venue, Horus, unique Déesse, la flamme contre mes enemis"; A. Burkhardt: "Ich bin gekommen als einziger (fem) Horus und speie Feuer gegen meine Feinde"; Redford: "I am come as Horus, the Unique One spitting fire against my enemies."

[370] It is in the nature of the verb *ii* , "to come" that the sentence refers first of all to Hatshepsut's arrival to kingship, but also her continuous holding it.

[371] Cf. *Pyr.* 819 c "Lo, he has come as Orion, lo, Osiris has come as Orion."

[372] In the setup of ancient Egyptian kingship, the position of "Horus" is a unique one and there seem to have been no provision to change it. It is significant that after the rapprochement between Hatshepsut and Thutmosis III only the former bears the designation "Horus."

[373] *Urk.* IV 160, 3. In both cases the designation *wꜥtt* for the uraeus is chosen to emphasize its uniqueness, a concern caused by the ambiguities in the power relationship between Thutmosis III and Hatshepsut. The text is clearly a belated affirmation of his sole rulership at a time when Hatshepsut had been dead for 20 years. Why Thutmosis III saw it necessary to emphasize his position at this point in time is not apparent at first sight, but might have something to do wih the persecution of Hatshepsut's memory; cf. Charles F. Nims, "The date of the dishonoring of Hatshepsut," *ZÄS* 93 (1966), 97-100.

[374] Cf. David Lorton, *The Juridical Terminology of International Relations in Egyptian Texts through Dyn. XVIII* (1974), 119-121.

[375] Gardiner: "I have banished the abomination of the gods, and the earth has removed their foot(-prints)"; S. Ratié: "j'ai chassé

17; de Buck, Reading Book 111, 11. Gardiner's "to banish" suits especially well the passage because of the implicit legal action against lawbreakers. The term *bwt-nṯrw*, lit. "abominations of the god,"[376] is a technical term when used for people who deserve the death penalty.[377] It applies here to a distinct group of people, who are denoted as *ḫftyw* "opponents" in the preceding sentence and earlier as "*šmꜣw*, among the people of Asiatic background in the area of Avaris."[378] The equation is important for realizing that Hatshepsut's actions were directed against a group of people of foreign extraction who had been dwelling in Egypt, specifically in the northeastern Delta with Avaris as its center.

It was after Hatshepsut had banished those disobedient people, that they suffered an additional blow, described as "the earth removed their foot-prints."[379] The removal of the footprints by the earth[380] amounts to an elimination from the living. Hatshepsut had not executed those who had disobeyed her, but had rather banished them from her realm. That they nevetheless came to grief was thus not her responsibility.

av) To evaluate this development serves the sentence *tp-rd pw n tf-tfw iww r sww.f hrw*. As a nominal clause it is atemporal in character.[381] The deed, namely the removal of the foot-prints by the earth, is an event unrelated to Hatshepsut. It was carried out by "the earth" (*tꜣ*) which had received the "instruction" (*tp-rd*)[382] to do so from an entity identified as *tf-tfw* lit. "father of fathers." It obviously has nothing to do with the person of Hatshepsut, not even her remotest descent, but also nothing with Reʿ as has been assumed.[383] While the royal designation *sꜣ-Rʿ* "son-of-Reʿ" might inspire the notion of a sonship from

l'abomination du Grand Dieu; la terre a porté leurs sandales"; A. Burkhardt: "Ich habe den Abscheu vor den Göttern vertrieben, und das Land hat ihre Fußspuren vertilgt"; Redford: "I have driven off the abomination of the great god, and the earth has removed their foot-prints."

[376]  can be understood in two ways: it is either a singular (*bwt*) followed by a plural (*nṯr*) as "abomination of the gods" or a plural of a compound term (*bwt-nṯr*) as "god's abomination." The first one would be collective for those who are abhored and those who abhore, the second would refer to a plural abhored by one god. Considering Hatshepsut's strong personal religious commitment to Amun, the latter would seem likely. Although *nṯr* has been used in the text in reference to her deceased father, a reference to Thutmosis I would here be out of place.

[377] Cf. Wolfgang Boochs, *Strafrechtliche Aspekte im altägyptischen Recht* (1993), 72; David Lorton, "The treatment of Criminals in Ancient Egypt," (1976), 29.

[378] See above, pp. 79 f.

[379] *Ini ṯbwt* "to carry off the foot-prints," corresponds to *ini rd* "to remove the foot" as closing act before leaving divine presence; for this ritual, see above , p. 40.

Although  could be a *sḏm.n.f* (see Gardiner, *Grammar* § 413, presumably by haplography) it does not affect the syntactic relationship between the two sentences. Only after the people were expelled, could the earth take away their foot-prints.

[380] For *tꜣ* "earth," see *Wb.* V 212-214.

[381] For the atemporal nature of the nominal clause, see, Gardiner, *Grammar* § 128.

[382] For *tp-rd* , "instruction," see *Wb* V 288 f. The idiom appears to be a favorite of the time, as demonstrated by Inana (*Urk.* IV 58, 1), Djehuty (*Urk.* IV 420, 17; 421, 8, 17; 422, 7, 15; 423, 7, 15, etc), but also Thutmosis I (*Urk.* I97. 6; 255, 13) and Rekhmireʿ (*Urk.* IV 1103, 14, etc. The term does not imply the absolute force of a "command" (*wḏ*) but is nevertheless authoritative. It does not only indicate the vehicle by which a deed is to be achieved, but also the concept which generates the "instruction." In this respect it requires a rendering "governance", for which *Urk.* IV 255, 13 *mꜣꜣ.ṯ tp-rd.ṯ m ʿḥ* "may you see your governance in the palace" is a good illustration dating to Hatshepsut.

[383] Former renderings are, Gardiner: "Such has been the guiding rule of the father of [my fathers]"; S. Ratié: "Ce fut le devoir du

Reᶜ,[384] there is nowhere any indication of a descent from Reᶜ by successive generations. While the god might be portrayed as a spiritual father, there is no myth of a physical procreation by him, leave alone is there a female companion as would be necessary for a descent. While "father of fathers" in the later Eighteenth Dynasty might be used euphemistically for the Pharaoh,[385] it cannot have any bearing on a political ruler. It is rather to be recognized as designation of the primeval entity the Egyptian conceived of.[386] This primeval father is not necessarily a spiritual numen, but can also be a material one, as clearly indicated in the creation account according to which Atum floated in Nun until their separation which set creation into motion.[387] It is in this sense, namely as reference to Nun, the primeval water, that *tf-tfw* should be understood here.[388]

This primordinal "father of fathers" is qualified as *iw r sww.f hrw 1*. The spelling does not allow a distinction between a present or past participle; the former would indicate a habitual coming "at his times," the latter has the historical implication of "who came at his time."[389] Of the two the second is preferable, because there is no conceivable schedule for the appearance of Nun at the human scene. Two aspects have to be elucidated: first, the implication of coming at one's own time, and second, the delineation of it. As for the first, to come at one's own time is, of course, unknown to the one who is been visited and thus a surprise. In short, the appearing of Nun is indicated as a surprise for those who were affected by it. The possible plural of occurrences might seem odd at first sight until one takes into account that the northeastern Delta was the scene of two major intrusions of the Mediterranean Sea as far as Avaris. The

---

père de mes pères"; A. Burkhardt: "Eine Weisung des Vaters der 'Väter' war es"; Redford: "that was (?) the instruction of the father of the father[s]."

384 The designation "son of Reᶜ" is widely seen as indicating divine origin of the king. is influenced by the political myth promulgated by or for Hatshepsut about her descent. This notion is rooted in the primarily physical evaluation of sonship in western cultures, while in ancient Egypt the emphasis seems to be rather on loyalty and fellowship. In its nature the term *sꜣ* should rather be seen to denote a "disciple," especially in the German "Jünger," indicating a spiritual association which has an implicit active value; in modern parlance rather a "confessor," i.e. someone who confesses a religious doctrin.

The religious nature of the designation is well demonstrated through its adaptation by every ruler from the Fourth Dynasty on, including the Hyksos-rulers of the Fifteenth Dynasty. It would make little sense to envisage for them a physical descent from Reᶜ as Hatsepsut had promulgated for herself.

385 See H. Goedicke, *BES* 3 (1981), 33 ff.; cf. also Wolfgang Helck, *"Vater der Väter,"* NAWG 1965,9 (1965), 173 ff.

386 Concerning such a numenous power the mention here provides a number of specification. It is not stationary, as it "comes." It does not carry out actions directly, but rather issues an instruction to the earth. Its presence in the human realm is temporary and not necessarily defined in advance.

While *it-itw* would seem the reading for 𓏏𓆑 𓏏𓆑 𓏏𓆑[𓏏𓆑] some observation deserves mentioning. The word for "father" had occurred twice earlier. Once (l. 26) as plural spelled i 𓇋𓏏𓆑𓀀𓏥 and in the open space at the end of l. 26 as 𓏏𓆑. The marked difference makes me wonder if f 𓏏𓆑 𓏏𓆑 𓏏𓆑 𓏏𓆑 should really be read *it-itw* "father of fathers" and not *tf-tfw*. Because of its four elements, it could be a superlative formation (cf. Gardiner, op. cit. § 112). The absence of any determinative makes it difficult to define *tf*. The removal of foot-prints and the earlier mentioned "water-torrent" (see above, p. 59) let one think of some hydrological term here as well. There is the word *tf* "spittle" in Pyr. 241 a which applies to some monster.

387 Cf. James P. Allen, *Genesis in Egypt*, YES 2 (1988), 4 f.

388 Nun denoted as "father of fathers" is attested in the reign of Ramesses II; see W. Helck, op. cit. 176

389 For *r sww.f* "at his time" cf. *Wb*. IV 57, 10; 13.

first happened prior to Amenophis I and is the event described in the flood-inscription of Ahmose.[390] This would make it a little over 70 years before Hatshepsut, a timespan easily remembered when it comes to devastating events. The other is the intrusion of the sea in her lifetime which is mentioned in the earlier part of the text as a reason for Hatshepsut's gratitude to Pakhet for diverting the "water-torrent into the wadis of the Eastern Desert without drawning her," scil. her realm.[391] In other words, there were two surprising arrivals of Nun in Egypt's perimeter. The second one happened when Hatshepsut, not long after her ascent as king, had banished those who had disobeyed her orders, so "that the earth removed their foot-prints."

Following *r sww.f* is 𓇳𓏤 which has been taken as a dangling apposition.[392] The removal of the foot-prints has nothing to do with Reʿ and even less with his timely appearance. As already pointed out before, the suffix after *r sww.f* can only refer to precedingly mentioned *tf-tfw* for whom a subsequent identification by an apposition makes no sense. The simple solution is reading *hrw* or *hrw 1* "by day" or "on one day."

Conclusion

"Just as the destruction of a command of Amun will not happen, my inscription shall last like the mountains!aw) As the sun-disc shines on the titulary of my Majesty, my falcon over the throne shall be elevated for all my duration."ax)

aw) That those opposing her were punished following their expulsion from Egypt, Hatshepsut takes as a confirmation by the divine of her reach for power. The remainder of the text is thus a request for continuous support of her rule and is not part of the preceding reflections.[393] As an outlook into the future it is, of course, beyond her control and can only have the form of an invocation of that power that had influenced her fate.

As she emphatically states her religious belief in Amun in the early part of her inscription[394] the god's mention as given in Davies copy should be prefered to Sethe's former reading and restoration. The closing

[390]See Hans Goedicke, *Studies about Kamose and Ahmose*, 121-166; cf. also Karen P. Foster and Robert K. Ritner, *JNES* 55 (1996), 1-14.

[391]See above, p. 59 f.

[392]Gardiner: "who came at his (appointed) times, even Reʿ;" S. Ratié: venus en leurs temps (comme) Rê;" A. Burkhardt: "die zu seiner Zeit, (nämlich) des Re, kam;" Redford: "who comes at his regular times, viz. Re."

[393]Previous translation did not separate this section from the main body of the text, nor did they reflect the two pairs of sentences of which it consists. Gardiner connected part of the first pair with the preceding as "and there shall never be the destruction of what Amun has commanded." S. Ratié changed the first part into a personal statement "Jamais il n'y aura de transgression à ce que j'ai ordonné." Similarly A. Burkhardt as "Nicht soll verletzt werden, was ich befohlen habe" as well as Redford "What I have authorized shall not be annulled."

[394]See above, pp. 45 f.

section is carefully styled. It consists of two wishes, both construed in the same fashion, namely as a model and its emulation.[395]

The model in the first plea is *nn ḫpr ḥḏt wḏ n ỉmn*. As for *nn ḫpr*, it can only be prospective;[396] the subject is *ḥḏt* "the destruction." *Wḏ n ỉmn* is obviously not a relative-form, which would have to be feminine. Consequently it has to be recognized as a noun followed by an indirect genitive.[397] This formulation is due to the fact that the absolutely used relative-form would refer only to a specific command, while here a global validity is intended. This allusion to the permanence of a command by Amun is, of course, a hardly veiled reference to Hatshepsut's elevation on account of an oracle by Amun.[398] This prototype "as a destruction of a command of Amun will never happen," is followed by the wish "my inscription shall last like the mountains." There is obvious punning between the "command of Amun," and Hatshepsut's inscription (*wḏ*); if there is also an alliteration between *ỉmn* and *mn* can only be guessed. The comparison with "the mountains" as metaphor of durability[399] has its basis in the nature of the rock-inscription.

ax) The second request has as premise "As the sun-disc shines and it throws rays upon the titulary of my Majesty."[400] The separation of *psḏ ỉtn* and *sš.f stwt* is curious and might be an attempt to inject a direct link to the inscription. The royal protocol to be illuminated by the sun's rays is the one written as opening of the text. Unfortunately there are no observations of the sun's impact on it, i.e. if the sun actually reaches it.

The correlated plea is *qꜣ bik.ỉ ḥr-tp śrḫ n ḏt ḏt*, "my falcon(-standard) over the palace shall be high for ever." Because the "falcon" (*bik*) is here most probably to be understood as a physical symbol of authority,[401] it is tempting to understood *srḫ* also as denoting a material reality.[402] Although *srḫ* depicts the

[395]This part has almost literary quality and one could consider it made up of two couplets.

[396]Cf. H. Satzinger, op. cit. § 57.

[397]Gardiner, note w, takes it as an irregularity for an absolutely used relative-form *wḏt.n*. Even the spelling with the determinative — after *wḏ* is more in line with the noun than the verb. Sethe had originally divided the text into *wḏ.n.ỉ mn [nḫbt.]ỉ mi ḏww* which has been followed by some despite Davies copy. The result is a meaningless repeated claim of Hatshepsut's personal act without any corollary to confirm it. Against Sethe's restoration speaks further the unlikely repetition of the word *nḫbt* "titulary" in close succession.

[398]The towering event during the great feast of Amun, which led to Hatshepsut's turn to a chapel from which she emerged crowned is literally ascribed to a "command" of Amun, which became the pivotal feature of Hatshepsut's kingship.

[399]Cf. H. Grapow, *Die bildlichen Ausdrücke des Ägyptischen*, 52 f.

[400]Disregarding the literary structure, Gardiner gave for it ". . . and the sun's disk shines and spreads rays over the titulary of my august person, and my falcon rises high above the kingly banner unto all eternity." S. Ratié follows it closely as "le disque Aton étincelle, il répand des rayons sur la titulature de Ma Majesté; mon faucon est haute sur la façcade du palais pour l'infini de l'éternité." A. Burkhardt divided the syntactic unit into separate sentences as "Die Sonne scheint und breitet ihre Strahlen aus über die Titulatur meiner Majestät. Mein Falke ragt hoch über den Thron meiner Person ewiglich." A somewhat differenmt division was offered by Redford: ". . . and when the sun-disc shines, he shall shed his rays upon the titulary of My Majesty! High shall be my falcon upon the *serekh* for all time!"

[401]appearances. The establishing of the "falcon over the palace facade" is also claimed by Thutmosis III in his inscription from year 42 about the building actiivity at Karnak *Urk.* IV 160, 11-14 "the one who wrote for me (my?) titulary himself, he established my

facade of the archaic palace, the word is not used to denote the palace itself. It is later rather commonly applied to the throne, i.e., the place from which the king makes binding pronouncements while acting as *nswt*. In other words, Hatshepsut emphasizes here her role as king of Egypt, different from her earlier position as Theban "patrician."[403] This plea for carrying the symbol of supreme authority has the qualification  . It indicates not an unlimited "eternity"[404] but rather "bodily duration," i.e., while being alive.[405] Hatshepsut's plea for holding the authority as king is aimed for the duration of her lifetiome. This is insofar remarkable as it implies the possibility of an abdication, either total or partially. It provides some hint what kind of a political deal apparently existed between her and Thutmosis III and his partisans.

To sum up, the closing of the text returns to the topic stated at its beginning. It is the plea that her "great name" as a symbol of her role as king lasts and that she will be remembered in the annals in a positive form.

---

falcon over the palace facade; after he made me strong as victorious bull, he caused that I appear inside Thebes . . ." See also P. Lacau–H. Chevrier, *Une Chapelle d'Hathchepsout*, 143 f.

[402]*Srḫ* denoting the throne begins with Amenophis III, which supports the identification here with the palace; cf. K.P. Kuhlmann, op. cit. 60 f.; 84 f., as does *Urk*. IV 896, 9.

[403]Her social status is only once defined as *bἰt* in conjunction with her musing before ascending the throne; see above, p. 44.

[404]*Wb*. V 506, 3 lists it under *ḏt* "body," but still renders it "eternally." The term is a compound of two word, namely "*ḏt* "body" and *ḏt* "duration." It conerns specifically the bodily duration, i.e., the physical lifetime. G. Thausing, *Mél. Maspero* I, 1934, 36 understood it as the forerunner of *nḥḥ ḏt* The situation in the Pyramid Texts (e.g., *Pyr*. 101 d) is not transparent enough to allow a conclusion. It does seem to emphasize the notion of "duration" in the sense of "body of duration."

[405]For the political implications, cf. below pp. 96 ff.

Running Translation

"[Life to the Horus: 'Powerful of Attributes'; the Two Goddesses: 'Flourishing of] Years'; Horus-of-Gold: 'Divine of Appearances'; the 'Good-God' Lord of the [Two] Lands *Kꜣ-Mꜣꜥt-Rꜥ*; Offspring of Reꜥ [Companion of Amun Hatshepsut, given life.] [She made this] lasting [monument] of perpetuating her great name like heaven, as she graces the annals, and as she prevails over the region of the Mountain-mistress eastward.

The Lord [of the glow] over the coast-line—(while) his flames were outside the Two Mountain-ranges (i.e. Upper Egypt)—braziers were distributed, which enlarged the (darkened) shrines [into] favorite places. Every god—each one away from the dwelling which he had loved—his Ka was satisfied about his (temporary) seats, which I had established for residence. [The heart] of [those in] their pillared halls were gladdened, as the hiding place inside the structure was reinforced up to the place of (the rite of) removing the footstep. Every [god] fashioned in his body from electrum of ꜥAmau, their permanent feasts in the cycle of the cult-year and the seasonal festive gifts were in observation of the regulation of my maker. The ritual in its arrangement which had been done for the predecessors of the (present) persons was reinforced.

When the stipulations of her being ruler were fulfilled, which he had made in the past to the chiefs, my divine heart was searching for the future, as the heart of the *bit* had thought of eternity upon the pronouncement of 'Him-who-splits-the-*ished*-tree': 'O Amun, Lord-of-Millions, I shall magnify the Maꜥat, which is desired for him! As one who lives on it knows: It is my bread! May I swallow its fragrance, when I am one flesh with him who has caused me to exist in order to cause his fame to be powerful in this land!'

I am a [belonging] one of Atum [through knowing] Khepri, who makes what is, one whom Reꜥ intended at his designing that the lands be united under my supervision, and that Egypt and Desert (Black Land and Red Land) be under my dread! My might be causing the foreigners to bow down, while the uraeus upon my brows making peaceful all the flat-landers for [me]. El-Shawet and [*M*]*iww*—they do not hide from my Majesty. Punt shall overflow for me on fields whose trees bear fresh myrrh. The (desert) tracks, which were closed because of the Two Ways, shall be trodden again. My troops which had been neglected shall be supplied with excellent things.

Since my appearance as king, the temple of the Lady of Qusae, which had fallen into oblivion, the earth had swallowed its noble sanctuary. A/the child could dance on its roof, as there was no tradition, which would cause respect. As crooks were accounting the 'damage' dishonestly, there were indeed not its date of appearances. I consecrated it, when it was built anew. I made her guiding serpent statue of gold in order to protect her city out of the ark for land-procession.

Pakhet, the Great, who roams the wadis in the midst of the East, [she opened] the roads for the water-torrent without drenching me, in order to catch the water. I made her a shrine by dig[ging a rock-chapel] for the Ennead of her gods. The doors were of acacia-wood inlaid with copper, in order that [it be closed except for the performance of the] seasonal [offering] as the priest has learned its time.

Hor-wer, Wenu and Sha-[ʿaa—all the people there were satisfied] after I gave provisions and consecrated the shrines (again). Their towns were settled with unwelcomed one from [. . . They went to] the storeroom while begging 'Give!'

Thoth, the Great, who came forth from Reʿ—may he instruct [me about finding the things of] his [house:] the altar of silver and gold, the chests of linen, all kinds of channels which are to remain in its place. (Even) the one who enters eye-to-eye with the leader of the Ennead of gods was ignorant of it. Of all the gods, there was none familiar with his house. The god's-fathers were in distress without recognizing the arm of (my?) father over my Majesty. May he give alertness to the supporters of the god (after) I built his main temple from limestone of Tura, its gates from alabaster of Hatnub, the doors of Asiatic copper, the inlays therein on fine gold. (As) one sanctified by 'the-one-high-of-plumes' (scil. Amun)—I [conducted] the statue of this god during the two festivals, (namely) the *nḥb-kꜣw*-feast and the Thoth feast, which I established for him anew, that they are in the calendar and not as seasonal ones. Since the feast celebration be one, I doubled for him the divine offerings beyond what had been done before as my acting for the Ogdoad, for Khnum in his forms, for Heqat, Renenutet and Meskhenet, who had joined together to form my body and [to] Nehmet-ʿway, my Nekhbet-ka, who said: 'Hers is heaven and earth!'

The 'followers-of-Horus' in *Ḥbnw*—their settlements were festive after I asserted that 'I don't know temporary shelters in my design!' After I establish it and after I adorn it, I shall give houses to their owners, (namely) everyone who does say on his own (i.e. voluntarily): 'One who shall act eternally is the one whom Amun had let appear as permanent king on the throne of Horus!'

Listen to him, you, namely all patricians and common folk in its multitude! I did these things by the design of my heart and the forgotten one shall not sleep for me! While I restored what had decayed, I levied the mayor's draft since Asiatics were in the region of Avaris of Lower Egypt. Resident aliens among them were disregarding the tasks (after) (I) ruled them, while thinking that Reʿ would not be blind when the god (scil. Amun) assigned the steering rope to my Majesty. When I was established over the thrones of Reʿ, I became known through a period of years as a born conqueror. And when I came as Horus, my uraeus threw fire against my opponents. And after I expelled the abomination of the gods, the earth removed their footprints! This was the governance of the *tf tfw*, who came at his time on one day.

Just as the destruction of a command of Amun will not happen, my inscription shall last like the mountains. As the sun-disc shines on the titulary of my Majesty, my falcon over the throne shall be elevated for all my duration."

Stylistic Comments

Hatshepsut's inscription on the Speos Artemidos is not an ordinary royal text. It does not follow recurrent patterns used for royal donations or pious deeds, but it is rather unique in its directness and candidness. Instead of describing royal acts in formulaic statements, it reflects personal thoughts and reactions hardly ever found in an official royal text of ancient Egypt. This unaccustomed frankness concerns not only the description of some particular actions, but is even more unusual in revealing personal thoughts of a ruler in connection with the ascent to kingship. In addition, the text also includes events which occurred before Hatshepsut became king.

Not only is this a rare chance of learning about personal thoughts of someone who ruled Egypt for 15 years, but it also provides the modern reader with a wide range of indications about the events marking a period of particular interest.

The text as inscribed on the front wall of the rock-cut shrine dedicated to the goddess Pakhet is not homogeneous. Those sections which report about deeds for specific cults in Middle Egypt closely follow formulations known from other royal inscriptions and might very well be the product of the royal chancery.[1] While they are historically of interest, they tell little about Hatshepsut herself and the political tensions marking her time. It is impossible to decide if those passages were specifically composed for the text displayed at the Speos Artemidos or if they were extracted from other documents.

The accounts about measures taken in the face of serious adverse conditions in part of the country are not only historically important[2] but seem to be formulated in a more individualistic fashion. There is a conspicuous feature in these formulations which occurs also in the part concerning Hatshepsut's personal thoughts. Again and again the important point in a statement is placed in anticipation. Although this form of emphasis is known from other texts as well,[3] it is the frequency of its application which is unique. Especially in those parts of the text which concern Hatshepsut's personal experiences this anticipatory emphasis dominates. Because of this association with her personal concerns and the frequency of its use, it

[1]The rare indication of the size ancient Egyptian administrative correspondence must have had it is quite clear that much of the process was carried out by the members of the staff without much, if any participation by the ruler. The consistency of the documentary forms is in itself a demonstration that the mechanics of the administration were well established, covering most activities of the crown.

[2]See below, pp. 98 ff.

[3]See Gardiner, *Grammar* §§ 147 ff.; Gustave Lefebvre, *Grammaire de l'Égyptien Classique*,2 BdE XII (1955), §§ 590 f.

seems justified to consider this way to formulate a direct reflection of Hatshepsut's individual style of speech.

As far as the anticipatory emphasis is concerned, it occurs in verbal and non-verbal clauses. Among them, two forms can be distinguished. One is the stressing of the subject, which is not only the most frequent form, but is also attested otherwise as well. The other is the focusing on an adverbial adjunct.

There are major sections of the text which show distinct literary qualities. They are either of syntactic or of semantic nature. The first is the frequent arrangement of thoughts in interconnected pairs; the second, the choice of words culminating in punning. Of particular finesse is the choice of verb-forms, to express progression of thought or time. Last but not least, it should be said that some of the vocabulary used is highly selective and quite beyond the usual display found in royal documents.

The impressive language of the Speos Artemidos text entails two further questions. One is the degree of Hatshepsut's participation in the formulation, the other, if the available text was the only version published, or if there had been other documents containing the same or related versions. As for the first, it would seem that the text reflects at least in part Hatshepsut's diction. If the inscription on the Speos is a reflection of her way of speaking or if it was dictated in this form is, of course, impossible to decide. As it seems at least doubtful that the person on the throne physically wrote a text, Hatshepsut's authorship would be more likely a secondary one. That it was solely composed for being inscribed on the Speos might be doubtful; its being edited for the particular publication is a more likely possibility.

The part pertaining directly to the shrine built by Hatshepsut might have very well been composed for the occasion, while others, especially the one concerning the temple of Thoth and the one about Qusae might have originally belonged to other documents. While this remains ultimately an academic question for which there is no sustainable answer, some of the topics broached in the text must have been very much on Hatshepsut's mind.

Behind these questions lies the problem, what instigated the building of the rock-cut shrine and why the inscription was displayed on its front. It is stated in the text that the shrine was carved out of gratitude to the goddess Pakhet, who is specified as "the great one, who roams the wadis inside the East." Granted that the broad wadi Batn el-Bakara might seem an appealing access, the only question is whence. There is no obvious place in the desert that could inspire a continuous access. This does in no way deny that some individuals at various times might have used the wadi to penetrate the desert, either for hunting or for prospecting, but neither one has the implication of continuity. In order to come to an understanding of Hatshepsut's shrine, which was not the only one, it is necessary to approach the question in a larger context. The worship of the goddess Pakhet antedates the New Kingdom and is regionally linked with Beni Hasan.[4] The famous tombs at the site do not seem to belong to members of indigenous nobility, but rather to people who had gained social significance due to their professional careers in the military. It is there that Pakhet is mentioned, which agrees with the connection of some of the people beyond the Nile Valley's confines.

[4]There are rare mentions in the Coffin Texts, such as *CT* V 388 f.; 399 a.

There is no known place of worship of Pakhet from the Twelfth Dynasty; Hatshepsut's activity might be a renewal of an earlier tradition without any direct link to those buried at Beni Hasan. Her motive, as stated in the text, is gratitude for protecting her realm from devastation by a water-torrent, scil. a tsunamis, by diverting the water into the desert. In other words, Pakhet is honored by the shrine not for a deed performed at the wadi Batn el-Bakara, but for her role as "roaming the wadis in the East." This suggests that some kind of sacred place of the goddess existed there and that it was used by Hatshepsut to express her gratitude. Even after the shrine was made it was not the locale of continuous worship, but the activity was limited to one specific day. Who was to perform the service then is not indicated. The rest of the year the shrine was to be closed. The cult activity could hardly have been the main motive for the shrine's making.

When it becomes necessary to see the Speos Artemidos as a monument of Hatshepsut's gratitude to the goddess Pakhet for diverting the waters away from the queen's domain into her own realm, the wadis of the East, the placing of the long text becomes understandable. If anybody should pass through the rather forlorn area, the religious deed could always be appreciated, provided the person could read, and also the political views of Hatshepsut. In other words, the Speos Artemidos has a double function. It is on the one hand a religious deed, but it is also a monument for Hatshepsut's political ambitions and her accomplishment.

When one considers these political motives, the location of the Speos requires some thoughts. The event for which Hatshepsut is grateful to the goddess Pakhet certainly had no direct impact on the choice of the site. The existence there of some previous place of worship for the goddess is feasible, but lacks corroboration. As far as the scene of the natural disaster can be delineated, it appears to have especially affected the northeastern part of the Delta, i.e., quite a distance from the Speos.

Hatshepsut's pious activity is concentrated in Middle Egypt. The restoration of the temple of Hathor at Qusae is the southernmost one, while the others are the planned rebuilding of Thoth's temple in Hermopolis and her support of other sanctuaries in the region. Her deeds there are connected with the northern disaster and its consequences, especially in the form of refugees begging for support. The emphasis on the two areas adjoining the Speos' location might seem a logical choice for a text which intends to reflect Hatshepsut's largess. However, this might not be the only reason.

As pointed out in the commentary,[5] the restoration of Hathor's shrine at Qusae, which had fallen into disuse, might not only be a pious act, but might also have a political aspect. During the later Seventeenth Dynasty Qusae was the delineation between the Thebans and the Hyksos. The curious remark that the conditions at Qusae had been such that a youngster might dance on its roof might possibly be a veiled reference to Thutmosis III, who in Hatshepsut's eyes might have been an obnoxious lad, tempted to overstep what seems to have been the point separating the realms of interest. Hatshepsut's interest appears to have been extended beyond this point to include the fifteenth district. Could it be that the inscription on the Speos Artemidos is a reflection of expanding her realm of interest northward? While it is clear that

[5] See above, pp. 55 f.

some political arrangements existed between Hatshepsut and Thutmosis III during the 15 years of their existence side by side, there is no pertinent information available.

Because the text on the Pakhet shrine at the Speos Artemidos has the distinct features of political propaganda, as extensively exercised during those years of political competition, the chance of intensive involvement of Hatshepsut in the formulation is highly probable.

The Historical Significance of the Text

Written on the front of the rock-cut shrine dedicated to the goddess Pakhet, the text is more than a religious dedication. Of course, the pious motives which instigated the building of the sanctuary play a major role in it, as does Hatshepsut's piety, especially in regard to Amun. However, beyond this immediate concern the text is also a historical source of unmatched importance. Two topics are particularly affected, one the political and in some way personal developments connected with Hatshepsut's becoming king. The other, its indications about the impact of nature on the lower Nile Valley during her time and its consequences to society.

Once it is recognized that the inscription on the Speos Artemidos is a fundamentally historical source, the first task has to be to date it as precisely as possible. Needless to say, the events mentioned in the text did not all happen at the same time, but the dating of the extant composition is nevertheless essential.

Although the text does not contain a calendar date, its issue can be established within a fairly narrow range. The events reflected in it are not confined to a specific point in time, but cover a certain span of time. Part of them fall before Hatshepsut's reach for kingship; others occurred after it. As a result, Hatshepsut's ascent to the throne can be taken not only as the pivotal event indicated[1] but also the basis for a chronological definition. It seems by now as good as certain that Hatshepsut's *coup d'état* occurred early in her seventh year.[2] As a result, some of the points raised in the text apparently happened prior to year 7, others either during that year or shortly thereafter. This chronological perimeter is corroborated by the mention of Hatshepsut's plans for an expedition to Punt.[3] Its return is ascertained for Hatshepsut's 9th year.[4] This endeavor is indicated in the text more as a plan than a task in progress. It results that the text was written well before the 9th year.

It is less defined to what extent the text reaches back before her becoming king. There are internal and external reasons to assume that this was a rather limited time. The external argument is that Thutmosis III in his 5th year appointed *Wsr-ḥ3t* as vizier in Upper Egypt, a clear sign that he was able to promulgate and

[1] See above, pp. 42 ff.

[2] See further, "Thutmosis III's Early Years," pp. 126 ff.

[3] See S. Ratié, op. cit., 139 ff.l

[4] Urk. IV 349-354; cf. also Peter Dorman, *The Monuments of Senenmut* (1988), 9.

exercise royal acts.[5] As for Hatshepsut's account, there is no mention of specific deeds prior to her contemplating the reach for kingship.[6]

Although no absolute certainty can be established, it would seem likely that the text does not reach back beyond year 5 or slightly earlier.[7] Putting the available indications together it can be concluded that the events mentioned in the Speos Artemidos inscription occurred between year 6 and year 8, i.e., in chronological terms between 1473 and 1471 B.C.[8]

In the early section, i.e., concerning the time before Hatshepsut became king, no political events are mentioned. Only emergency measures at sanctuaries are talked about, and these will concern us later. The role Hatshepsut played during these events is not entirely clear, partly due to the lack of geographical specification of the affected places. She does claim participation in restoration measures, but neither extent nor motivation is clarified. It gives the appearance that she performed those acts alone and on her own volition, but at the time Thutmosis III was ruler, especially in the North. As a result, I wonder if Hatshepsut is not presenting her participation in needed emergency restorations as her independent action without necessarily being involved in them.

It is apparently during this time that her decision to reach for the kingship in the country was made,[9] culminating in the "pronouncement of 'Him who splits the ished-tree.'" That Amun is invoked at this point is, of course, in reference to the support she had received in carrying out her reach for power.

Her political program is clear. Its main objective is the acceptance of her rule by all people living in Egypt, the natives as well as those of foreign extraction. The second point emphasized in the program is the revival of commercial links, which had been disrupted. It is in this connection that Punt and the need for myrrh is mentioned, which provides a chronological indicator. The third point of her political program concerns the military. It is mostly a promise of future riches, after the claim that the military had "been without income." That this point follows the description of her commercial ambitions might reflect a link between the two. The concern for the military is certainly more than humane compassion and might very well be one of the avenues of her success in staging her *coup d'état*. This notion is strengthened by another

[5] It is not unlikely that this very appointment triggered Hatshepsut and her Theban allies to reach for kingship; cf. p. 127.

[6] The commonly assumed regency of Hatshepsut turns out to be based on an untenable division of a passage in Inana's biographical inscription; see the detailed discussion of Thutmosis III's ascent (pp. 115 ff.).

[7] It was apparently in year 6 that preparations began for the *coup d'état* in year 7, as demonstrated by the beginning of work on the obelisks which were ready for Hatshepsut's coronation.

[8] The dates use the chronological computation established by Jürgen von Beckerath, *Chronologie des pharaonischen Ägypten*,[2] MÄS 46 (1997).

[9] It is totally unknown what happened to Thutmosis III at this time. While her motives are cast in strongly religious terms, her political ambition cannot be overlooked. However, the events affecting especially the northeastern Delta could also have been interpreted as a divine revelation concerning the political situation. If we can trust Manetho that the Hyksos left Avaris voluntarily after the Mediterranean Sea had penetrated the Delta as far as this town, a renewed intrusion of the Sea could have inspired Hatshepsut's political ambitions; for the impact of the Sea on the northeastern Delta, see further H. Goedicke, "The End of the Hyksos in Egypt," L.H. Lesko, ed., *Egyptological Studies in Honor of Richard A. Parker*, 1986, 37-47; idem, "The Chronology of the Thera/Santorin Explosion," *Ä&L* III (1992), 57-62.

detailed statement about her attitude to the members of the professional military. According to it[10] she promised anyone the ownership of a house in return for a pledge of unwavering loyalty. Another aspect of her military policy seems to allow independent dwelling, i.e., not to insist on quartering soldiers in fortified garrisons.[11]

Concerning the time after her ascent to kingship, the indicated facts are basically of religious nature. How much of this is due to the religious setting of the inscription and how much it reflects the absence of other noteworthy events is impossible to decide. That the first project mentioned is the temple of Hathor at Qusae might be, as already pointed out,[12] more than a pious act in view of the role of Qusae in the past as the dividing point between North and South. It is curious that Hatshepsut's account makes special reference to a "guiding serpent statue of gold" for the specific purpose of "protecting her city."

Aside from having the rock-cut shrine made for Pakhet, Hatshepsut's main activity was her promise to build a new temple for Thoth at *Ḫmnw* (Ashmunein), although the place is not specifically mentioned. There is no mention that the temple was destroyed, only that it was in dire straits due to social problems. Hatshepsut provides no reason for her interest in this particular sanctuary, except that it apparently had been deprived of its inventory. Not only was she personally to take part in the consecration, but also to use the opportunity to install some religious services for her own spiritual benefit.[13]

Of even greater interest than Hatshepsut's religious deeds in Middle Egypt are the indications in the text about adverse natural phemomena affecting Egypt and theIr social consequences. These indications fall into two parts, one concerning the time prior to her becoming king, the other after this pivotal event. The importance of the latter for Hatshepsut is such that it can be used safely as a fixed point for dating events in her reign. After introducing Hatshepsut as the king responsible for the inscription, the first describes a number of phenomena and their impact on Egypt. As Hatshepsut's reflections about the future follow immediately thereafter, it seems justified, while assuming a roughly chrononlogical sequence in the mention of the topics in the text, that they occurred prior to Hatshepsut's maneuvers that led to her takeover. As they commenced sometime in her 6th year, the events mentioned in the early part of the Speos Artemidos inscription can be dated to the 5th/6th year, i.e., 1475 B.C.

The first reference is to the source of the phenomena which impacted parts of Egypt. It could be observed "over the coast-line," which can only refer to the Mediterranean littoral, because of the remoteness of the Red Sea to the Nile Valley.[14] The adversity is attributed to an anthropomorphically conceived entity identified as "lord of." Unfortunately, the qualification is lost in a lacuna. However, the potential danger is indicated as "his flames," whose visibility "over the coast-line" is the basis for the

[10]See further, pp. 72 ff.

[11]Concerning this particular promise, cf. further below, p. 102.

[12]See above, p. 13.

[13]The worship of a number of deities is clearly connected with the myth about her divine origin, which apparently was conceived shortly after her becoming king, if it had not been promulgated before; cf. further, pp. 70 ff.

[14]See above, p. 36.

proposed restoration *nb-iꜣḫw*.[15] While the "flames" could be observed "over the coast-line," the impact of the phenomenon, i.e., "his flames," remained "ouside the two mountain ranges." While Egypt's Delta is a wide open expanse, the Nile Valley south of modern Cairo is narrowly defined by a mountain range on either side. Thus the indication of the area not affected by the phenomenon beyond the littoral should be understood as Middle and Upper Egypt.

While the physical impact, i.e., "his flames," left Middle and Upper Egypt unaffected, this did not exclude other consequences. The text reports about the setting up of braziers, i.e., lamps, in darkened sanctuaries, making them "favorite places" again. The latter denotes the place where the day is spent, so that it implies that sanctuaries were in the dark during daytime. Next, mention is made of cases where "gods" had to be evacuated from their accustomed cult-places to temporary shelters. Others had their cult-places reinforced so that they could remain in there. These phenomena are not ordinary and can only be understood as part of a major natural disaster that impacted Egypt. That under such conditions special emphasis was paid to the performance of ritual obligations would seem only the expected.

It was apparently after Hatsepsut's ascent that another calamity befell Egypt. This is indicated as the reason for her devotion to the goddess Pakhet and the carving of the Speos Artemidos. The goddess, who is said to "roam the wadis in the midst of the East," is thanked that "she opened the roads for the water-torrent without drenching" Hatshepsut. Pakhet has no specific place of religious residence, but she is rather conceived to dominate the wadis of the East, i.e., the mountainous desert between the Nile Valley and the Red Sea. That the goddess is credited with diverting a "water-torrent" without drenching Hatshepsut means in geographical reality that devastating water was diverted from Egypt into the Eastern Desert. Two aspects have to be defined: one is the affected area, the other the extent of the devastation. If Hatshepsut's claim to have remained unscathed by a "water-torrent" is correct, it can only concern the eastern fringe of the Delta in order to become diverted into the realm of the goddess Pakhet. Geographically, this requires identification with the area of modern Port Said as its center. Anything substantially further west would have caused serious harm in the realm under Hatshepsut's kingship. The southern limits of any water calamity affecting Egypt's northeastern fringe is defined by the geographical features of the area, i.e., the gradual elevation would have stopped any water long before it could reach the Wadi Tumilat.

Hatshepsut's text says nothing about the nature of the dangerous "water-torrent." While cloudbursts happen occasionally in the desert, it is inconceivable that such an event would have posed a threat to Egypt. On the other hand, the area which could be established as the theater of calamity has the Mediterranean Sea as its northern border. The phenomena described as affecting Egypt in the beginning of the text had their origin outside of Egypt proper, beyond the coast-line of the Mediterranean. Linking this information with the reference to a "water-torrent" that narrowly passed Hatshepsut's realm to the east, the latter has to be envisioned as a flood-wave which rolled into Egypt's very northeast. It is not the only time a Mediterranean flood-wave penetrated into this area. There is information about another flood which apparently occurred

[15]The available space is limited, which has its impact on the possibilities for restoring the lacuna. Another possibility would be *iḫḫw*, "shine": see *Wb.* I 126, 3-5.

shortly after the death of Kamose in his attempt to storm Avaris,[16] and which is also mentioned in a prayer against pestilence of approximately the same time, i.e., 1550 B.C.[17]

A flood-wave of disastrous size is not a common phenomenon of the Mediterranean Sea. This rules out a climatological cause for it and requires a specific instigation. To define it, the text provides the following indicators: the cause was located north of Egypt in the Mediterranean. In addition to a flood-wave, it also caused darkness by day and required the removal of cult-statues from their usual places, either into safe areas within a building or to temporary shelters. Some fiery reflections could be observed from Egypt, but these "flames" did not affect Egypt directly. Adding up these indicators, there is only one possible explanation for them as a natural phenomenon, namely, the explosion of Thera/Santorin, located 70 kilometers north of eastern Crete.

Volcanologists operate with chronological definitions which are not always applicable to human nature. Nevetheless, a number of them have dated the Santorin explosion to the early Fifteenth Century B.C.[18] The same date was also promulgated by Minoan archaeologists concerning the destruction of Akroteri, which is located on the island of Santorin.[19] While I am neither the person nor is this the place to discuss the complex problems associated with the volcanological questions surrounding the Santorin explosion or the intricacies of Minoan archaeological chronology, there are two indisputable facts concerning the impact of Santorin on Egypt's northeastern Delta. One is the establishing of volcanic ash from the Santorin explosion in several spots in this area.[20] Even without any archaeological context, it is a demonstration that at least this part of Egypt was affected by Santorin. In this connection, of further significance is the size of the ash flakes; it has been shown that they had to be blown to a height which made the event discernible from Egypt over the earth's curvature.[21]

The impact of Santorin on Egypt is further demonstrated by the discovery of pumice that unquestionably originated from Santorin. The majority came from recent finds in the excavations at Tell ed-Dabʿa; although inscriptional evidence is lacking, the excavator has dated this material on the basis of ceramic seriology to the earlier Eighteenth Dynasty, ± Thutmosis III.[22] Such a date is in accord with a piece

[16]See Hans Goedicke, *Studies about Kamose and Ahmose* (1995), 135-145.

[17]Hans Goedicke, "The End of the Hyksos in Egypt," L. Lesko, ed., *Egyptological Studies in Honor of Richard A. Parker* (1986), 37-48; also H. Goedicke, *Studies in Kamose and Ahmose*, 170 ff.; idem, "The northeastern Delta and the Mediterranean," *The Archaeology of the Nile Delta* (1987), 165-175.

[18]For the complex problem of dating the Thera explosion, see H. Goedicke, *Ä&L* III (1992), 57 ff. with extensive lieterature; cf. also P. Warren, "The Minoan Civilisation of Crete and the Volcano of Thera," *JACF* 4 (1991), 29-39; P. Warren and V. Hankey, *Aegean Bronze Age Chronology* (1898), 141 f.

[19]Chr. Doumas, *Thera Pompei of the Ancient Aegean* (1983), 138 f.

[20]Daniel J. Stanley and Harrison Sheng, "Volcanic sherds from Santorin in the Nile Delta," *Nature* 320 (1986), 733-35.

[21]D. M. Pyle, "New Estimates for the Volume of the Minoan Eruption," *There and the Aegean World*, III, 2 (1990), 113-121.

[22]Manfred Bietak, *Avaris: The Capital of the Hyksos* (1996), 78 f.; pl. 34 B; Manfred Bietak, et al., *L&Ä* IV (1994), 35, Tf. 10 B.

of pumice which Petrie found at Kahun and which dates to Thutmosis III.[23] A chemical analysis made it clear that the pumice is from Santorin.[24]

In sum, the clearly volcanic events, including a tsunamis, indicated in the inscription on the Speos Artemidos, can be attributed to the activity and eventual explosion of Santorin/Thera. By its mention in Hatshepsut's inscription the event can be dated with stunning precision.[25] It did not happen in one single stroke, but stretched over some time, seemingly two years. The darkness, presumably due to volcanic ash and causing some peril or destruction to buildings, presumably by tectonic movements, is mentioned prior to Hatshepsut's becoming king, while the "water-torrent" which mostly missed her realm happened after it, i.e., approximately two years later, i.e., 1473/2 B.C.[26]

While Hatshepsut claims that she was not affected by the "water-torrent" generated by what can be defined as the explosion of Santorin, she does mention it again in her text as a demonstration of the divine support of her rule. She draws this conclusion from a specific episode that happened probably not too long after her becoming king. The setting is against her efforts to "restore what was destroyed." Although no specific project is identified at this point, its nature emerges in pulling the various bits of information together. Despite the seemingly all-encompassing nature of the reference to destruction, it is certainly not a kind of national clean-up campaign. The "Hyksos," whom later xenophobia likes to make responsible for devastations, were neither that barbaric, as Egyptologists sometimes like to portray them,[27] nor is it likely that almost 70 years since their departure had passed without any improvements, had they been necessary, especially under such beneficial reigns as that of Amenophis I or Thutmosis I. Hatshepsut almost immediately after her becoming king did not set out to tackle old decays, but the same recent damage mentioned in the opening section of her text should be envisioned here as well.

In order to cope with what should be seen as an emergency, at least as far as the Delta was concerned, she instituted a measure which apparently allowed local administrators to draft people to perform labor in the public interest. This kind of forced labor, which is attested in the later Old Kingdom[28] and which existed until modern times,[29] had apparently not been summoned for a very long time, at least for the northeastern Delta region. The reference to the presence of "Asiatics in the region of Avaris of Lower Egypt" covers approximately 300 years.[30] That the unfamiliar drafting for physical labor did not meet with

[23]W. M. Flinders Petrie, *Illahun, Kahun and Gurog* (1891), 23.

[24]The pumice, now in the Petrie Museum, University College London (U.C. 27929), was most graciously supplied by Mrs. Barbara Adams. The analysis was performed by the Smithsonian Institution, Washington under the supervision of Dr. Daniel Stanley.

[25]Hans Goedicke, "The Chronology of the Thera/Santorin Explosion," *Ä&L* III (1992), 57-62.

[26]The picture evolving from Hatshepsut's text helps in unraveling a puzzle which has mystified the archaeologists working at Akroteri. The absence of any human remains, as well as the lack of any luxury goods, makes sense when the catastrophe of Santorin is seen as a gradual development which gave the people enough time to flee.

[27]E.g., Sir Alan Gardiner, *Egypt of the Pharaohs* (1962), 163 -170; Wolfgang Helck, *Geschichte des Alten Ägypten* (1968), 134; Donald B. Redford, "The Hyksos," *Or.* 39 (1970), 1-51.

[28]See Hans Goedicke, *Königliche Dokumente aus dem Alten Reich*, ÄA 14 (1967), 244.

[29]The latest case of corvée in modern times was for the digging of the sweet-water canal in conjunction with the Suez Canal.

[30]The presence of "Asiatics" certainly antedates the arrival of the "Hyksos" of the Fifteenth Dynasty and should not be conflated with the latter; see above pp. 78 f.

universal cheer should hardly come as a surprise. It is a specific group among those living in the Avaris region who particularly opposed the assigned tasks. They are identified as "resident aliens," i.e., people who had lived in the country for a while but had not assimilated with the rest of the population Their obstruction, at least in Hatshepsut's eyes, stems from the belief that she would not be able to carry off her plan to become king.

Once she had reached her aim and had become king, she did not hesitate to turn against those who had been disobedient to her orders. For their obstruction such people deserved death in her eyes, i.e., they had become "abominations of god" or "abomination of the gods."[31] However, instead of prosecuting them, she "expelled" them. No reasons are given for this change in legal venue. The association with Hatshepsut's ascent to kingship provides the chronology for this development, namely, her (early) 7th year, i.e., 1473/2 B.C. The story did not end there, but according to her, those people perished during her expulsion of them, because "the earth removed their footprints" due to a decision by "the father-of-fathers," scil., Nun, the primeval water, that had come unexpectedly.

What might seem an ephemeral incident is not only the culmination of Hatshepsut's lengthy inscription but also proof for her that her reach for kingship found sanctioning by the divine. Upon closer inspection, the episode takes on a surprising new dimension. In order to make it more distinctive, the different elements will be highlighted. The people concerned were originally of foreign extraction and had been residing in Egypt for some time. These people apparently had some connection with the authority, because they held their own opinion about the holder of kingship in the land. No professional pursuit is identified, although a membership in the professional military is not unlikely. In the wake of devastations caused by nature, specifically by the impact of volcanic activity on Thera/Santorin, Hatshepsut had called up the corvée, i.e., the drafting of people for physical labor. No such tasks had been performed for a very long time and the possibility had been forgotten. Those resident aliens when drafted opposed the tasks assigned to them. For reasons not specified they were allowed to depart from Egypt, or in the eyes of the authority were expelled from there. After departing they were eliminated by water to the point that "the earth removed their footprints," i.e., they were washed away. The water is apparently the same which had threatened but spared Egypt, i.e., the reported elimination of the people was attributed to the tsunamis which happened in the area beyond Egypt's border.

When reviewed in this fashion, the similarity to the Biblical account about the departure of the Children of Israel from Egypt is so striking that it is difficult to overlook it. In order to make the similarity even more distinct, let me highlight the events associated with the Exodus in the same way as was done with the section in Hatshepsut's text. The Children of Israel are unquestionably foreigners who had resided in Egypt for more than one generation. After enjoying privileged status, they are drafted to perform hard physical labor,[32] which not only caused their frustration but also led to the decision to exit the contract

[31] Wolfgang Boochs, *Strafrechtliche Aspekte im altägyptischen Recht* (1993), 72.

[32] One of the curious details in the Biblical account is the nature of the work to which they are drafted. The making of bricks (Ex.1:13) never develops into specific constructions.

under which they were in Egypt and to leave for the ancestral home at Mamre. The desire to leave Egypt leads to protracted negotiations with the authorities for permission to do so. The need for it demonstrates that the people had not just strayed into Egypt, as is frequently assumed, but that they were there in a legally structured way. During the negotiations various adversities take place in Egypt. Among them some are of special interest: according to Ex. 9:8-11 Moses and Aaron are to "take handfuls of soot from the kiln and throw it toward the sky . . . It shall become a fine dust all over the land of Egypt, and cause an inflamation." It is followed (Ex. 9: 23-5) by "it rained down hail upon the land of Egypt, the hail was very heavy—fire flashing in the midst of the hail—such as had not fallen on the land of Egypt." And further, "Thick darkness descended upon the land of Egypt for three days" (Ex. 10:22). These have been considered before[33] as literary references to volcanic phenomena, either as ash-flow, or as tephra.

When finally permission to depart was granted, the Children of Israel set out for their intended goal, namely, Mamre near Hebron. Beyond the Egyptian border point at Tjel, modern Abu Sefeh near Qantara, there was one road, the *via maris*, to get there. In order to reach Egypt's border, there were two roads, a southern one near the Wadi Tumilat and a northern one along the southern edge of what is now Lake Menzaleh, but which was open to the Mediterranean in the middle of the Second Millennium B.C. It was the latter, "the way of the wilderness at the Sea of Reeds" (Ex. 13:18), which was apparently chosen after Pharaoh "will drive you out of here (scil. Egypt) one and all" (Ex. 10:1).

For reasons detailed in Ex. 11:2 the Egyptian king sent police after the departing ones, presumably with the intention to reach them before they had left Egyptian territory. It was at their first stop, indicated as Etham,[34] that the people became aware of being pursued, and that they changed their route for a point defined as "before Pi-hahiroth, between Migdol and the Sea, before Baal-zephon" (Ex. 14:1). Unfortunately, the indicators cannot be geographically identified with certainty, except that the people were facing the Sea of Reeds, i.e., they were at the southeast of what is now Lake Menzaleh. What happened next is in poetical terms the equivalent of a description of a tsunamis:[35] "There was the cloud with the darkness, and it cast a spell upon the night" (Ex.14:20) "and drove back the sea with a strong east wind all that night, and turned the sea into dry ground" (Ex. 14:21); "the waters turned back and covered . . . Pharaoh's entire army that had followed after them" (Ex. 14: 28).

Of course there are differences between the two accounts due to the different viewpoint. For the Egyptians the departed aliens had disappeared, because they had taken a turn into Sinai and it must have been a long time before any news about any survivors reached the Egyptian authority. For the Biblical account only the fate of the pursuers is of interest, not even the reason for the move into Sinai, obviously an attempt to be safe from any recurrence of an incursion of water. Despite this diametrically opposed evaluation, as is frequent when two parties are involved, the central feature is identical, namely, the

[33]E.g., Dorothy B. Vitaliano, *Legends of the Earth* (1952), 254 ff.

[34]This word is a distorted rendering of the Egyptian *ḫtm*, "fortress," which is probably identical with the place mentioned in Egyptian writing as "Migdol."

[35]An impressive ancient description can be found by Ammianus Marcellinus, XXVI, 15 ff.

annihilation by an unexpected water-torrent which can be identified as a tsunamis due to the accompanying volcanic phenomena.

While there cannot be any question that the event described in Hatshepsut's text on the Speos Artemidos occurred in Egypt's Northeast, the identifiable indications in the Biblical account also point to the northeastern fringe of the Nile Delta. Assuming that the latter reflects a mundane historical happening makes an equation of the two accounts unavoidable. In other words, the historical reality mirrored in the Biblical report about the Exodus of the Children of Israel should be dated to the commencing single reign of Hatshepsut, in chronological terms 1473/2 B.C.

The tsunamis that saved them can only have been generated by the explosion of Thera/Santorin, after the volcano had been active for approximately 2-3 years. There is no other instance in the Mediterranean basin where volcanological, literary and historical information jell in such perfect harmony, which would seem the most persuasive corroboration.

Related Discussions

Thutmosis III's Early Years

The history of the early Eighteenth Dynasty is widely seen as a veritable family drama.[1] It commences with the unexpectedly successful patriarch Thutmosis I. He has a beautiful, proud daughter. And then there is Thutmosis II, who does not directly belong to the family's main-line,[2] but as son-in-law becomes king of Egypt. From the marriage with Hatshepsut emerges only one daughter, Nofrureᶜ. Thutmosis II also has a son with a harem girl, Isis, who is named Thutmosis after him. This situation Redford[3] formulated in romantic terms, as "Thutmosis II penetrated into a dark corner of the harem to bring forth another concubine's son." It would not require many Victorian moral precepts to envisage Hatshepsut's pride hit in the heart. Although she could not prevent the succession of Thutmosis' son, she ultimately took late revenge when her "unfaithful" Thutmosis II died early.[4] According to the commonly held view, the two half-siblings were not only joined together in their early childhood, but Hatshepsut as regent took over the reins of the state and totally pushed aside the child Thutmosis III from his rights. The assumption of her murder by the frustrated Thutmosis III,[5] prevented for years from exercising the rulership he was awarded at the death of Thutmosis II, would seem not only a dramatic necessity, but is also assumed to be true by some historians, such as Helck. Only after her death did Thutmosis III gain the full rulership and began almost immediately a major military campaign against "Asia," in order to stave off by a preventive action the danger of an impending invasion seriously looming from there.[6] By his strategic talent he succeeds to

[1]James H. Breasted, *A History of Egypt* (1905), 266-83; the most dramatic interpretation is, of course, Kurt Sethe's efforts (*Die Thronwirren unter den Nachfolgern Königs Thutmosis' I*, UGAÄ 1 [1896]) to cope with Hatshepsut; cf. also William C. Hayes, *The Scepter of Egypt* II (1959), 74 f.; idem, "Internal affairs from Thutmosis I to the Death of Amenophis III," in *The Cambridge Ancient History*^{3} (1973), 315 ff.; Sir Alan Gardiner, *Egypt of the Pharaohs* (1961) 178 ff.; Donald B. Redford, *History and Chronology of the Early Eighteenth Dynasty* (1967), 57 ff.; W. Helck, *Geschichte des Alten Ägypten*, HdO (1968), 143 ff. Suzanne Ratié, *La Reine Hatchepsout*, Orientalia Monspeliensis 1 (1979), 67 ff.; Peter F. Dorman, *The Monuments of Senenmut* (1988), 18 ff.

[2]Wolfgang Helck, *Geschichte Ägyptens*, HdO (1968), 151; Edward F. Wente, in *An X-Ray Atlas of the Royal Mummies* (1980), 130 f.

[3]D. B. Redford, op. cit., 73.

[4]E. F. Wente, op. cit. 248 f., envisages it as 24 + x to 26 + x years; there seems to be general agreement that Thutmosis II, not a healthy person, died of natural causes; cf. also C. Eliot Smith, *Royal Mummies* (CCG) (1912), 29.

[5]W. Helck, op. cit., 155; but the *opinio communis* is in favor of a natural death; e.g., Redford, op. cit., 87; S. Ratié, op. cit., 296 f.; Charles Nims, "The Date of the Dishonoring of Hatshepsut, *ZÄS* 93 (1966), 97 ff. Dorman, op. cit., 46 ff.

[6]Cf. Wolfgang Helck, *Die Beziehungen Ägyptens zu Vorderasien im 3. und 2. Jahrtausend v. Chr.*^{2} (1971), 118 ff.; idem, *Geschichte des Alten Ägyptens*, 154 f.; D. B. Redford, op. cit., 86 f. The notion of an impending attack on Egypt from the Levant is

surprise and destroy the hostile coalition still in the process of assembly. He must, however, conquer the town of Megiddo, whence the enemy's leader, the Ruler of Qadesh (on the Orontes),[7] could retreat to. The latter escapes, but Thutmosis III becomes the absolute lord of the Levant as a consequence of the surrender of Megiddo.[8]

These are the basic ideas of the family drama in their more or less accepted form, which could be translated into a TV show of dynastic fascination. Kurt Sethe in his inimitable fashion projected the dynamics in a still more complicated way,[9] which found general acceptance until William Edgerton[10] radically deflated fusions and confusions in his famous discussion of "the Thutmoside Succession."

As all historical evaluations should begin with the sources, let us see what the Egyptian ones have to say, starting with Thutmosis I. After the last event in the replacement of the Hyksos-lords residing at Avaris by the Thebans,[11] namely, the advance of Ahmose as far as "Sharuhen"[12] between his 17th and 20th regnal year, i.e., ± 1530 B.C., no bellicose controversies occur north of the *nahal bezor* (= Brook of Egypt)[13] during the remaining years of Ahmose, or during the reign of his son Amenhotep I (1526-1511 B.C.). The Thebans had more than enough problems in the traditional extent of rulership, i.e., Egypt,[14] in addition to efforts to consolidate the southern border at Buhen. There are no indications of any kind of contact with the Levant during this time. What happened there we do not know in detail, but the notion of an all-out war is tempting, especially when taking into account Josephus' tradition[15] that the Hyksos-rulers of Avaris retreated to Palestine on the basis of an agreement, and that they founded there the city of Jerusalem. For

---

basically due to a conflation of the town Kadesh, whose chief is the principal opponent of Thutmosis III. It was erroneously identified as the town with this name located on the Orontes, which is the site of the confrontation between Ramesses II and Muwatallish II. The town Kadesh and its chief against which Thutmosis III conducted his campaign was, however, Kadesh Naphtali located less than 10 kilometers from Megiddo: see Hans Goedicke, *The Battle of Megiddo* (2000), 35 f.

[7]Qadesh is, as far as I am aware, universally identified with the town on the Orontes where Ramesses II fights his battle against Muwatallish. As I discuss elsewhere, the opponent of Thutmosis III is actually the ruler of Kadesh Naphtali, who apparently headed some kind of amphictiony in the area of the Jezreel Plain.

[8]The political and military significance of Megiddo is pronounced by Thutmosis III when he decides to besiege it as "the taking of 1000 places is the taking of Megiddo" (*Urk.* IV 660, 8).

[9]Kurt Sethe, *Die Thronwirren unter den Nachfolgern Königs Thutmosis' I.: Ihr Verlauf und ihre Bedeutung*, UGAÄ 1 (1896), 1 ff.; idem, *Das Hatschepsut-Problem, noch einmal untersucht*, AAWBerlin 1932, 4 (1932).

[10]William F. Edgerton, *The Thutmosid Succession*, SAOC 6 (1933); see also William C. Hayes, *Royal Sarcophagi of the XVIII Dynasty* (1935), 3; Étienne Drioton et Jacques Vandier, *L'Égypte*[4], 381 ff.

[11]Although it is universally assumed that Ahmose conquered Avaris in a military action, there is no written evidence supporting it. On the contrary, Manetho reports that the Hyksos left the northeastern Delta following an agreement giving them free way. Kamose, the older brother of Ahmose, had apparently made an attempt to storm Avaris. He was not only unsuccessful but also lost his life during the operation; cf. Hans Goedicke, *Studies about Kamose and Ahmose* (1995), 167 ff.

[12]Ahmose, son of Eban (*Urk.* IV 4, 10), reports only of the "looting" (*ḥ3q*) of Avaris, but not of a conquest of the place. As for "Sharuhen" it should be recognized as a region and not as a specific place. There Ahmose conducted warfare in three different years; for "Sharuhen," cf. Hans Goedicke, *The Battle of Megiddo* (2000), 18 ff.

[13]For the identification of the *nahal bezor* as the Biblical "Brook of Egypt," see Nadav Na'aman, "The Brook of Egypt and Assyrian Policy on the Borders of Egypt," *Tel Aviv* 6 (1979), 68 ff.

[14]There is good reason to assume some form of a major epidemic during this time; cf. Hans Goedicke, "The Canaanite Illness," *SAK* 11 (1984), 91 ff.

[15]Josephus, *Contra Apionem* I 26.

Egypt proper the reign of Amenhotep I is over-all a good time during which the country made a rather quick economic recovery.[16] The evaluation in Inana's biography[17] is "His Majesty passed a lifetime in success and years in peace."

In the 4th year of his reign (1507 B.C.) we find his successor Thutmosis I engaged in a move through the entire Levant, which brings him to the Euphrates.[18] There are no indications that it was a specifically military campaign from the outset, nor even that Thutmosis I was accompanied by any sizable Egyptian military units (beyond some kind of bodyguard).[19] Only after reaching the Euphrates does fighting with the Mitanni develop, in which, in all likelihood, locally provided "troops" were used almost exclusively. For the understanding of the new political situation, several reused blocks of a door-frame from Karnak which Donald B. Redford has published are of special importance.[20] Among others, Tunip and Zion are depicted as bringers of food donations. It is of utmost importance that the representation of the places uses the traditional type of depiction of a supporting social unit going back to Snofru, and not the one typical of a subdued enemy.[21] From the idiosyncrasies of the representation it follows that the indicated lands were not forced into their role, but that their attitude rather corresponded to that of estates supporting the king, i.e., that they voluntarily accepted the king as their lord. For the understanding of the political situation and the position of Thutmosis I, especially in the Levant, this is of utmost importance. Although we have no detailed relevant information, in my opinion it is necessary to view Thutmosis I as sovereign over the Levant on the basis of political treaties or agreements.[22] How these came about is obscure in detail; the driving force appears to have been the disintegration of the internal situation in the Levant to the point of general anarchy.[23] In order to end the battling of everyone against everyone, one returned to the

[16]W. Helck, op. cit. 117; Franz-Jürgen Schmitz, *Amenophis I.*, HÄB 6 (1978), 131 ff.; 182 ff.

[17]*Urk.* IV 54, 14; see my discussion of the passage in FS Altenmüller forthcoming.

[18]*Urk.* IV 85, 14; W. Helck, op. cit., 115.

[19]The claim of Ahmose-Pennekhbet that he brought in "21 hands" (*Urk.* IV 36, 10) is not necessarily an indication of an extended bloody military campaign. He was an officer closely associated with the Crown and might as such been a personal companion of Thutmosis I.

[20]Donald B. Redford, "A Gate Inscription from Karnak and Egyptian Involvement in Western Asia During the Early 18th Dynasty," *JAOS* 99 (1979), 272; for the suggested identification of Zion, see Mordechai Gilula, "*D*ꜣ*IWNY* = ZION?," in Sarah Israelit-Groll, ed., *Pharaonic Egypt* (1985), 48 f.

[21]For the early Eighteenth Dynasty the number of pictured subjugated foreigners is mostly in the area of symbolic representation. It is only in the later Eighteenth Dynasty that this topic appears in the Egyptian canon to be fully developed in the Ramesside period.

[22]This does not exclude the local application of force, but concerns rather the overall picture. It is not sufficiently recognized how much of this development is an extension of the political concept introduced by the "Hyksos" into the Fertile Crescent. Egyptian kings have had foreign vassals since the Old Kingdom, as in the case of Dakhleh, or the late Middle Kingdom situation of Byblos, but the extent and variation demonstrated by the "Hyksos" rulers is different.

[23]Thutmosis III also claims political chaos in the Levant as a belated justification for his First Campaign. For *Urk.* IV 648, 2-7, see Hans Goedicke, "The Background of Thutmosis III's Foreign Policy," *JSSEA* 10 (1980), 201-13; Donald B. Redford, "The Historical Retrospective at the Beginning of Thutmose III's Annals," ÄAT 1 (FS Elmar Edel) (1979), 338-342; William J. Murnane, "Rhetorical History? The Beginning of Thutmose III's First Campaign in Western Asia, " *JARCE* XXVI (1989), 183-189.

international concept of sovereignty introduced or promulgated by the "Hyksos," i.e., one opted for an "overlord" in order to protect the local political interests.

Thutmosis I was presumably quite flattered and impressed by the offer to be made "sovereign" and accepted. This shift of the political picture had, of course, its consequences. For the new "overlord" numerous problems presumably developed in holding the various differences in the Levant to an acceptable level. This required in all probability his extended personal presence in the Levant, and simultaneously his absence from Egypt proper.[24] The Thebans, especially the group of people associated with the cult of Amun, could react only negatively to this. After all the efforts to become again the political center of Egypt as in the later Eleventh Dynasty, a shift of the political equilibrium in favor of the Levant was synonymous with a decline in the role of Thebes.[25] The negative reaction as well as the attempts to mollify those parochialists began to take place in short order.

We know as good as nothing about the later years of Thutmosis I,[26] or about the shorter reign of Thutmosis II. Two reasons appear to be responsible for this: 1st) the two rulers did not reside in Thebes; 2nd) a local Theban opposition emerged especially against Thutmosis II. The center of this opposition was apparently the Theban priesthood, which, as once before, namely, in the Twelfth Dynasty, saw itself relegated to insignificance. On the opposite side stood military interests, which were rooted in the emerging professional soldier class.[27] A heretofore side-stepped secondary source in the historical discussion, the inscription on the el-Arish naos, brings some light.[28] It contains an indication of an attack from the East which was repelled by Thutmosis (II) acting for Thutmosis I. Subsequently, this brought about the establishing of military centers or garrisons in the Wadi Tumilat and along the eastern Delta, presumably at Nebesheh and Tell el Yahudiyeh.[29]

[24]As far as I am aware, it is generally assumed that Thutmosis I spent his reign in Egypt aside from the campaign that led him to the Euphrates. There are reasons which point to considerable interest by the king in the northern part of his realm including the possibility of a delegation of power to Thutmosis II prior to his becoming king; cf. further below.

[25]It is in some way a forerunner of the inner Egyptian antagonism which overshadowed the Ramesside period and led eventually to the splitting up of the country: cf. Jürgen von Beckerath, *Tanis und Theben*, ÄF 16 (1951), 20 ff.

[26]The highest attested date is year 4, but it has been convincingly argued that a considerably longer reign, maybe twice as many years, might be more likely. Equally uncertain is the length of Thutmosis II's reign and his relation to his predecessor. Although there does not seem to have been a formal co-regency between the two, the text on the shrine from el-Arish seems to indicate that Thutmosis II acted in lieu of his predecessor when defending it against an onslaught by *Š3sw*. His description as *bik imy šsi* (*Urk.* IV 58, 15) would support such a notion rather than pointing to infantility at the time of his ascent: cf. also further below, p.   For the chronological problems besetting this section of Egyptian royal history, cf. Jürgen von Beckerath, *Chronologie des pharaonischen Ägypten*, MÄS 46[2] (1997), 120 f.

[27]We are still a long way off from an understanding of the internal social development during Egypt's long history. A guiding beacon for possible work in this vein was Wolfgang Helck, *Politische Gegensätze im alten Ägypten*, HÄB 23 (1986); see also Andrea Maria Gnirs, *Militär und Gesellschaft*, SAGA 17 (1996).

[28]Ulrich Luft, *Beiträge zur Historisierung der Götterwelt und der Mythenschreibung*, Studia Aegyptiaca IV (1978), 219 ff., who sees it as a myth about gods, "der Mythos als Göttergeschichte (ist) ein Ersatz für die fehlende eigene Geschichte"; similarly, Donald B. Redford, *Pharaonic King-lists, Annals and Day-books* (1986), 94 f.

A study of the text and its historical reflections is forthcoming.

[29]The two places appear to have originated in the "Hyksos" period, but nothing is known about the occupational history during

It was apparently these military interests which saw to it that Thutmosis II, who did not belong to the main line of the ruling family, became king. For reasons which are still unclear in detail, he "marries" Hatshepsut at this point in time,[30] after he had been associated earlier with a certain Isis. From this pairing had originated a son, who then was presumably already at least 8-9 years old.[31] The association with Hatshepsut does not seem to have been love at the first or last look, and it is not at all certain in how far the two were ever together. Hatshepsut at this time was possibly already allied with Senenmut,[32] a member of the Theban particularists. On the basis of the information available to us, it is futile to ponder if Hatshepsut became a proponent of the Thebaïs on account of her personal interests, or if her personal interests were the consequence of Theban plotting.

Although Hatshepsut sports a number of times the designation *ḥmt-nswt wrt*, "great king's wife,"[33] there is no case known to me where she is shown together with Thutmosis II, who would be the presumable spouse. A seeming exception was until recently a stela in Berlin, Inv. Nr. 15699, depicting Thutmosis II, Ahmose and Hatshepsut.[34] Originally only the text was published in a copy.[35] Through the good services of Dr. Wildung I received an excellent photograph of the object, which made it likely to be a fake. My suspicions were fully corroborated by recent investigations which Dr. Kischkewitz pointed out to me.

---

the early Eighteenth Dynasty due to a lack of pertinent archaeological investigation beyond the work of Naville, Griffith and Petrie in 1887.

[30]D. B. Redford, *History and Chronology*, 65 ff., ascribed it to a matriarchal concept, for which there is hardly any evidence from ancient Egypt. That it was a political rather than a personal, or even emotional, choice can be taken for granted. This would suggest that it was an effort to reconcile the opposing trends in the country on a personal basis, similar to the joining of Thutmosis III with Nofrureʿ, the daughter of Hatshepsut. The difference between the two moves lies in their direction, but the aim is still the same.

[31]Although it is widely assumed that Thutmosis was a small infant at the death of his father, there is nothing to support this notion. The results of recent investigations of the king's mummy produced an estimated age of 35-40 years, which is, of course, in blatant variance with the known historical facts; cf. James E. Harris and Edward F. Wente, *An X-Ray Atlas of the Royal Mummies* (1980), 210 f.; 246 f.

[32]The beginning of the association of Senenmut and Hatshepsut is difficult to pinpoint exactly, but in view of his Theban position it is likely that it dates to the reign of Thutmosis II if not even earlier; cf. Peter F. Dorman, *The Monuments of Senenmut* (1988), 171, who allows this possibility without defining it.

Suzanne Ratié, op. cit. 64 f., supports Senenmut's advance to significance under Thutmosis II, but is not certain about the notion of A. R. Schulman, "Some Remarks on the alleged 'Fall of Senmut,'" *JARCE* 8 (1969-70), 33 f.; W. Helck, *Zur Verwaltung des Mittleren und Neuen Reichs* (1958), 356 f.

[33]*Urk.* IV 192, 11, 14; 193, 2. It is impossible to assign those attestations to a specific date, although it might seem likely that they fell into the time after Thutmosis II's death and, of course, before her ascent as king. All attestations are on alabaster vessels and it seems likely that they all belong to the same find. One of them makes reference to a deed for the deceased *Iʿḥ-ms*, the mother of Hatshepsut.

[34]*Urk.* IV 143-145; Günther Roeder, *Aegyptische Inschriften aus den Staatlichen Museen zu Berlin*, II (1924), 103; Dietrich Wildung, "Zwei Stelen aus Hatschepsuts Frühzeit," *Festschrift zum 150jährigen Bestehen des Berliner Ägyptischen Museums* (1974), 255 ff.; Tf. 34. The piece has been declared not genuine by Rolf Krauss, "Der Denkstein Berlin ÄGM 15699—eine Ägyptologen-Fälschung," *Jahrbuch Preussischer Kulturbesitz* (1998), 204-220. After receiving a good photograph through the kindness of Dir. Dr. Dietrich Wildung, I am inclined to accept his verdict. As a consequence, the only instance depicting Thutmosis II and Hatshepsut together is no longer valid.

[35]*Urk.* IV 143-145; Günther Roeder, *Aegyptische Inschriften aus den Staatlichen Museen zu Berlin*, II (1924), 103, who included a caveat doubting the genuineness of the piece. A poor photograph of the object was published by D. Wildung, *Festschrift zum 150jährigen Bestehen des Berliner Ägyptischen Museums* (1973) 255-268.

According to Christian Goedicke and Rolf Krauss, "Der Denkstein Berlin ÄGM 15699" is "eine Ägyptologen-Fälschung."[36] This discovery eliminates the only direct evidence for a "marriage" between Thutmosis II and Hatshepsut. Her holding the designation "great king's wife" is not necessarily a reflection of a personal relationship and can also be understood as an indication of her social position.[37]

Nothing is known about the circumstances of Thutmosis II's death.[38] At this time his son Thutmosis (III) was presumably about 12 years old.[39] On the basis of the el-Arish text it would appear as if Hatshepsut attempted a *coup d'état* at this moment, or else the late report conflates two events.[40] I suspect that Thutmosis III as a teenager was put on the throne by the professional militaries of his father without the participation or consent of Thebes. By this *fait accompli* the intentions of Hatshepsut and of the Theban particularists were thoroughly crossed, because one seems to have considered the possibility of regicide unthinkable.[41]

Despite the universal notion of Hatshepsut's acting as regent for the envisioned infant Thutmosis III, there is no written evidence reflecting her in such a role. On the contrary, there are several dated texts of the early years of Thutmosis III and none of them makes any reference to Hatshepsut whatsoever. It is only after Year 15/16 that the two appear in joint inscriptions, which obviously date to a time when Thutmosis would have to be seen as fully grown up even by those favoring his becoming king as a child.[42]

Information about Thutmosis III and Hatshepsut dating to these years is minimal. The earliest is the[43] dedicatory inscription at the temple of Semna dated to "Year 2, 2nd month of *šmw*, day 7."[44] It contains no

[36]*Jahrbuch Preussischer Kulturbesitz* (1998), 203-220.

[37]The title "great king's wife" occurs late in the Eighteenth Dynasty as a social indicator for the daughters of Amenophis III and others as well.

[38]The mummy of Thutmosis II does not provide any clue as to the cause of the king's death; see E. Smith, op. cit., 29. It is remarkable that his demise is noted in Inana's biography (*Urk.* IV 59, 13-14) in the shortest possible form, which is likely to be a reflection of the political climate in Thebes at the time the text was written, presumably shortly before Hatshepsut's becoming king.

[39]It is widely assumed that he was a small infant at the time, for which there is no corroborating evidence. It seems that the notion of an assumed "extramarital" liberty of Thutmosis II might be the only cause, for which, however, there is no support. Not only is Thutmosis III's mother Isis later treated quite honorably, e.g., in Cairo 34015 where she is denoted as *ḥmt-nswt*, but the undoubtedly later tradition about the divine selection of the young Thutmosis speaks against it. He is described there (*Urk.* IV 157, 7-9) as introduced into the temple, though before he had become a "priest" (*ḥm-nṯr*); although vague, it would seem to suggest the reaching of some age, especially as the attaining of priesthood before becoming king is implied. The envisioned age is based on the notion that Thutmosis III was born before his father occupied the role of representing Thutmosis I.

[40]Hatshepsut's Speos Artemidos inscription does not indicate such a dramatic move, but makes it nevertheless clear that she aspired to become king as soon as Thutmosis II had died.

[41]The sanctity of kingship is well illustrated by such cases as Ay, who lived to his natural end despite the mighty opposition of Horemhab. Regicide is reported by Manetho for Teti and central in the tradition conveyed by The Teaching of King Amenemhet I; for the former, see Wolfgang Helck, "Gedanken zum Mord an König Teti, *Essays on Egyptology* (1994), 103 ff.

[42]Edward F. Wente in James E. Harris, ed., *An X-Ray Atlas of the Royal Mummies* (1980), 246 f. in deliberating the age of Thutmosis III at the time of his ascent finds it likely that he was "between 10 and 13 + x years" of age and "between 63 and 66 + x years" at death, which would seem reasonable for acting without tutelage.

[43]*Nṯrw*, "gods," refers here specifically to the deceased kings and should not be seen as a reference to any royal divinity; cf. H. Goedicke, "God," *JSSEA* XVI (1988), 57-62. The point is to delineate the military service to the past kings and to exclude Thutmosis III from them.

[44]Ricardo A. Caminos, *Semna-Kumma*, I (1998), 43-47, pl. 25; cf. also P. Dorman, op. cit., 29.

mention of Hatshepsut. On the exterior face of the West Wall[45] was once a royal lady, but her picture was subsequently obliterated. There is no reason to identify her as Hatshepsut, but her daughter *Nfrw-Rʿ* might be a more likely possibility.

The stela mentioning a donation to Senenmut[46] by Thutmosis III has the date "Year 4, 1 *šmw,* day 16 "under the Majesty of King *Mn-ḫpr-Rʿ*." Although the text was extensively restored under Sety I, there is no reason to question the validity of the indicated date including the role of Thutmosis III as principal authority in the country.[47] On the left side of the stela, unquestionably an addition, is a mention of Hatshepsut denoted as "king" (*nswt-bit*). The very fact that Thutmosis III is mentioned as king in the date makes it clear that Hatshepsut's ascent must have occurred later.

Two biographical inscriptions by officials have to be discussed in this connection. Ahmose-Pa-ny-Nekhbet commences his biography with a summary:[48] "I served the Kings, (namely) the 'gods' under whom I existed, at their moves on the southern and northern foreign land, at any place in which they were: King *Nb-pḥty-Rʿ*, the blessed, King *Ḏsr-kꜣ-Rʿ*, the blessed, King *ʿꜣ-ḫpr-kꜣ-Rʿ*, the blessed, King *ʿꜣ-ḫpr-n-Rʿ*, the blessed, up to this *nṯr-nfr* King *Mn-ḫpr-Rʿ*, given life eternally, when I reached a good old age. I am (still) one who lives for and through the king, as my honors with their Majesties (still) are and my being beloved in the palace exists. The God's wife, great king's wife *Mꜣʿt-kꜣ-Rʿ*, may she be blessed, repeated for me favors, as I brought up her great daughter the king's daughter *Nfrw-Rʿ*, may she be blessed, while she was a nursing child."

[45]Caminos, op. cit., 81-84, pls. 81-84. There was once a depiction of a lady of stature, whose name was in a cartouche. Nothing is left of her, as she was subsequently completely obliterated. The traces of the accompanying text reflect a benediction quite similar to the one for Thutmosis; however, it should be noted that the cartouche is not preceded by any designation, a point quite different in the male text. There is also the curious *iwʿ.k mnḫ ḥmt-nṯr ḥmt-nswt wrt sꜣt pw prt m [ḥʿw].k* . . . "your beneficent heir, the god's wife, great king's wife. It is (my/a) daughter, who came forth from your limbs . . ." which hardly would suit a mention of Hatshepsut, especially in view of the following *wnn.n.k si m ib mrr sꜣt.k pw n [ḫt.k] ir.s n.k mnw*, "after you have reared her with loving heart, it is your bodily daughter, she will make for you monuments . . ." The aspect of upbringing and the emphasis on the daughterly role would seem more appropriate for *Nfrw-Rʿ* than for Hatshepsut, who was older than Thutmosis III. This notion could draw support from another very fragmentary mention of Hatshepsut on the same wall (ibid., p. 76 ff.; pl. 38), speaking about the renovation of the temple dedicated to *Ddwn* and Sesostris III. Only Thutmosis III is credited with the deed: "the *nṯr-nfr Mn-ḫpr-Rʿ*, he made as his monument for his father Dedwen, residing in Nubia (and) for king *Ḫʿ-kꜣw-Rʿ* to make for them a temple out of limestone of Nubia: lo, (My) majesty had found it in greatly dilapidated brick, as a son acts with loving heart for his father who granted to him the two shores who reared him for (being) Horus, lord of this land; who gave in my divine heart to make his monument, that I cause that he be important as he has caused that I am important . . ." It is followed by two now almost completely defaced columns. The first commences . . . *wrt ḥswt* and after a gap of ± 12-13 squares follows *ḥmt-nṯr ḥmt-nswt wrt Ḥꜣt-špswt ir.n.s m mnw.s n it.s Ddwn ḫnt Tꜣ-Sti ir si ʿnḫ.ti ḏt* ". . . the god's wife, the great king's wife Hatshepsut, after she made as her monument for her father Dedwen, residing in Nubia, who made her, may she live eternally." I find it difficult to unify the text over the large gap and wonder if there are not two ladies mentioned, namely *Nfrw-Rʿ* and her mother Hatshepsut. Such a view would best account for the queenly title *wrt-ḥswt*, otherwise not used by Hatshepsut as dowager queen.

[46]Louis A. Christophe, *Karnak-Nord* III (1951), 86-89, pl. XV; Wolfgang Helck, "Die Opferstiftung des *Sn-mwt*," *ZÄS* 85 (1960), 23-34; idem, *Historisch-biographische Texte der 2. Zwischenzeit und neue Texte der 18. Dynastie* (1983), 122-26; cf. also P. Dorman, op. cit. 29-31.

[47]Edward Brovarski, *JEA* 62 (1976), 67, note 12, favored reading "Year 3," while R. Tefnin, *CdE* 48 (1973), 236 thought even of "Year 12."

[48]*Urk.* IV 34, 5-9; cf. P. Dorman, op. cit. 37 f.

Although Pa-ny-Nekhbet was obviously associated with Hatshepsut in connection with the upbringing of *Nfrw-Rᶜ*, there can be no doubt that Thutmosis III was the official authority in the country. The assignment to *Nfrw-Rᶜ* might very well have occurred before Thutmosis III became king, another indication that Hatshepsut had no official status, which does not rule out her exercising control in southern Upper Egypt.

The most important source for the evaluation of Thutmosis III's early years is the biographical inscription in Inana's tomb, which conveys a general picture of the mood in the country, in particular among some of the old guard at Thebes. Inana, upon whom Hatshepsut continued to heap high honors, was apparently a traditionalist and not a particularist, i.e., he was more concerned about the good of Egypt than with that of Thebes and its community. He reports the death of Thutmosis II in taciturn fashion in his autobiography:[49] (*Urk.* IV 59, 14-60, 2):

"May he ascend to heaven."

In contrast to it, he describes in some detail the ensuing ascent of Thutmosis III and the political situation behind the surface: (*Urk.* IV 59, 15-60, 11)

"After he had joined among the gods,
his son was set up in his place as King of the Two Lands.
While he ruled from the throne of him who begat him,
his sister, the god's-wife Hatshepsut made plottings: The Two Lands according to her plans—Egypt shall be made serviceable to her with bent head, as the glorious divine seed came forth before him. As the bow-rope of Upper Egypt has moored the southern lands, the excellent stern-rope of Lower Egypt is a mistress of commanding words. As her plans are excellent, the two banks will be pleased according to her saying."

This crucial passage has been repeatedly translated, but not all the translations will be discussed in the following.

Kurt Sethe, *Urkunden der 18. Dynastie, deutsch* (1914), 32:

"Er stieg zum Himmel empor und vereinigte sich mit den Göttern. Sein Sohn trat an seine Stelle als König der beiden Länder, er herrschte auf dem Throne dessen, der ihn erzeugt hatte. Seine Schwester, das Gottesweib Hatschepsut, sorgte für das Land, die beiden Länder lebten nach ihren Plänen, man diente ihr, indem Ägypten in Demut war; der vortreffliche Same des Gottes, der aus ihm kam, das Vordertau Oberägyptens, der Landepflock der Südvölker, das vortreffliche Hintertau Unterägyptens

[49]For a comprehensive comparison of various descriptions of a king's death, cf. now Hans Goedicke, "Sinuhe R 5-8," FS Altenmüller.

war sie, eine Herrin des Befehlens, deren Pläne vortrefflich waren; die die beiden Länder beruhigt, wenn sie redete."

James Henry Breasted, *Ancient Records*, II § 341:[50]

"His son stood in his place as king of the Two Lands, having become ruler upon the throne of the one who begat him. His sister the Divine Consort, Hatshepsut, settled the 'affairs' of the Two Lands by reason of her plans. Egypt was made to labor with bowed head for her, the excellent seed of the god, which came forth from him. The bow-rope of the South, the mooring-stake of the Southerners; the excellent stern-rope of the Northland is she; the mistress of command, whose plans are excellent, who satisfies the Two Regions, when she speaks."

Sir Alan Gardiner, *Egypt of the Pharaohs* (1961), 181:

"Having ascended into heaven, he became united with the gods, and his son, being arisen in his place as king of the Two Lands, ruled upon the throne of his begetter, while his sister, the god's wife Hatshepsowe governed the land and the Two Lands were under her control; people worked for her, and Egypt bowed the head."

Suzanne Ratié, *La reine Hatchepsout* (1979), 73:

"Il sortit vers le ciel et s'unit avec les dieux. Son fils se leva à sa place, en Roi des Deux Pays. Il gouverna sur la thrône de celui qui l'avait engendré. Sa soeur, l'Epouse du Dieu Hatchepsout, dirigeait les affaires du pays selon sa propre volonté. On travailla pour elle, l'Egypte étant tête baissée . . ."

William J. Murnane, *Ancient Egyptian Coregencies*, SAOC 40 (1977), 32:

"(Thutmosis II) went to heaven and joined the gods. His son stood in his place as King of the Two Lands, and he began to rule on the throne of him who had begotten him, (while) his sister, the God's wife Hatshepsut, managed the affairs of this land. The Two Lands were governed according to her plans, and work was done for her."

Eberhard Dziobek, *Das Grab des Ineni: Theben Nr. 81*, AVDAIK 58 (1992), 54:

"Als er aufstieg zum Himmel, vereinigte er sich mit den Göttern. Sein Sohn wurde erhoben auf seinen

[50]His rendering is closely followed by P. Dorman, op. cit., 38.

Thron als König der beiden Länder. Dass er auf dem Thron dessen, der ihn gezeugt hatte, herrschte, war, indem seine Schwester, die Gottesgemahlin Hatshepsut, in Verantwortung für das Land herrschte und indem die beiden Länder unter ihrem Ratschluss waren. Dass man ihr diente, war, indem Ägypten das Haupt beugte. Die vortreffliche Saat des Gottes, welche aus ihm kam, das Bugtau von Oberägypten, der südliche Landepflock, das wirksame Hecktau ist es von Unterägypten. Herrin des Befehlens, ausgezeichnet an ihren Beschlüssen. Eine, durch deren Worte die beiden Ufer zufrieden gemacht werden."

There are, aside from Dziobek's brief comments, no detailed grammatical discussions available of the text. It is obvious that the mention of the succession of Thutmosis II[51] has a close parallel in the wording of the succession following Thutmosis I.[52] In both cases Sethe considered them as conclusive statements in his edition of the text. In order to clarify the structure, the parallel statements are placed here side by side:

iw ḥswt.i mn.ti m ʿḥ nrwt.i ḫr šnyt	*iw.i m ḥswt ḥm.f m ẖrt-hrw*
sꜣḥ.n wi ḥm.f m mrt	
ʿqw.i ḥr šnwt nt pr-nswt	*snm.tw.i ḥr ṯt nt nswt*
m ẖrt-hrw nt rʿ nb	*m tꜣ n ʿbw rꜣ-nswt* (etc.)
	iw nḏ.tw ẖrt.i m snb ʿnḫ
	m ḏd ḥm.f ḏs.f ny-mrt

The parallelism transpires instantly and applies to the three areas covered by this part of the text. First is the emphasis on continuous enjoyment of the king's favor (and also that of the officialdom). Second, the consequences of this favored state in the form of material rewards, especially in the form of food, one in a more general, the other in a more specific fashion. Third, as far as Thutmosis II's reign is concerned, the material appreciation is augmented by a social one, which consists of two parts: one is the general concern with Inana's condition, in particular his health, the other, the king's personal inquiry. Both contain a direct quote, not only the first, as Sethe[53] had assumed. The commonly accepted interpretation entails grammatical and semantic problems. If the impersonal *nḏ.tw* is understood as a reference to the king,[54] an additional specific reference to a royal saying would be tautological and superfluous. It would require assuming here a construction *m* + *sḏm.f*, which, however, has conditional connotation.[55] It makes better sense to see the two

[51]*Urk.* IV 58, 7-13.

[52]*Urk.* IV 59, 5-14.

[53]Op. cit., 32. "Man erkundigte sich nach meinem Befinden mit (dem Wunsche) 'Gesundheit und Leben,' indem der König selbst es aus Liebe zu mir sagte." For the salutation *snb ʿnḫ*, see Hermann Grapow, *Anreden* . . ., III, 96, 102.

[54]It is a Late Egyptian idiosyncrasy to allude to the king in impersonal fashion; see Jaroslav Černý–Sarah Israelit-Groll, *A Late Egyptian Grammar*, Studia Pohl: series maior (1975), 30.

[55]Gardiner, *Egyptian Grammar*^{3} § 163.11. It would require a theoretical rendering *"when (or as far as) His Majesty himself

occurrences of the preposition *m* as being parallel, i.e., both qualifying *nḏ.tw*. Consequently, I consider *ḏd* an infinitive, i.e., "in His Majesty's own saying," followed by the quotation of the statement "one inquired my condition as *snb ꜥnḫ* through His Majesty's saying to a favorite."[56] The latter I see as *ny-mrt.i*, "the one belonging to my love," with an implicit possessive aspect, i.e., "possessor of love," or as *n mrty*, "to (a) favorite."[57]

The parallelism between the description of the two reigns ends with a reference to the termination of either reign. As far as Thuthmosis I is concerned it is *ḥtp nswt m ꜥnḫ pr r ḥrt*, "then the king rested from life." For the idiom *ḥtp m ꜥnḫ*, cf. *Wb.* III 191, 20; it reflects the theological concept that the end of the physical existence is not termination, but a station in life, hopefully followed by a new cycle.[58] The form of *ḥtp* is a narrative infinitive, used to indicate timelessness.[59] Curious is the use of the designation *nswt* in reference to the dead king. The term usually reflects the office conceived as permanent and not the individual holder.[60] Its use here might be due to the somewhat unusual situation in the holding of authority. As is further demonstrated later on, Thutmosis II was already actively involved with the affairs of Egypt without holding a/the royal title while Thutmosis I was alive.[61] In other words, Thutmosis I was the only holder of the designation *nswt* at the time, although the later Thutmosis II played an active, almost king-like role in Egypt. To emphasize that Thutmosis I was the one to "rest from life" *nswt* seems to be used.

The mention of the king's death is followed by the wish *pr.w r ḥrt*, which occurs first in the Story of Sinuhe (R 7) and is used in Inana's inscription following every mention of a royal demise.[62] It is apparently a formalized idiom, "may he go forth to heaven," like other hortatives following the mention of the living king.

What follows, possibly influenced by the distribution in Sethe's edition, has universally been considered a part of the description of Thutmosis I's reign.[63] The result is a rather strange sequence of statements opening with the king's death, followed by the wish for his heavenly ascent and finally the completion of his lifetime. It also leads to a grammatical inconsistency, as it would leave the ensuing

---

spoke for love of me," which has no meaning. There is no justification to supply an object here, as Sethe did, especially not in view of the qualification *ḏs.f*.

[56]Sethe's notion of the king's speaking "out of love to me" (i.e., Inana) makes little sense, because it could be expected that the king's amiable saying would be quoted verbatim. Without it, the reference to the king's personal speaking "for love of me" makes hardly any sense.

[57]See *Wb.* II 103 f.

[58]This cyclic notion is found already in Pyr. 305n-306b in "W. be guided the ways to Kheper, as W. rests from life in the West. May the ones of the underworld guide him, that W. shines anew in the West." It also transpires in the inscription on Hatshepsut's obelisk (*Urk.* IV 366, 9-12) "As Reꜥ exists for eternity like an imperishable star, I shall rest from life like Atum (i.e., the setting sun)."

[59]Cf. Gardiner, op. cit. § 306.2.

[60]Hans Goedicke, *Die Stellung des Königs im Alten Reich*, ÄA 2 (1960), 17 ff.

[61]This situation did not, however, have the form of a co-regency, i.e., a formal recognition of a junior partner in the royal office. What the exact form was is impossible to decide because of lack of information.

[62]See further, H. Goedicke, "Sinuhe R 5-8," FS Altenmüller.

[63]Dziobek, op. cit., 53, "Der König ging im Leben zur Ruhe, indem er zum Himmel ging, nachdem er seine Jahre vollendet hatte mit zufriedenem Herzen."

pseudo-verbal clause without introduction. As in the parallel section concerning the transition from Thutmosis II to his son, the opening *sḏm.n.f* is a time clause, defining the pseudo-verbal clause following it. The pronoun *.f* does not refer to the deceased, but rather stands in anticipation and concerns Thutmosis II. Literally, "(after) he had completed his years in appreciation," the passage refers to the time when the later Thutmosis II had taken care of the affairs of Egypt as representative of the presumably absent Thutmosis I. The term *rnpwt.f*, "his years," does not refer to a lifetime but to a specific period of time. *Nḏm-ib* is less a reference to a joyous time, but one which was met with "appreciation," presumably by the ruling king but also by the populace in general.[64] The focusing on the quality of the years the later Thutmosis II had spent in taking care of the affairs of Egypt might surprise initially. The context shows that it is given as the reason for his becoming king, but possibly also as a contrast to the later description of Hatshepsut's behavior.

At the time of Thutmosis I's demise, Thutmosis II was already *bik imy šs*, lit., "falcon who is in the nest." It is the subject in a pseudo-verbal clause and corresponds to the *s3.f ꜥḥꜥ m st.f m nswt t3wy*, "his son was established in his place as king of the Two Lands." Although ultimately derived from ornithology, the denoting of Thutmosis II as "falcon who was in the nest" should be recognized as more than just an expression of his being young at the time. It rather seems to indicate that Thutmosis II at the time of Thutmosis I's demise was already close to or included in the political power center of Egypt for a period of years.[65] In other words, his becoming king (*nswt-bit*) was not an event *ab ovo*, but steps had been previously taken to assure his eventual assumption of kingship or his successful activity had made him a candidate of choice for being king. Such a thesis is in accord with an indication that Thutmosis II acted as a kind of junior partner of Thutmosis I during the latter's later years as contained in the el-Arish inscription,[66] in addition to a Karnak inscription of the Eighteenth Dynasty suggesting a kind of power sharing between Thutmosis I and II of 7 years.[67]

The opening statement about Thutmosis II's sole reign is marred by a lacuna, which Sethe gives with 2-1/2 squares,[68] while the earlier publications[69] indicate it as much smaller. Using the parallelism between

[64]For *nḏm-ib*, cf. also *Wb.* II 380, 24-25.

[65]The legal relationship between Thutmosis I and II is difficult to define. It was not a coregency of the kind exercised during the Twelfth Dynasty and thus it is not included in Murnane's important discussion of this phenomenon. At the same time, the el-Arish text suggests some dominant role of (the later) Thutmosis II in Egypt while Thutmosis I was apparently attending to business in the Levant in his role of sovereign. There are no records preserved which would shed light on the situation, probably due to its occurrence in Egypt's north.

Sethe, *Das Hatschepsut-Problem. Noch einmal untersucht*, APAW 1932, 4, p. 60 has envisioned a coregency on the basis of various erasures, which was rejected by D. B. Redford, *History and Chronology of the Eighteenth Dynasty of Egypt* (1967), 53, 11. While the notion of a "coregency" might not be applicable, it would nevertheless appear that he exercised a major role in Egypt during the later years of Thutmosis I.

[66]The text indicates that Thutmosis II, though not necessarily as king, defended Egypt against an attack of migrant people from the East. It is probably the same event which he later reports as an attack by *Š3sw*-people; for it, cf. Raphael Giveon, *Les bédouins Shosou des documents égyptiens* (1971) 7 ff.

[67]Such a possibility is suggested by the inscription from Hagar el Merva, dividing the reign of Thutmosis I into two parts. For the inscription, cf. Anthony J. Arkell, "Varia Sudanica," *JEA* 36 (1950), 36-8; Jean Vercoutter, "New Egyptian Texts from the Sudan," *Kush* 4 (1956), 66 FF.; Cf. also Karola Zibelius-Chen, "Die ägyptische Expansion nach Nubien," BTA B/78 (1988), 165.

[68]Sethe suggested *ḫꜥw ḥr st-Ḥr*, which is too long even for the lacuna indicated by him. This restoration was followed by

the description of the ascent of Thutmosis II and that of his son Thutmosis III, a possibility for restoration can be envisaged. It requires a specification for Thutmosis II's exercise of rulership over the two lands and the basis for doing so. As a result I would restore (*Urk.* IV 58, 15) thus: *bik imy sš*   *ʿ3-ḫpr-n-Rʿ*, "the falcon in the nest while leading the Two Lands appeared as King ʿAa-kheper-en-Reʿ." For *sšm t3wy*, "to lead, i.e., administer, the Two Lands," see *Wb.* IV 286, 14; *Urk.* IV 250, 8; *Deir el Bahari* I, pl. XXIII; for *ḫʿi m nswt-bit*, see Margit Schunck, *Untersuchungen zum Wortstamm* ḫʿ (1985), 44-47. The proposed reading would explain why the later Thutmosis II was already taking care of Egypt's affairs before his ascent. The aim of the ascent is described as "that he rule Egypt and that he administer the Red-land, after he had taken possession of the Two Lands properly." To summarize the transition from Thutmosis I to Thutmosis II Inana says: "Then the king rested from life—may he ascend to heaven. After he had completed his years in appreciation, the falcon, which was in the nest while [guiding the Two Lands, appeared as] King ʿAa-kheper-en-Reʿ, that he rule Black-land and administer Red-land." It emphasizes the orderliness of the transition of power and the resulting authority of Thutmosis II as king of Egypt.[70]

As indicated earlier, the transition of rulership is stated in principally identical terms in regard to Thutmosis II's following Thutmosis I and also concerning the ascent of Thutmosis III with one striking difference: Thutmosis III is not named in any form. The insights gained in analyzing the former help in understanding the latter. Accordingly, *pr.w r pt* should be understood as a wish attached to a statement about a king's demise.[71] It can only be seen as a reflection of the spirit prevailing at the time Inana's biography was written, that the king's death is not stated *explicit verbis*. That the wish for the deceased's ultimate ascent to heaven is retained might be a reflection of Inana's personal loyalty to Thutmosis II, whose memory had otherwise been suppressed.

As in the description of Thutmosis II's becoming king, there are two sentences, one a temporal clause, the other a pseudo-verbal one. The former, namely, *ḫnm.n.f m nṯrw*, "after he had joined among the gods," introduces the main clause *s3.f ʿḥʿ m st.f m nswt t3wy*, "his son was established in his place as king of the Two Lands." The statement about the joining of the *nṯrw* is, of course, a reference to the completion of the burial of Thutmosis II, which was the prerequisite for having a new king.[72] Syntactically, it is obviously

Dziobek, op. cit. 51, note 158.

[69]U. Bouriant, "Une stèle du tombeau d'Anna," *RT* 12 (1890), 107; Hyppolite Boussac, "Le tombeau d'Anna," *MMAF* 18, 1 (1896), 10.

[70]The clause *iṯi.n.f idbwy m ʿ3ʿ ḫrw* is more likely the introductory temporal clause for the statement about Inana's elevated relationship with Thutmosis II. Thus, a rendering "After he had taken possession of the two banks orderly, I was a confident of the king in all his places. Greater was what he had done to me than the ancestors."

[71]As the king's fate was beyond human reach, any statement about it could only be hortative.

[72]Cf. *Urk.* IV 895, 13-896, 8 with a detailed account of the passing from Thutmosis III to Amenophis II; cf. also Winfried Barta, *SAK* 8 (1980), 35.

a pseudo-verbal clause with the Old Perfective expressing a completed action[73] as all translators, though with some leeway, have taken it. There are two details in the formulation which deserve notice. One is the omission of the newly installed king, i.e., Thutmosis III. Like the suppression of an explicit mention of his father's demise, it should be attributed to Hatshepsut's stance against Thutmosis II and his son. The other noteworthy feature is the establishing of the latter as *nswt tȝwy*, "King of the Two Lands," instead of the formal designation *nswt-bit*.[74] Prior to Amarna this is the earliest occurrence of this descriptive designation which is, indeed, not a formal title.[75] The reason for its use for Thutmosis III appears to be an emphasis on his being king of both parts of the country, presumably in salient opposition to Hatshepsut's *de facto* control of the southern part of the realm.

, has been generally understood as a narrative *sḏm.n.f* clause.[76] Such a notion, however, has important consequences. Inana wrote his autobiography before Hatshepsut became king (*nswt-bit*). This results clearly from the specification of Hatshepsut as *ḥmt-nṯr* and not as *nswt-bit*, which would have been inappropriate before the "Year 7," when Hatshepsut assumed the kingship.[77] From the way Hatshepsut is identified, it results that in Inana's late years up to his death[78] Thutmosis III was the sole and only "king" in the country. In view of this unambiguous political situation the *sḏm.n.f*  cannot be a narrative main statement, but should rather be taken as a temporal specification of the adjoining pseudo-verbal clause[79] in the same syntactic structure as before. Murnane seems to have been conscious of this grammatical aspect, which would explain his translation, "he began to rule." In as far as the *sḏm.n.f*-form is used in reference to the commencing point of an action in the past, this action has also to be completed in the past; otherwise a construction with *šȝʿ* would be in place.

"After he ruled from the throne of his begetter," i.e., in direct succession of his physical father, this not only contradicts the historical situation, but also contradicts the widely held notion that Thutmosis spent his early years under a regent, with Hatshepsut envisaged in this role. Aside from the passage under discussion,

[73]Gardiner, op. cit. § 311; Wolfhart Westendorf, *Der Gebrauch des Passivs in der klassischen Literatur der Ägypter*, VIO 19 (1953), 79 ff.

[74]See, e.g., *Urk.* IV 58, 15; 896, 7.

[75]See *Wb.* II 327, 10. The reasons for the vacillating use of the term, presumably reflecting changing political situations in the country, have not been investigated.

[76]Dziobek's "Sein Sohn wurde erhoben auf seinen Thron als König der beiden Länder. Dass er auf dem Thron dessen, der ihn gezeugt hatte, herrschte, war, indem seine Schwester die Gottesgemahlin Hatshepsut, in Verantwortung für das Land herrschte . . ." interprets features into the text which it does not contain. This concerns especially the rendering of *ḥqȝ.n.f* and its relation to the adjoined pseudo-verbal clause.

[77]See William C. Hayes, "Varia from the Time of Hatshepsut," *MDIK* 15 (1957), 78-80; Peter Dorman, *The Monuments of Senenmut*, 44 f.

[78]The use of the term *ḥmt.s* for Hatshepsut is not necessarily an indication of her being "king" as the use of the word for the dowager queen Aḥhotep (*Urk.* IV 31, 7) shows. The reference to Inana's "excellence" (*iqrw*) in the "palace" (*stp-sȝ*) most probably refers to the esteem he enjoyed under the previous reigns.

[79]As long as the situation that Thutmosis III at the time of the making of the inscription was, at least nominally, the "King of the Two Lands," as which he had been established following the death of his father had remained unchanged, the fact of his rulership could not be expressed as a past event, but only as a temporal indicator.

there is no other evidence which would support the thesis of a regency during the early years of Thutmosis III.

In addition to providing a clear description of the official political situation in the country, the text also talks at length about Hatshepsut. Although he admits her patronizing him, Inana, who had been a trusted follower of Thutmosis II, was not blind to what was going on in Thebes, where Hatshepsut's influence was initially concentrated. Her social position is exclusively defined in relation to the past king, i.e., Thutmosis II. It consists of calling her "his sister" and also *ḥmt-nṯr*, "god's wife."

The latter designation appears first for Ahmose-Nofretari, the widow of Ahmose, the founder of the Eighteenth Dynasty, and the rather influential mother of Amenhotep I.[80] It is commonly equated with the designation "god's wife of Amun," which plays a major role at Thebes during the Third Intermediate Period and into the beginning of the Twenty-Sixth Dynasty.[81] In its early use the designation is limited to *ḥmt-nṯr* and lacks a specific association with Amun;[82] it also has to be noted that it is used not for the reigning queen but rather after the demise of her royal spouse. As a result, it seems necessary to abstain from envisaging excessive religious connotations, especially in view of the absence of any indication of a belief in an *hieros gamos*, despite Hatshepsut's personal notions in this vein.[83] Instead, the original meaning should be recognized as denoting the "dowager queen," i.e., the wife of the late king who had become "god."[84]

The main statement about her is in the form of a pseudo-verbal clause; this verbal construction, *ḥr* + infinitive, expresses contemporaneity and continuity,[85] which at the time of the statement still prevailed. The second point deserving our attention is *tꜣwy ḥr sḫrw.s*, which Sethe indicated as an independent sentence. How Gardiner got to its translation as "the Two Lands were under her control" mystifies me, as does Murnane's "the Two Lands were governed according to her plans" or Dziobek's "in Verantwortung für das Land herrschte und indem die beiden Länder unter ihrem Ratschluss waren." Ratié's rendering "Hatchepsout dirigeait les affaires du pays selon sa propre volonté" is, of course, the only possible one, except that she does not explain how she attained it. The facts are remarkably simple. The object of the infinitive *ỉrt* is not an undefined word **mḫrw-tꜣ*, but Sethe's text contains an epigraphic error, either his or Bouriant's. *Ỉrt mḫrw* is a paralleled idiom[86] containing *mḫrw* written with  as determinative, which

[80]Cf. Michel Gitton, *L'épouse du dieu Ahmes-Néfertary* (1975); Franz-Jürgen Schmitz, *Amenophis I*, HÄB 6 (1978), 41 ff.; Lana Troy, *Patterns of Queenship*, Boreas 14 (1986), 107 ff.

[81]C. E. Sander-Hansen, *Das Gottesweib des Amun*, Det Kongelige Danske Videnskabernes Selskab, Hist.-filolog. Skrifter, I, 1940; Erhart Graefe, *Untersuchungen zur Verwaltung und Geschichte der Gottesgemahlin des Amun vom Beginn des Neuen Reiches bis zur Spätzeit*, Äg. Abh. 37 (1981), II, 101 ff.

[82]For a listing, cf. *LÄ* II 802 ff.

[83]Hellmut Brunner, *Die Geburt des Gottkönigs*, ÄA 10 (1964), 194 ff., in contrast to a widely held political interpretation of Hatshepsut's cycle about her birth, envisions it as a late manifestation of a much older myth.

[84]It is essential to recognize the wide use of *nṯr* in reference to a ritually buried dead one; see Hans Goedicke, "God," *JSSEA* XVI (1988), 57-62.

[85]Gardiner, op. cit. § 319.

[86]*Wb.* II 135, 1; Faulkner, op. cit. 116.

should be recognized here as well. In other words, *t3wy ḥr sḫrw.s* is not a separate sentence, but is rather part of the pseudo-verbal clause describing Hatshepsut's goal and reflecting her intention to direct "the matters of the Two Lands according to her designs." It does not indicate that she had any legal basis for what she was doing, but instead emphasizes that she acted according to her will, and this while Thutmosis III was legally ruling.

The "designs" (*sḫrw*) of Hatshepsut for "doing the matters of the Two Lands" are further specified by Inana. Although he might give the impression of being a follower of Hatshepsut, he seems to have had a clear vision of what was happening in the country. This is summarized in one sentence, *b3k.tw n.s Kmt m w3ḥ-tp*, which Sethe in his edition split into two lines. The sentence is, of course, a *sḏm.tw* passive.[87] The object of this submission as well as the recipient of the service are additionally specified. As for the first it is *Kmt m w3ḥ-tp*, "Egypt submissively," lit., with "bent head,"[88] and concerns the attitude desired of Egypt. The justification of this demand is given as *prt-nṯr 3ḫt pr.ti m-ḫnt.f*, "the glorious god's-seed has come forth before him." This statement concerns Hatshepsut and formulates her conviction that Egypt should serve her, because she was older than Thutmosis III.[89] Her "designs" (*sḫrw*) have nothing to do with a role as "regent" or similar; they rather smell of attempted political takeover. This is particularly implied by the desire for Egypt's submission (*w3ḥ-tp*), which is an attitude more appropriate for subdued foreign territories than for Egypt proper.[90] It can be inferred from Inana's formulation that Hatshepsut, from the moment of Thutmosis II's death, was ambitious to assume the power in the country, despite the installation of Thutmosis as "King of the Two Lands."[91]

The reason for her power-hungry attitude is supported by a pair of statements in which her controlling role in the South is juxtaposed with the need of Lower Egypt for such guidance in the form of a decisive mistress:

> "As the bow-rope of Upper Egypt has moored the Upper Egyptians;
> the excellent stern-rope of Lower Egypt is a mistress of decision."

The grammar of the explanatory pair of statements corresponds to the different situation as far as the two parts of the country is concerned. The pseudo-verbal clause indicates the accomplished and still prevailing achievement, while the nominal clause with *pw* states an unquestionable principle.

The reference to Hatshepsut as "mistress of decision" is augmented by a further pair of short sentences

[87]Because Hatshepsut at the time was not "king" (*nswt*), the formulation could not be an impersonal *.tw*.

[88]*Wb.* I 257; *Urk.* IV 166, 5; 324, 3.

[89]Dziobek's "Die vortreffliche Saat des Gottes, welche aus ihm kam" misses the intended references and thus also the political implications.

[90]It is a basic tenet of Egyptian iconography, descriptive or pictographic, that foreigners and foreign countries are shown as submissive to Egypt and her ruler; cf. Cyril Aldred, "The Foreign Gifts Offered to Pharaoh," *JEA* 56 (1970), 105 ff.

[91]For the previous translations of the passage, see above, pp. 114 f.

about "the excellence of her designs and that the two banks are always pleased with her saying."[92] According to the various complements, Hatshepsut was already "the bow-rope of Upper Egypt," i.e., she exercised control in Upper Egypt. Concerning the Delta the situation was still different at this time. She did not yet control it, but had the intention to do so. In her eyes the Delta needed a "mistress of decisions, excellent in her designs," who, of course, meant nobody else than herself.

Through an exacting analysis of one relatively short text passage a number of essential insights into the domestic situation following the death of Thutmosis II can be gained. They are: 1) Thutmosis III did not ascend to the throne as a minor but as a fully righted "King of the Two Lands," who ruled independently in the succession of his father. 2) There had not been a regent who took care of the affairs of state, neither Hatshepsut nor anybody else. 3) Already at the time of Thutmosis II's death Hatshepsut was playing an active role in the politics of the country. At that time her influence was limited to Upper Egypt, but she already had the intention to expand her role so that all of Egypt would be serviceable to her.

This situation, namely an official "King of the Two Lands" whose power was limited to the Delta, and Hatshepsut, who *de facto* controlled all or most of Upper Egypt, lasted for some time. On the basis of block 287 of the *Chapelle Rouge*[93] Schott had assumed that Hatshepsut was crowned as king on "day 29, 2nd month of *peret*, Year 2."[94] This thesis originally found some acceptance, but was met with early doubts by J. Yoyotte,[95] and more recently by R. Tefnin,[96] S. Ratié[97] and P. Dorman [98] The fragmentary text is part of a lengthy account of various oracles of Amun, in which he prophesized Hatshepsut's future role as king. Such a statement is incompletely preserved, as the date is lost. It commences:[99] ". . . a very great [miracle] in front of this 'good-god' by the announcing of the kingship of the Two Lands for me, with Upper and Lower Egypt in respect for me, and about the transfer to me of all foreigners after the enlightenment of the *nḫtw* about my majesty." A second "miracle" is mentioned immediately following it, including the date "Year 2, 2nd month of *peret*, day 29, the third day of the feast of Amun during the litanies for Sakhmet: the second time of promising me the Two Lands—in the court of the Southern residence." Although no details are given, the implication of the statement is that an oracle of Amun in favor of Hatshepsut happened during the celebration of specific parts of the "feast of Amun."[100] The "litanies for Sakhmet" (*nt*

[92]The reference to the "two banks" does not concern Egypt in general, but applies only to the narrow part of the Nile Valley where the embankments and the desert lining are close, i.e., Upper Egypt. It is in this particular sense that *idbwy* occurs in Hatshepsut's reign in *Urk*. IV 383, 15; cf. above p. 36.

[93]Pierre Lacau et Henri Chevrier, *Une Chapelle d'Hatshepsout à Karnak* (1977), 133-15; pls. 1 and 6.

[94]Siegfried Schott, *Zum Krönungstag der Königin Hatschepsut*, NAWG 1955, 6, 195-219.

[95]Jean Yoyotte, "La date supposée du couronnement d'Hatshepsout," *Kêmi* 18 (1968), 86-91.

[96]Roland Tefnin, "L'an 7 de Touthmosis III et d'Hatshepsout," *CdE* 48 (1973), 232-42.

[97]Op. cit., 83-85.

[98]Op. cit., 22-28.

[99]For the reading, see P. Lacau–H. Chevrier, op. cit. 134; cf. also P. Dorman, op. cit. 22.

[100]It should be kept in mind that Hatshepsut's final reach for power was also staged at Amun's great feast. This is not only a sign of a particularly strong religious motivation on her part, but equally an indication of the participation of those associated with Amun's cult in the political process. That forebodings of Hatshepsut's call to power happened in connection with Amun's feast shows how much the Amun priesthood was interested in seeing her as ruler of the country.

Sḫmt) might not necessarily be a devotional act for Amun, but could rather be part of a political aspect of Amun's cult, as a religious rendering of political authority seen under the auspices of Thebes and its religious establishment. Sakhmet is not associated with the cult of Amun,[101] so her invocation in connection with the "feast of Amun" should be seen as a political rather than a religious act. The nature of Sakhmet suggests that it had something to do with the military, without our being able to define it any closer.[102] While the text in the *Chapelle Rouge* was apparently an enumeration of the signs anticipating Hatshepsut's reach for power, it is also clear that in the 2nd year after the death of Thutmosis II Hatshepsut was still a long way from attaining the goal of her desire, namely, formal rulership over all of Egypt.

That Hatshepsut could not possibly have been crowned King of the Two Lands in "Year 2" can be demonstrated beyond doubt. There are several documents of the period which make it clear that the chronological annual count was based on the regnal years of Thutmosis III. One of them is the date "day 1, 1st month of *akhet*, year 5" at the opening of the decree of appointment of the "scribe of the god's treasure," *Wsr*(*-ỉmn*), as vizier.[103] The document is an important demonstration that acts of state such as the appointment of the vizier, namely, the one at Thebes, were still in the hands of Thutmosis III as king.[104]

Dating to "Year 5" are two more stelae found at Serabit el Khadim[105] commemorating an expedition on behalf of Thutmosis III. The latest dates of Thutmosis III are "day 16, 3rd month of *shemu*, Year 6"[106] and "day 9, 2nd month of *prt*, Year 7."[107] This is a rather coarse ink inscription of a scribe, possibly with the name *Ṯmḥy*. The origin of the piece is unknown, which diminishes its significance as a historical source. However, the fact remains that one is still dated in "Year 6" to Thutmosis III, who has to be seen as the constitutional lord of Egypt at this time. What the *de facto* situation was, especially at Thebes, has nothing to do with it.

According to Ianana's inscription, which presumably was composed not too long after the death of Thutmosis II, Hatshepsut already then had clear aspirations to become "King of the Two Lands." Her patience and that of her followers must have been rather strained towards the end of "Year 6." How great the impatience was, while she still hesitated to take the final step to grasp the position of "King of the Two

[101] Cf. Sigrid-Elke Hoenes, *Untersuchungen zu Wesen und Kult der Göttin Sachmet* (1976), 197 ff.

[102] I surmise that it had somewhat the character of a review of military installations, i.e., the confirmation of contractual agreements with professional military units. Because of our almost total ignorance of the workings of the military establishment in the Eighteenth Dynasty (or, for that matter, any other period of Egyptian history as well), it is impossible to grasp the "ceremonial" event any more specifically.

[103] A copy of this document is preserved in Papyrus Turin 1878; see also W. Helck, "Die Berufung des Vezirs *Wsr*," *Ägyptologishe Studien* (FS Grapow), VIO 29 (1955), 107-117; Dorman, op. cit. 33 f.

[104] Helck, *Zur Verwaltung des Mittleren und Neuen Reichs*, 291, assumes that *Wsr* was appointed vizier under Hatshepsut's rule. If this were correct, she would have had to appoint him. It rather seems that this appointment was an attempt by Thutmosis III to strengthen his position in Thebes, by having a partisan there in the key-position and by doing so, to curb the power of the Amun priesthood. *Wsr* (who seems to have dropped the reference to Amun from his name) was obviously not a protege of Hatshepsut, as results from the fact that he was (again ?) vizier several years after Hatshepsut's death.

[105] Gardiner–Peet–Černý, *Inscriptions of Sinai*, I, nos. 175-6; J. Černý, *The Inscriptions of Sinai*, II (1955), 150 f.

[106] OMichaelides 59 = Hans Goedicke–Edward F. Wente, *Ostraca Michaelides* (1962), no. 59, Taf. XLI.

[107] W. C. Hayes, *MDAIK* 15 (1957), 78-80.

Lands," is exemplified by an inscription left by Senenmut at Aswan.[108] He was there to direct the work on a pair of obelisks which arrived punctually in Thebes for the celebration of Hatshepsut's kingship.[109] Despite the fact that the inscription bears no date, it can nevertheless be assigned to the later part of "Year 6."

The text had originally been recorded by Lepsius[110] and next copied by de Morgan.[111] More recently Labib Habachi made a new copy of it.[112] For historical inquiry it is the annotation of the representation of Hatshepsut which is of significance.[113] Four translations will form the basis of the discussion:

L. Habachi: "The princess, great of praise, great of favor, and much beloved, the one to whom has been given the real kingship among the Ennead, king's daughter, king's sister, divine wife and great king's wife, the King of Upper and (Lower Egypt), Hatshepsut, may she live, beloved of Satis, mistress of Elephantine, and beloved of Khnum, master of the Cataract region."

S. Ratié:[114] "La princesse grande en louanges, la charmante, la bien-aimée . . . celle qui est vraiment dans le coeur de l'Enneade, la Fille Royale, la Soeur Royale, l'Epouse du Dieu, la Grande Epouse Royale, Hatchepsut, qu'elle vive!"

A. Burkhardt:[115] "Grosse Fürstin, gelobt an Beliebtheit, gross an Liebe, [der ihr] Vater Re das Königtum [gegeben hat], die wahr in der Meinung der Götterneunheit ist, Königstochter, Königsschwester, Gottesgemahlin, grosse königliche Gemahlin Hatschepsut, die leben möge, geliebt von Satis, Herrin von Elephantine, geliebt von Chnum, Herrn des Katarakten Gebietes."

P. Dorman:[116] "heiress, great in favor and charm, great in love . . . king's daughter, king's sister, god's wife, king's great wife [mistress of the two lands]."

The premise for reviewing this text must be the fact that Hatshepsut at the time of its composition was not "king" in a formal or constitutional sense. Such a role would require the use of the traditional designation *nswt-bit*, as it is later borne by Hatshepsut. The fact that she was not "king" at this time makes Sethe's restoration **di(t).n n.s it*[*.s*] *R*ᶜ untenable, despite Habachi's apparent epigraphic confirmation of it. There is good reason to question his reading at this point: in all passages in which the sign *n* occurs, it is written as a zigzag line except in this case—which justifies doubts. The proposed text would require the translation "to whom her father had given kingship," which presupposes a political development that had not occurred when the text was written. In as far as the passage concerns the assigning of kingship to Hatshepsut by Reᶜ, this event can only have been a future one at the time Senenmut was at Aswan. While I

[108] S. Ratié, op. cit. 81 f.; Christine Meyer, *Senenmut: Eine prosopographische Untersuchung*, HÄS 3 (1982), 129-131.

[109] *Urk.* IV 356 ff.

[110] *LD* III 25 bis.

[111] *Catalogue des monuments* I, 41; see also *Urk.* IV 396 f.

[112] Labib Habachi, "Two Graffiti at Sehel from the Reign of Queen Hatshepsut," *JNES* 16 (1957), 92. There is, of course, the earlier translation by Henry James Breasted, *Ancient Records*, II, § 150 f.

[113] She is denoted as "king's daughter, king's sister, great king's wife," but does not hold the king's title.

[114] Op. cit. 81.

[115] Adelheid Burkhardt, et al., ed., *Urkunden der 18. Dynastie, deutsch* (1984), 50.

[116] P. Dorman, op. cit., 115.

agree with Sethe in principle, I can envisage this assigning of kingship only as a wish and not as an accomplished fact.

M3ʿt cannot qualify the mention of *r3-pʿt*, as in such a case the specified word would have to be identified by a determinative. It can only serve, as Habachi had already realized, as an adjective to *nswy*(*t*), i.e., the promulgated wish concerns the awarding of "true kingship."[117] This formulation is very revealing. It shows that Hatshepsut at the time exercised a role that in the eyes of Senenmut was comparable with that of being "king," except that it lacked the official awarding of kingship to her. Of special interest is the mention of "the wish of the Ennead of gods," which is perhaps to be understood that Hatshepsut's political intention was supported by Amun, his priesthood, and the temple establishment.

Despite the symptoms of impatience in Senenmut's Sehel graffito, Hatshepsut did not wait much longer before her intentions and desires finally materialized. The work on the pair of obelisks was in all probability coordinated with the plans for her becoming king. The final date for Thutmosis III is quite late in "Year 6."[118] A "Year 7, 1st month of *akhet*, day 16" is mentioned in an inscription of Thutmosis III, which bears the date "Year after the 23rd, 1st month of *shemu*, day 2."[119] The text describes the king's deeds for Amun in gratitude for the success earlier in the same year, when he conducted the First Campaign into the Levant, leading to his recognition as "sovereign," i.e., as Levantine overlord. The text is unfortunately full of lacunae, which greatly mars the understanding. In his publication of the text, which is actually in the Festival Hall of Thutmosis III and thus is of a much later date,[120] Gardiner[121] was of the opinion that "the purpose of this date is quite obscure." Helck in his translation[122] expresses the notion that the date refers to the setting up of a foundation under Hatshepsut which Thutmosis III subsequently enlarged. The endowing by Hatshepsut of a great "offering" (i.e., income) for the cult of Amun leads to the question, what could have inspired Hatshepsut's deed at that date. The question becomes especially interesting when we consider that Thutmosis III is still attested as "king" late in his 6th year, and that there are indications that Hatshepsut assumed the role of "king" in "Year 7."[123] When the enormous endowment for Amun is viewed against this background, the conclusion seems unavoidable that Hatshepsut had become "king" shortly before making the deed. This date is principally confirmed by two inscriptions which name of the day of Hatshepsut's crowning as "New-Year's-day, 1st month of *akhet*."[124] With this event the problems between Hatshepsut and Thutmosis III receive a momentary resolution. After her crowning Thutmosis III disappears completely from any known sources.

For the historian two questions remain to be asked, even without a possibility to answer them at this

[117] In contrast Thutmosis III emphasizes the duration of his kingship; cf. *Wb.* II 333, 4.

[118] OMichaelides 59 = Hans Goedicke–Edward Wente, *Ostraka Michaelides* (1962), pl. XLI.

[119] *Urk.* IV 1256, 8; Wolfgang Helck, *Urkunden der 18. Dynastie* (1961), 18, note 1, assumes that this "year 7" refers to Hatshepsut.

[120] The festival hall was possibly planned at the very end of Thutmosis III's 23rd year; cf. C. Nims, *ZÄS* 93 (1966), 97.

[121] Sir Alan Gardiner, *JEA* 38 (1952), 6 ff.

[122] *Urkunden der 18. Dynastie, deutsch* (1961), 18, note 1.

[123] Cf. P. Dorman, op. cit., 43-45.

[124] *Urk.* IV 262, 71; 261, 8; cf. also J. von Beckerath, op. cit., 200 f.

point of research. One is what triggered Hatshepsut's final reach for power, the other what happened to Thutmosis III and his initial supporters. In view of the indication that he not only became king but also ruled (*ḥqꜣ*) following the death of his father, he was no longer that young by the time Hatshepsut pushed him aside; if one assumes his age at becoming "King of the Two Lands" of at least 12 years, he would have been 18 or 19 years old when Hatshepsut took over. In other words, he was no longer an infant who was easily pushed aside. This makes it necessary to see his abdication not only as a personal fate but also as a political one in the loss of support. As indicated earlier, it would seem likely that he was originally supported by the professional military; his fall from power can only mean that the military, either generally or at least partially, no longer favored him. In Hatshepsut's inscription at the Speos Artemidos is at least one indication that she tried to attract the members of the military by offering them house ownership as a reward for unwavering loyalty.[125] She appears to have been mostly successful[126] except for a special group of soldiers of originally foreign extraction whom she expelled after her takeover. There is no indication that Thutmosis III shared the group's fate, although it would seem most likely that he left Egypt as well.

While the few available indications point to Hatshepsut's becoming king in Year 7, it was hardly as sudden a development as her account about the miracle during the feast of Amun would suggest. Not only does the choice of the particular moment imply careful planning, but even more so the manufacture and completion of the pair of obelisks in her honor coinciding with the event. It should have taken a year to accomplish the latter so that Hatshepsut's decision to stage the *coup d'état* must have occurred in Year 6 at the latest. Considering it a date *ante quem* for Hatshepsut's decision makes it come close to year 5, the date of the appointment of *ꞽImn-wsr* by Thutmosis III as vizier in Thebes. Unfortunately nothing is known about his activities during the crucial years 6 to 22, except that he died in year 28, i.e., when Thutmosis III had been again sole king for several years.[127] That a Thutmosis III appointment in Hatshepsut's own bailiwick could have given her the impetus for usurping kingship would seem a feasible hypothesis.

Thutmosis III's first renewed mention is in "Year 13 at Serabit el Khadim,"[128] i.e. after the passing of seven years. The stela does not point to any great love between him and Hatshepsut, who is also depicted; on the contrary, the strict separation of the two antagonists would seem quite indicative. From "Year 16" dates a stela at Wadi Maghara[129] which depicts the two, but looking in opposite directions. Only Hatshepsut bears the designation *nswt-bit*, while Thutmosis III is denoted as *nṯr-nfr*.[130] It seems that this reflects the formula of some form of political compromise between the two. Hatshepsut retains the formal position, while Thutmosis III becomes something like a "junior partner." This rapprochement I surmise was fully

[125] *Urk.* IV 389, 14; see above p. 75.

[126] For a supposedly peaceful reign, the representation of military units in Hatshepsut's temple is rather surprising. In the controversy between her and Thutmosis III, the control of power was certainly a major factor and might have provided the basis for the kind of Rapprochement achieved in year 15.

[127] See Wolfgang Helck, *Zur Verwaltung des Mittleren und Neuen Reichs* (1958), 290-293.

[128] Gardiner–Peet–Černý, op. cit., no. 179, pl. LVIII; cf. also Jaroslav Černý, *The Inscriptions of Sinai*, II (1955), 151 f.

[129] Gardiner–Peet–Černý, op. cit., no. 44; pl. XIV; Černý, op. cit., 74.

[130] While the implication of this designation can be guessed in this case with some success, the fundamental meaning of it is, however, an unresolved problem.

achieved in "Year 15" and celebrated in the form of a *ḥb-sd*. The relations between the two remain tense, but are somewhat softened by the physical separation of the antagonists. Thutmosis III most likely resided in the Delta (possibly at Nebesheh), while Hatshepsut held court at Thebes. Over the years the relationship loses its militant antagonism, as demonstrated by an inscription from "Year 20."[131]

There is good reason to assume that during those missing years Thutmosis III devoted himself primarily to the establishing of a professional military.[132] Among them he apparently had a unit with an especially close attachment to him, which played an interesting role as *nḫtw* in his First Campaign. It is not unlikely that Thutmosis III during these years conducted minor military operations for Hatshepsut,[133] having nothing to do with the Levant. There the "sovereignty" that had emerged under Thutmosis I had collapsed. What the political situation was like can be grasped only to a very limited degree. The "Egyptian" interests were, as previously under Amenophis I, limited by the *nahal bezor*. There were three garrisons there, namely Tell Faharah, Tell Ajjul and Tell Jamnah. In the north of Palestine existed a loose political conglomeration with a sanctuary as its center. It was ultimately the pressure by those garrison troops, who were dissatisfied with their living conditions to the brink of mutiny, which inspired Thutmosis III to a military advance north ending with the taking of Megiddo.[134] With this deed Thutmosis III followed in the footsteps of his grandfather Thutmosis I and became "overlord" of the Levant. In contrast to the earlier sovereignty, Thutmosis III had achieved his by war, which determined the fate of the Levant for the next 400 years.

[131] Gardiner–Peet–Černý, op. cit., no. 18; pl. LVII; Černý, op. cit., 152 f.

[132] The level of military preparedness displayed by Thutmosis III at this First Campaign makes it virtually certain that the organization must have been established well in advance of this event. It is especially the professional elite-troop denoted as *nḫtw* that might have its beginning in the years before Thutmosis III became again sole master of Egypt; cf. H. Goedicke, *The Battle of Megiddo* (2000), 154 ff.

[133] A. R. Schulman, *JARCE* 8 (1968), 29 ff.

[134] See Goedicke, op. cit., 132 ff.

Comments on the Tomb of the Great Herald Antef (TT 155)

In its present paltry state tomb 155 at Draᶜ abu Naᶜga gives only a lamentable impression of what it once must have been. The damage was apparently done a long time ago, because the records made of it by Burton and Hay in the 1820s reflect somewhat more than what is left now, but still indicate large-scale destruction.[1] The only full survey of the tomb was made by Torgny Säve-Söderbergh on the basis of copies made originally by Davies in 1930.[2] The comments offered here are made with the help of this publication and no independent investigation of the extant remains was conducted.

The earlier recordings concerned primarily the recurrent "hunting and fowling," which will stand without much comment.[3] Basically unparalleled is a sequence of pictures pertaining to the making of wine as well as decorative elements with presumably political significance. The date of TT 155 is generally agreed upon as belonging to the reigns of Hatshepsut–Thutmosis III.[4] In their totality they span a stretch of 54 years and comprise distinct inner-political developments, which make a more precise dating desirable. Among the decorations in the tomb there are two potentially indicative scenes, which will concern us later.[5] Both are highly incomplete and thus do not offer a simple answer. One consists of a reference to a "jubilee" (*sd*-festival) depicted on the two sides of the doorway leading into the inner part of the tomb. The other is an otherwise unparalleled man-sized rendering of a "palace-facade" containing a royal Horus-name; it is opposite the picture of a man identified as "Great Herald Antef," who holds a large staff towards the Horus-name.

To begin with the wine-making depictions, they fill the right half of the hall's back wall adjoining the "fishing and fowling" scene. On the opposite side of the central passageway are the representations of arms-carrying men and the bringing of "tributes" by Asiatics.[6] The division appears to be of significance, as the one side seems to depict the official military exploits; the other is assigned to non-belligerent matters.

[1] Porter and Moss, *Topographical Bibliography*, I^2 (1960), 263-265; the location of the tomb explains the early interest in it.

[2] T. Säve-Söderbergh, *Four Eighteenth Dynasty Tombs*, Private Tombs at Thebes (1957), 11-21; pls. X-XX.

[3] Säve-Söderbergh, pl. XIV; cf. also Luise Klebs, *Die Reliefs und Malereien des neuen Reiches*, AHAW 9 (1934), 79 ff.; Max Wegner, MDIAK 4 (1933), 108.

[4] For his prosopography , cf. Wolfgang Helck, *Zur Verwaltung des Mittleren und Neuen Reichs* (1958), 495.

[5] See below, pp. 140 ff.

[6] Säve-Söderbergh, op. cit. pl. XIII.

Since they apparently comprise the full range of the tomb owner's activities, the two sides deserve to be recognized as a balanced, intertwined display of Antef's life. In order to better grasp the scenes' purport, it is necessary to keep in mind that their main aim was not a purely descriptive one, but that they are rather to be understood as statements rendered with the help of pictures.[7] This is especially transparent in the case of the "fishing and fowling scene", as it seems rather unlikely that ancient Egyptian high-ranking officials spent their time primarily in sportive pursuit. As pictures of significant mundane activity the "fishing and fowling scene" should instead be interpreted as a summary of adult life.[8] In this vein, the setting in the swamp is most meaningful as an expression of life's locale, namely, in a surrounding dominated by nature and prone to man's activity therein. This activity is divided into two kinds: on the one side is the overcoming of what dwells in the amorphous, i.e., the water, and it is indeed significant that the prey is frequently depicted as a *bwt* -fish,[9] *bwt* being the Egyptian word for what is to be rejected. The occurrence of the hippopotamus in this scene is most likely not an ideal of a leisurely pastime, especially when the spearing is performed by the gentleman himself.[10] It is rather to be seen in ritualistic terms as the overcoming of chaos or evil, which has its historic roots in the hippopotamus hunt, but which by the end of the Old Kingdom had become entirely ritualistic,[11] just as it still is in the Triumph of Horus.[12] The second activity, also placed in the same swampy scenery, is the chase after the lofty as represented by the birds. In the water a monster or a crocodile is lurking, while the proper gentleman tries to get hold of the flying birds, though with limited success, judging by the birds he holds.[13]

After this digression into literary symbolism of scenes seemingly reflecting daily life, we can now turn to the scenes which are exceptional in Antef's tomb. The depiction of "wine-making" is subdivided into four panels with an additional self-contained panel inserted into it, which is not directly part of the making of wine. The first scene (fig.1) is an elaborate depiction of the grape harvest in an arbor. The two vines are depicted so far apart that two men can stand there in addition to two others squatting at the vines. The original annotations are almost completely lost. The man at the left seems to begin his speach (*ḏd.f*) with

[7]For the principally didactic character of Egyptian representation beyond mere descriptiveness, see H. Goedicke, "*Rwty* und andere Tiergötter," *Zwischen den beiden Ewigkeiten (FS Thausing)* (1987), 35 ff.

[8]It is widely assumed that the ancient Egyptians were passionate hunters and that they desired to project their favorite pastime into the Hereafter; cf. e.g., Wolfgang Decker, *Die physische Leistung Pharaos* (1971), 120 ff.

[9]For the identification of the fish, cf. Irmgard Gamer-Wallert, *Fische und Fischkulte im Alten Ägypten*, ÄA 21 (1970), 36; 128 f. Needless to say, there is a variety of fish in the Nile system, so the insistence on the *bwt* fish is a clear indication that this fish has a symbolic significance.

[10]For the hunting of the hippopotamus by a gentleman, see L. Klebs, *Die Reliefs des neuen Reiches*, 77. The participation of servants, sometimes to the point that the gentleman is only observing, appears to be a reflection of an increasing awareness of a social role in advancing order in the society.

The same notion, namely, representing evil as dwelling in the amorphous, has not only the *bwt*- fish and the hippopotamus as symbols, but also the turtle. For the latter, see Henry G. Fischer, *Ancient Egyptian Representations of Turtles*, MMA Papers 13 (1968).

[11]Cf. Torgny Säve-Söderbergh, *On Egyptian Representations of Hippopotamus hunting as a Religious Motive*, Horae Soederblomianae 3 (1953); Almuth Behrmann, *Das Nilpferd in der Vorstellungswelt der Alten Ägypter*, I, Europäische Hochschulschriften XXXVIII/22 (1989), Dok. 161 a-j.

[12]H.W. Fairman, *The Triumph of Horus* (1974).

[13]In most of the scenes, the gentleman holds only one or two birds, while the number of alighting ones is substantial.

Figure 1

ỉw.n ỉr.n . . . "we shall make . . .", the rest is lost. The foreman, of course, does not work himself; it is interesting that he holds a whip in his left hand, which would be more befitting for the driving of animals than the supervision of workmen.[14] His words to the man working in front of him are badly worn. As a possible reading I conjecture *ỉỉrp šw pꜣ* . . . "as the wine is empty, o . . ."

The second panel (fig. 2) shows the treading of the grapes by four agitated men, while a fifth adds grapes to the treading floor. His action is accompanied by *n kꜣ n* [*wḥ*]*mw* "for the ka of the herald." If the name was included is uncertain; the available space is limited. The wish might be part of a singsong between those treading the wine and those serving them.[15] The caption which is written to the right of the scene is highly incomplete; it was originally arranged in two lines, which have been incorrectly run together.[16] It begins with *ḥny* . . ." singsong . . ." with a possible mention of the workers involved.[17] The song reads *hy n nbt*[*.n Rnnwtt*] [*ỉr.*]*s ḥr.n m kꜣt tn n* [*nb.n*] *swr st nb.n m-wḥm* [*m*] *ḥswt.f ḫr nswt*, "hail to [our] mistress [Renenutet! May she act] for us in this work for our lord! May our lord drink it again in his favor with the king!" Considering the uncertainties in regard to the reading of the text, it cannot be determined if the inscription consists of one or two lines of the workers' "singsong." Säve-Söderbergh and Guglielmi have divided the signs somewhat differently due to their conflation with the part written to the right of the treading scene. Instead of their assuming a very unusual orthography * for the interjection,

[14]Säve-Söderbergh, *Eighteenth Dynasty Tombs*, pl. XIV C. I am not aware of another representation of the foreman in the picking of grapes holding a whip.

[15]For the kind of singsong during work, cf. Hermann Junker, *Zu einigen Reden und Rufen auf den Grabbildern des Alten Reiches*, SAWW 221 (1943), 6 ff.

[16]Säve-Söderbergh, op.cit. 17, apparently ran the lines together, so that he read "A song (?) to [our] Lady (Ernutet): 'O may she remain with us at work,'" in which he was followed by Waltraut Guglielmi, *Reden, Rufe und Lieder auf altägyptischen Darstellungen* . . . , TÄB 1 (1973), 87 f.

[17]In its full form it is probably *ḥn n wšb*, *Wb.* III 289, 10.

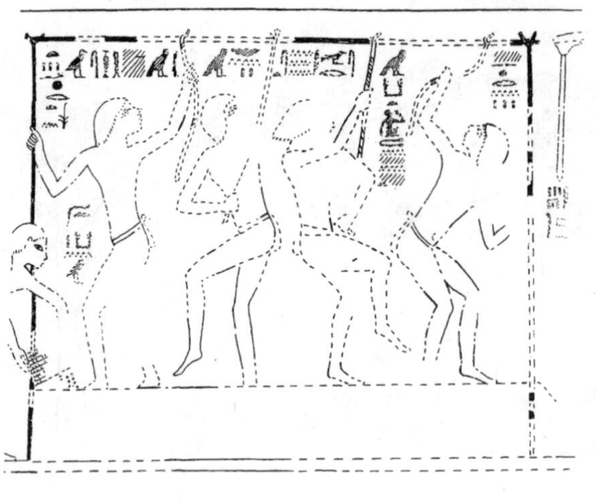

Figure 2

the difficulties disappear when one realizes that the word is spelled , as is usual.[18] The invocation of Renenutet on the occasion of treading the grapes is paralleled.[19] Although the restoration of the goddess's name is not certain, a female should be invoked in view of the feminine suffix in the ensuing text. What is requested or hoped for is to be conjectured because there is a lacuna in the text. Since only a small space is available, a sign like or has to be imagined. There is no object among the textual remains, thus pointing to an intransitively used verb. This rules out *dỉ*, but supports a restoration *ỉr.s*, "may she act." The goddess's support is requested for the ongoing task, i.e., the treading of the grapes. The end of the line is again lost; the demonstrative *tn* is certain and has been accepted by the previous translators. What closed the invocation is surmised here as **n nb.n*, "for our lord"; it results that it closes a self-contained section and that the remaining text is entirely separate because it contains also a mention of *nb.n*, "our lord." The renewed reference to the men's master requires a division into two lines. This second line not only anticipates the result of the ongoing effort, but links it with a wish for the lord: "May our lord drink it again in his gracefulness with the king." Säve-Söderbergh's "May our Lord . . . drink it as one who is repeatedly praised by the King" is grammatically untenable, as is Guglielmi's "Möge unser Herr ihn trinken als Wiederholung seiner Gunst beim König!" The latter disregards the lacuna between *m wḥm* and *ḥswt.f*; the former took *ḥswt* verbally. *M wḥm* is either adverbial,[20] i.e., "again," or a participle (*m wḥmw*), "as one who repeats his favored status with the king." Both have a double meaning, one being mundane, the other eschatological. The second would be a wish that Antef should partake in the beyond in the wine that is

[18]*Wb.* II 482 f. Guglielmi's notion of an exceptional misspelling of *ỉh* (*Wb.* I 117, 12-14) seems unfounded.

[19]Cf. TT 100: Norman de Garis Davies, *The Tomb of the Vizier Rekh-mi-Reʿ* (1943), pl. XV; cf. also J. Broekhuis, *de godin Renenwetet* (1971), 72 f.

[20]Cf. *Wb.* I 343, 4; it would be an early occurrence, like *Urk.* IV 1073, 17; also Hildegard von Deines–Wolfhart Westendorf, *Wörterbuch der medizinischen Texte*, Grundriss der Medizin der Alten Ägypter VI, 1 (1961), 206.

being made; the first indicates that Antef may regain favor with the king, a statement which implies that he had lost it at some time.

The third episode in the wine-making (fig. 3) shows two pairs of men wringing out the crushed grapes with the red liquid running from the sack. The process and its significance is quite obvious. The first step is designed to crush the grapes, after which they have to ferment in their juice. This step is necessary to produce fully red wine, different from the rosé resulting from straight pressing and fermenting of red grapes. In other words, the actual pressing of the wine is shown in the thrid step of the production, after which the juice is poured into jars.[21] It is not clear where the actual fermentation process took place. The representation apparently omitted this step, because it had no bearing on the message the series of pictures was intended to convey. The focal point appears to be the production of the red juice, which is carefully colored.

The accompanying annotation has been discussed at some length by Säve-Söderbergh[22] and has inspired numerous references.[23] It says [*ʿṯḫ*] *ỉrp in ʿprw n wḥm ỉIntf*, "pressing of wine by *ʿprw*- people for the herald Antef." There is no indication that the depicted people are directly related to Antef, but rather that he is the recipient of their activity. The scene has a virtual parallel in the tomb of Puyemreʿ (TT 39)[24] where, however, no reference to the tomb's owner is made. Another essential variant between the two representations is the differing spelling of *ʿprw*. In Puyemreʿ the designation is spelled , while Antef has  . As the indication in Puyemreʿ lacks any implication of ethnicity, Helck should be heeded in his misgivings against drawing extensive ethnic conclusions from the mention of *ʿprw* in the two pictures of wine-pressing.

The term *ʿprw* occurs in Egyptian inscriptions since the Old Kingdom, especially in connection with riverine navigation,[25] but also with laborers in a more general fashion.[26] The specific feature expressed by the designation *ʿpr* is the fact that those people were remunerated for the services they rendered. It appears that the term underwent a narrowing in its application by becoming restricted to professional military, i.e., a specific kind of mercenary. In the large inscription of Amenophis II (*Urk.* IV 1309, 1) a limited number of *ʿprw* is listed between local chieftains and their relatives and the general population. Later occurrences, such as Pap. Harris I 31, 7 or Hammamat 12, 17 corroborate the military employment of those designated as *ʿprw*, with Pap. Harris also suggesting a difference between them and those denoted as *maryannu*. While the exact meaning of the term is still elusive, it can nevetheless be insisted on the fact that it has no

[21]Although the representation gives the impression that the juice is fermented in closed jars, this is technically impossible. The gases developing during fermentation would cause an explosion, either blowing off the closing or shattering the jar.

[22] "The *ʿprw* as Vintagers in Egypt," *Orientalia Suecana* 1 (1952), 5-14.

[23]Jean Bottero, *Le Problème des Ḫabiru* (1954), 166 f.; Moshe Greenberg, *The Hab/piru* (1955); Wolfgang Helck, *Die Beziehungen Ägyptens zu Vorderasien im 3. und 2. Jahrtausend v. Chr.*2 (1971), 486.

[24]Norman de Garis Davies, *The Tomb of Puyemre*, I (1922), pl. XII.

[25]*Wb.* I 181, 6; Eckard Eichler, *Untersuchungen zum Expeditionswesen des ägyptischen Alten Reiches*, GOF IV/26 (1993), 163-168.

[26]Wolfgang Helck, *Untersuchungen zu den Beamtentiteln des ägyptischen Alten Reiches*, ÄF 18 (1954), 99, takes it as primarily an organizational indicator. For *ʿprw* working in quarries, see especially JdE 49623 (*ASAE* 25, 1925, 242 ff.)

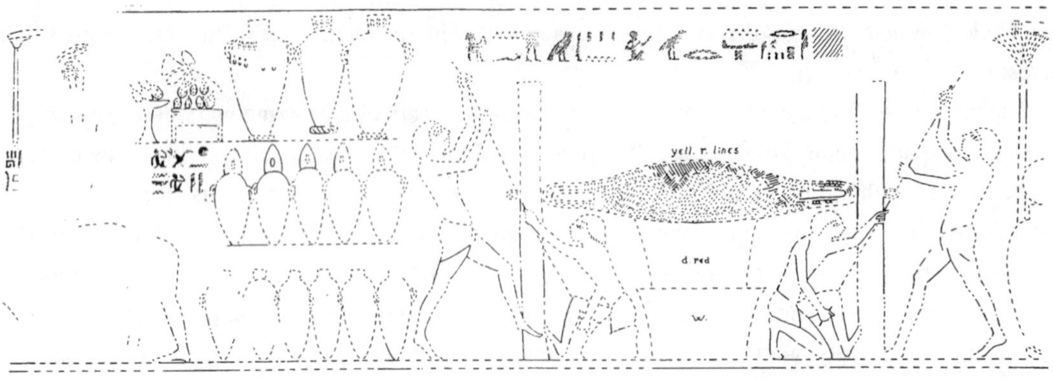

Figure 3

ethnic but exclusively professional connotations, which is in the general context of military employment. There is no indication that the term has anything to do with viniculture, which like most other forms of agriculture was largely the task of unskilled labor, with the possible exception of the wine-making itself. To pick grapes or to crush them does not require any skill whatsoever, nor does the final pressing of the wine. To have the people doing the latter denoted as *ʿprw*, which is otherwise applied to professional soldiers of some kind, makes sense only when taking the scene not at face value but considering it metaphorically. When seen in this vein the representation can be interpreted as showing professional soldiers producing dark red juice, namely, wine, instead of making blood run. In sum, the viniculture sequence should be interpreted as having symbolic value, the particular scene of pressing the wine as a demonstration of the peacefulness of the times, when professional militaries had nothing else to do but to squeeze the red liquid from grapes rather than from humans.

Adjoining the wine-pressing scene is a small panel (fig. 4), which should be seen as an insert. It is not an integral part of the sequence depicting the making of wine, but has its role in the symbolism connected with it. This scene, which is framed as if it were occurring in a small shelter, shows a heavy-bodied old man seated before a small table. In front of him stands a naked young girl. She has a string of beads around her hips as her only cover.[27] Her headdress ends in a long single pigtail. She extends her right arm towards the old man and apparently holds a flat drinking cup in her hand. She accompanies her gesture with the words *n k3.k šsp [tp-]nfr m p3 k3 n wḥm 'Intf*, "For your health! Take the prime for the herald Antef!" The annotation has one small gap, which Säve-Söderbergh, and following him Guglielmi, have restored as *[bw-]nfr*, thus reading "Receive the good thing with the *ka* of the Herald Antef!" and "Empfange [etwas] Gutes mit (durch) den Segen (Ka) des Grabherrn!" respectively. *N k3.k* is a widely used greeting[28] and could be compared with the French *à votre santé*. The proposed restoration is unconvincing for epigraphic and

[27]Young females in minimal habit are a reflection of the *joi du vivre* prevailing in the Eighteenth Dynasty, but ultimately squelched in the reaction to Amarna.

[28]Hermann Grapow, *Anreden* III (1942), 86 ff.

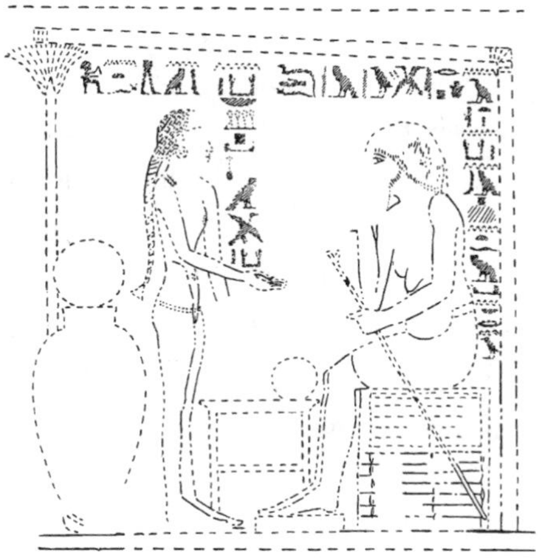

Figure 4

semantic reasons. The available space is less than half a full square, which speaks against restoring **b*, as does the terse spelling *[𓃀]𓄤 for a mid-Eighteenth Dynasty occurrence.[29] A general reference to "the good thing" or "etwas Gutes" remains too indistinct to be meaningful. Thus I propose restoring *tp nfr*, lit. "good head," as referring to the first pressed juice, still a cherished delight for vintners. 𓅓 seems to have caused problems for the previous translators, but finds an easy explanation when the ensuing *pꜣ* is taken into consideration as the well-known phenomenon of changing *n* to *m* before bilabials. *Pꜣ kꜣ*, which might originally have had a determinative which is now lost, is not a reference to the *ka* of the tomb's owner, in which case there should not be a definite article introducing it, but rather the word for "food, nourishment" (*Wb*. V 91). Antef at this time is not the owner but the intended recipient of the food, thus requiring that the 𓈖 introducing his mention is datival.

The response of the old man, obviously after tasting the sample, is *nḏm wy pꜣ ỉrp n [t]ꜣ ỉst n kꜣ n wḥm ỉntf m dỉ(.ỉ) n.k rnpwt* (?), "how sweet is this wine-for-the-cellar! For the *ka* of the herald Antef as I give (?) to you the young (wine)!" The interpretation offered here differs from previous ones and thus requires an explanation. That the speech of the old man, presumably the keeper of the cellar, consists of two separate statements has been likewise assumed by Säve-Söderbergh and Guglielmi. The first saying is in response to tasting the freshly pressed grape juice, the second a toast to the owner of the tomb. As for the first one, both translators rendered "How sweet is the wine of the workers" and "Wie [süss] ist dieser Wein der (Winzer-)Truppe!" respectively, both emending the article *tꜣ* before *ỉst*. However, two aspects have to be taken into consideration in order to grasp the meaning fully. First, at this point in the process the grapes have just been pressed and no fermentation has as yet taken place. Second, any pressing would have been done by

[29]The hieroglyphic restoration was introduced by Guglielmi, op.cit. 88, while Säve-Söderbergh had a transcription. *Urk* IV 339, 7 of Hatshepsut's time could be used as an argument in support of the restoration **bw nfr*. The meaning would change little in either reading.

workers, so that a reference to them at this point is gratuitous or meaningless. When the first results of pressing become available, it is the moment of tasting its sweetness which will determine the eventual quality of the wine. The situation demands that specific reference be made to the preliminary state of the grape juice prior to its fermentation and maturing. As a result, I do not consider *tꜣ ỉst* a reference to those who pressed the crushed grapes but rather to the destination of the juice, namely the cellar where it is to ferment and age. Consequently, I take *ỉst* not as the word for "crew" (*Wb*. I 127, 11 ff.), but rather as the homophon denoting an installation connected with food and drink, suggested by Sethe[30] on the basis of Pyr. 560b-c. In view of the adjoining depiction of a wine cellar, a renderng "this wine for this cellar" seems appropriate. The use of the article is noteworthy and might function here in reference to the installation which the old man supervised but did not own. "This wine for this cellar" anticipates the final product after the freshly pressed juice is handed over to the keeper of the cellar.

The second statement salutes the herald Antef in anticipation of the delight he will eventually have from the grape juice after it had been properly matured. The opening *n kꜣ.k* is in parallelism to the salutation the old man receives from the young girl. As in the latter case, the ensuing saying concerns the person addressed in the salutation. I thus see no reason to worry about the suffix *.k* which concerned Guglielmi, who envisaged the possibility that it was addressed to the girl, or Säve-Söderbergh, who read *m dỉ n.k Rnnwtt* , "as a gift to you (?) of Ernutet (?)." It rather anticipates the moment when the old man can toast his lord with the new wine. I thus read "as I give to you the young (wine)." This interpretation is supported by the recurrent use of *m dỉ (.ỉ) n.k* "as I give to you."[31] The last word, the object of *dỉ(.ỉ)*, is incomplete; it begins with *rnw* . . . and was considered part of the name of Renenutet. This seems improbable not only for orthographic reasons, but also because the goddess has given nothing to the owner of the tomb. The incomplete *rnw* I propose restoring into a derivate of *rn* "young" denoting the "young wine." Since *ỉrp* is masculine, *rnw* might only lack the determinative. The meaning of the statement is clear; it anticipates the moment when the wine has completed its fermentation and is ready for consumption, which is, of course, a moment of pride for the cellar master.

The last panel of the sequence (fig. 5) shows the delivery of the filled jars under the supervision of a guardian of a building which is closed by a door. Inside the structure, whose layout can not be made out from the drawing, jars are arranged in three lines. At the gate squats a man supporting his head and presumably sleeping. There are two types of jars, one with handles, the other without. Each jar is closed with a large stopper, which seems to have a circular "ornamentation" in its center. As far as I am aware no comments have been made about this, but from the point of oenology this detail is of significance. The jars which are brought, and which are apparently in the same stage of ripening as those inside the cellar, do not contain wine, i.e., fermented grape juice, but only the result of the pressing before it has turned. During the

[30]Kurt Sethe, *Übersetzung und Kommentar zu den altägyptischen Pyramidentexten*, III, 54 f.

[31]*Urk*. IV 1498, 17; Säve-Söderbergh, op. cit. pls XXV-XXVI; for the construction *m +sḏm.f* , see Gardiner, op.cit. § 444.3. The suffix first person seems generally omitted for reasons of politeness. Guglielmi's rendering "mit dem, was dir Renenutet gegeben hat" would require an absolutely used feminine relative form.

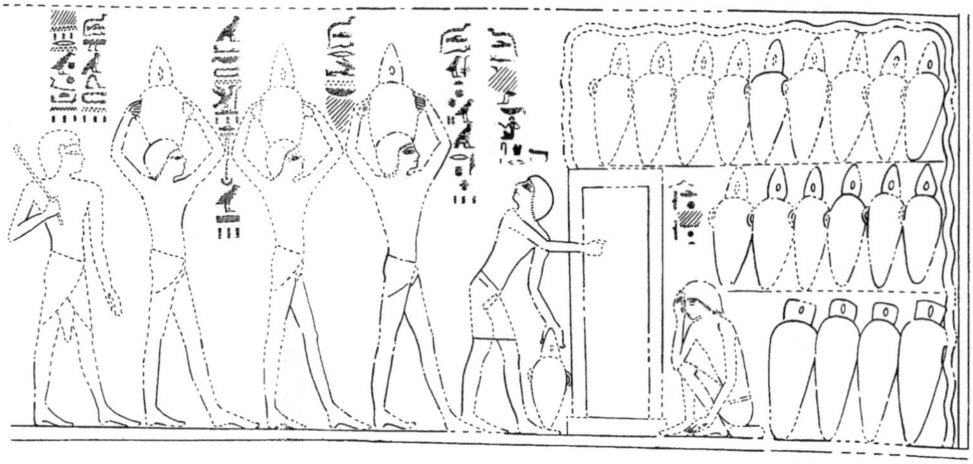

Figure 5

fermentation considerable quantities of gases develop, which would blow out the closure or shatter the jar. In order to relieve them, one apparently diverted them through an opening in the stopper; if and what conduit led to it cannot be determined. However, it is important to realize that the jars contain fermenting juice, a point which is significant for the man present in the room. The gases are highly toxic, a point reflected in the guard's statement.

The most advanced man of the delivering party knocks at the door and turning around says to the one behind him, "The servant is asleep!" The opinion of the latter is "He is drunk from the wine!" The words of the next in line are unintelligible in the form published. Säve-Söderbergh[32] entertained the notion that it might be emended to *r wn mꜣꜥ*, "really," in which Guglielmi (89) followed him. Such an isolated adverbial expression would be an unusual statement. I wonder if the emendation should not be done into **ir wn.k*, "make your haste!" if nothing else is missing, or else *ir wn nb* ... , "do! hasten! the master is ... "[33] The admonition to hasten fits well the saying of the next man, "See, the loads are heavy!"[34]

The comments of the foreman, walking as the last one, are puzzling when rendered "Go on, (or) we shall be scorched (?)" with Säve-Söderbergh or "Eilt! Wir werden (sonst) versengt werden!" with Guglielmi. There is no indication that particular heat prevailed at the time, nor does it have any bearing on the particular topic. Säve-Söderbergh expressed misgivings about the rendering partly on orthographic grounds, as the spelling of the envisaged word **nwḫ* "would be quite abnormal," while Guglielmi entertains

[32]Op. cit. 18, note 6.

[33]For the conjunction *ir wn*, see *Wb.* I 313, 12. The expression appears to be an old one and not necessarily common vernacular.

[34]Säve-Söderbergh offered "Lo, the numbers (= quantities) are heavy!" with the interpretation "lo, (= everybody) are heavily loaded!, repeated by Guglielmi. It would seem much simpler to link *tnw* with the verb *ṯni* , "to lift up." As *irp* is masculine the use of a term of this gender would make sense here.

a possible parallel to the German colloquial idiom "Senge kriegen." Obviously, the supervisor had little cause to be worried about receiving blows, especially as there was no one to mete them out but him. All other statements in the sequence are, as far as they are intelligible, concerned with the earliest stage of wine-making. To begin with, *šm.ṯn*, "may you go," opens the supervisor's statement and there is no reason why the saying should turn without reason to the "we"-form. The main theme of the scene is the transfer of the bottled juice to the place where it is to ferment. In order to accomodate this circumstance, I surmise as a possible restoration *šm.ṯn di.ṯn mw ẖm.ṯn*, "May you go and may you give the young wine your fetter!" The tenor is the intended transfer. *Rnw* is taken here as the same word used by the old man in the adjoining scene; it was considered there as a term for "young (wine)," to some extent anticipating the outcome of the next process. The puzzling  is interpreted here as related to *ẖm*, "to secure," captured birds, with specific application to the secure bottling of the wine-juice ready for fermentation. This is, of course, primarily a guess, but it suits the prevailing context.

The guard in the "cellar" has a response to the accusation by the fellow knocking at the door: *n qd (.i) qdt* which was read "I did not sleep at all!" (lit. I did not sleep a sleep!"). The copy of the text is not certain and as a result the translation is not beyond question. Two points have to be mentioned. If the man is in the place where the wine ferments, as is obviously the case, he would be well advised not to try to stay there too long because of the toxic fumes. Epigraphically, there seems an excessive space between the assumed two words. In view of the uncertainties of the text any suggestion can only be hypothetical. To envisage or deny the possibility of sleep would seem unfitting for the context. A possible reading would be*n (n) qd m-qd.i,* "there is no sleep around me", referring to the fermentation going on. However, no definite interpretation can be established.

Despite the descriptive nature of the sequence, it nevertheless appears to have also a symbolic side to it. One concerns the people identified as performing the pressing of the grapes, when the red juice flows from the sack. To denote them as *'prw* has certainly no ethnic connotation. It is also unlikely that specialists were employed for the pressing, which requires no skill but only strength. It would thus seem appropriate to equate the *'prw* identified in the scene whence the red grape juice is produced with the other use of the term in the professional military as paid, i.e., professional soldiers. On the basis of this equation the scene can be interpreted to show that the circumstances were such that the professional military spent its time making red grape juice flow rather than blood. The wine, its harvest, processing, storing, and fermentation to a new purport seems also to serve as a simile for life and its ending which leads to death and burial, and to a hoped-for new life. This circle, implicit in life and wine, is also the theme of the inserted scene with the old man and the young maiden, as she presents him with the promise of the first pressing, while he looks forward to its transformation into new wine.

Although wine and its cultivation are depicted in Egypt from the late Fourth and early Fifth Dynasty onwards, the symbolic value of wine seems to develop only in the New Kingdom. If it is connected with the more intensive experience with wine during this period is hard to decide. To have the entire interior of the tomb decorated as an arbor[35] is an unequivocal indication for the eschatological symbolism connected with wine.[36]

The thickness of the gateway into the inner section of the tomb is decorated on both sides with a matching picture (fig. 6). Although lamentably preserved it is nevertheless of considerable significance for its political implications. Each side shows the owner of the tomb dressed in formal garb in front of a "heraldic assembly." It is made up of an inscriptional column lined by a decorative band on either side and supported by a panel showing the emblem of *smꜣ-tꜣwy*, "the Uniting of the Two Lands," to which in either case two captives are attached. The difference between the two panels is that in one case the captives are African, in the other Asian. Neither one provides any identification. The panel is a standard symbol for the basis of the execution of kingship, namely the integration of Egypt leading to its subdual of foreigners.[37] Despite the formal basis, there is no royal representation above it, as found later, nor are there any remains of a reference to a ruler in the form of a royal name. What is left is not only highly fragmentary but also unusual in its formulation. Nevertheless, a point of major significance can be established: the passage uses the male suffix *.f* so that it can be concluded that it refers to a male ruler. Given the historical background of Antef this can only be Thutmosis III.

On the basis of similar or parallel formulations[38] the text can be restored as [*ỉr.*]*f ḥḥ*[*w*] *m ḥb-sd ꜥšꜣ wrt mỉ Rꜥ*. It is unquestionably a wish concerning an established king, in our case Thutmosis III. It is generally assumed that this wish concerns the celebration of "millions of Sed festivals."[39] Although many details about the Sed festivals are still a topic of debate, there is nevertheless a consensus about the fact that in principle the jubilee is celebrated first after thirty years of reign, and that it can be repeated afterwards at three-year intervals.[40] Even with an ideal lifetime of 110 years,[41] the Egyptians could not expect that any

[35]L. Klebs, *Reliefs des neuen Reiches*, 51 ff.

[36]Mu-chou Poo, *Wine and Wine Offering in the Religion of Ancient Egypt* (1995), 147 ff.

[37]The topic commences in the Archaic Period and continues into Roman times; for the former, cf. Hermann Junker, "Ägyptologische Studien," *VIO* 29 (1955), 162 ff., for the latter, William K. Simpson, *ZÄS* 100 (1973), 50 ff.

[38]The earliest attestation is for Pepi II (*Urk*. I 115), *dỉ.n.(ỉ) ỉrt ḥḥ m ḥb-sd ꜥnḫ.tỉ snb nb ꜣwt-ỉb nb mỉ Rꜥ*, "I give to you the doing of *ḥḥ* during the jubilee while you are alive [in] all health and all joy like Re'"; the most influential appears to be a stela of Sesostris III at Deir el Bahari concerning the cult for Menthuhotep-Nebhetep-Reꜥ (Edouard Naville, *The XIth Dynasty Temple at Deir el Bahari*, I, pl. XXIV), *nṯr-nfr pn dwꜣw rḫyt nb ꜥnḫ. sn rꜥ-nb ỉr.f ḥḥw m ḥbw-sd ỉr.f ꜥšꜣ wrt*, "This 'good god' whom the commoners praise while they live every day: may he make *ḥḥw* during jubilees very many and may he make many!" For Hatshepsut (*Urk*. IV 300, 7-9) exists the divine promise *wḥm.n.(ỉ) n.ṯ ỉrt ḥḥw m ḥbw-sd ꜥšꜣ-wrt ḫꜥ.tỉ m nswt-bỉt ḥr st-Ḥr n ꜥnḫw nb mỉ Rꜥ ḏt* , "I reported for you the doing of *ḥḥw* during jubilees very many, while you had appeared as king on the Horus-throne-of-all-living like Reꜥ eternally." Similarly (Edouard Naville, *Deir el Bahari*, I, pl. XI), *sỉ.n.(ỉ) n.ṯ wḥm ḫꜥ m nswt-bỉt ỉrt ḥḥw m ḥbw-sd ꜥšꜣ-wrt*, "I gave to you the appearing as King and the doing of *ḥḥw* during jubilees very many." Others are Hammamat no. 110 (Menthuhotep II) *ỉst grt ỉn ḥm n nṯr pn nb ḫꜣswt rdỉ mꜣꜥ n sꜣ.f M. n-mrwt ꜣw-ỉb.f wnn.f ꜥnḫ ḥr nswt.f nḥḥ ḥnꜥ ḏt ỉr.f ḥḥw m ḥbw-sd*, "it was the majesty of this god, the lord of the deserts, who did the revelation for his son M. in order that he be joyous as long as he is alive on/over his seats forever and eternally and that he make *ḥḥw* during jubilees very many."

[39]See *Wb*, III 153, 3; Säve-Söderbergh, op. cit. 19 interpreted the passage as ". . . [may] he [give ?] millions of Sed festivals, very many, like Reꜥ," which disregards the related formulations quoted above. In addition, there is no other agent who could grant the celebration of jubilees.

[40]Erik Hornung und Elisabeth Staehelin, *Studien zum Sedfest*, Aeg. Helv. I (1974), 54 ff.; 62 ff.

[41]Jozef M.-A. Janssen, "On the Ideal Lifetime of the Egyptians," OMRO 31 (1950), 33-43.

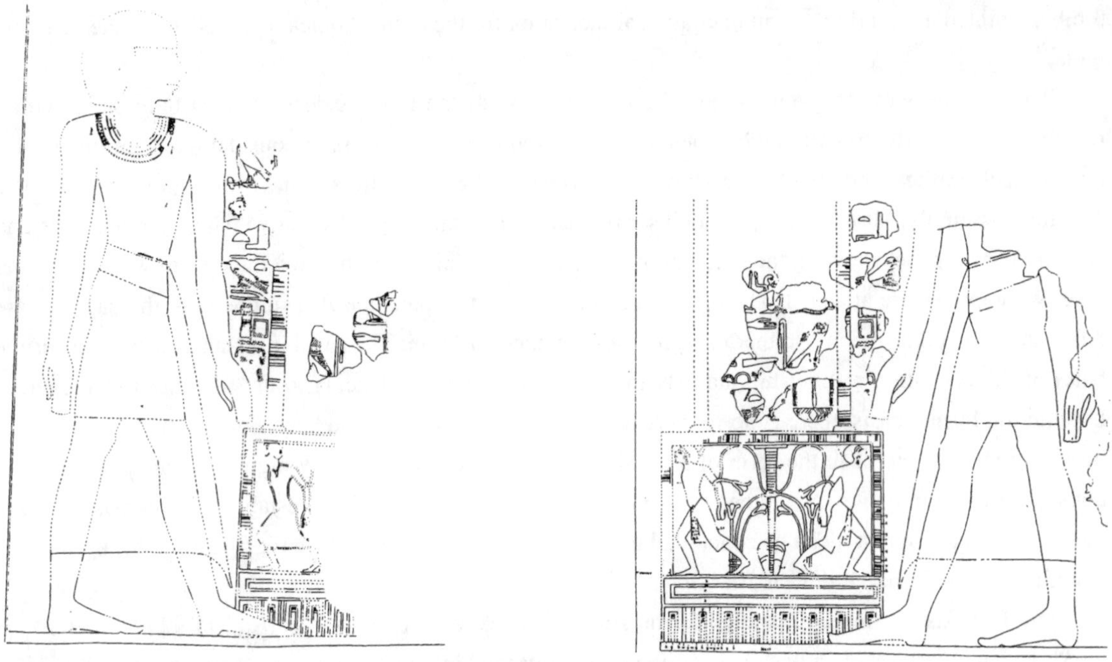

Figure 6

human could celebrate "millions of jubilees." Either they lacked any sense of reality, or there is something wrong in the commonly held interpretation. Of these alternatives, the latter seems the more likely. Such a notion is supported by the consistent use of the preposition *m* before *ḥb-sd* and also by the formulation found on Sesostris III's stela, which mentions the wish "may he make very many" (namely, jubilees) immediately after "may he make *ḥḥw* during the jubilee feasts." It makes sense only if 𓁨𓁨[𓁨] is not taken as an indication of infinite number, but rather as something specific which is done during the jubilee celebration(s). Although the word sign is always written with a squatting person, I wonder if it should not be identified with 𓎛𓂝𓀠 and thus read *ḥꜥw*, "jubilants." The wish thus reads "may he make jubilants at very many jubilees,"[42] in which case the occasional comparison with the sun god, namely, "like Reꜥ" also makes sense.

For the understanding of the historical setting of Antef's life, some major insights can be gained. It results that the decoration in the tomb (TT 155) was made at a time when a jubilee was anticipated. It was to see Thutmosis III at its center and from him positive consequences for numerous people were expected. It is important to note that the jubilee had not yet taken place, but was in the offing. This prospect is of even greater significance when the column of text written adjoining the heraldic display is taken into

[42]The adverbial adjunct "very many" can be linked with the mention of the jubilee and also with that of the jubilants.

consideration. Likewise incomplete, only "... Horus (?) *ḥr st.s wrt m ꜥḥ n nwb* "... Horus (?)[43] on her great throne in the palace of gold" is preserved. Two points can be established: 1) the passage concerns someone holding royal authority; 2) the person was female. In view of the time period of Antef's life, the female whose throne is mentioned here can only be Hatshepsut. She celebrated a jubilee in her 15th regnal year, i.e., 1464 B.C. Thutmosis III participated in the celebration, although it was not his jubilee, as results from scenes on the *Chapelle rouge*. The wish that "he may make jubilants at the jubilee very many" suits this situation nevertheless.

The way the reference to Hatshepsut and to Thutmosis III are related to each other sheds light on Antef's personal feelings in the political dilemma of his time. That Thutmosis III's name is displayed in a heraldic fashion, supported in the traditional manner fit for a ruling king, can only mean that Antef considered him the royal lord. At the same time Hatshepsut is referred to as well, which can be taken as a sign that the relationship between the two bearers of authority was not totally antagonistic, but that a certain *modus vivendi* prevailed, as is indicated repeatedly by the joint appearance on the decoration of the *Chapelle rouge*.[44] This political accommodation, by which Hatshepsut was accepted as nominal senior partner (*nswt-bỉ*), while Thutmosis III was junior partner (*nṯr-nfr*), applied also to their personal followers, as Antef appears to have been a partisan of Thutmosis III.

The unique political situation in the country and how it affected Antef is also implicit in another scene from the tomb (fig. 7). Its place is at the left jamb of the passageway leading into the inner part of the tomb, next to the scene discussed above. Although badly preserved, a fairly complete recovery of the various elements of the scene has been possible. The scene juxtaposes two elements: to the right is a representation of a "Horus-name," i.e., an elaborate schematic drawing of a palace facade is surmounted by a falcon. Unfortunately, nothing is preserved of the name which once was written in the display. From what is known about this period from other sources, and in view of the fact that Hatshepsut is apparently referred to as "feminine Horus" in the adjoining scene, it appears most likely that the formal display of the Horus-name represents her as supreme ruler of Egypt.

Opposite the Horus-name Antef is depicted wearing a formal long kilt, long wig and broad collar. However, what is most remarkable about this representation is the fact that Antef is not shown with the gestures of respect or devotion, as found in the tomb of Senenmut (TT 353).[45] Instead of holding his arms in adoration or down as a sign of respect, Antef holds a long staff with both hands, extending it towards the Horus-name, i.e., the Horus mounting the *srḫ*- frame. The upper end of the staff is now lost, but Säve-Söderbergh has restored it as a ram's head on the basis of miniscule remains. The accompanying text is reduced to some pitiful remains which provide no meaningful information. Above Antef's head are parts of  ,which Säve-Söderbergh considered as possibly being part of *wrt-ḥkꜣw*, "great of magic," denoting the

[43]It is not clear in what form reference is made to the ruling person. The sign  is possibly a determinative but it could also be used in the writing of "feminine Horus" (*Wb.* III 124, 10) for Hatshepsut.

[44]Pierre Lacau–Henri Gauthier, *Une Chapelle d'Hatchepsout à Karnak* (1977), pls. 40; 126; 169; 273; 300, etc.

[45]Peter F. Dorman, *The Monuments of Senenmut* (1988), 80 ff.; idem, *The Tombs of Senenmut* (1991), pl. 82 b.

Figure 7

name. The masculine *wr-ḥkȝw* is attested as the designation of ritual objects[46] but not the feminine one. There is also an epigraphic point which makes one doubt this suggestion; if an object were denoted here, a determinative identifying it could be expected, for which sufficient space would be available in the arrangement of the *kȝ-* signs. Considering the uncertainties marring the reading it seems best to abstain from any forced interpretation. The end of the annotation, aside from identifying the ower of the tomb as "the Herald Antef," has as its closing words . . . *n* (?) *nb.f sw* (?) *m* "*ꜥḥ*". . . for (?) his lord while/that he (?) is in the palace." In the context "his lord" and the adjoined mention of "the palace" can only refer to Thutmosis III and his presence in the royal palace. While these two points seem certain, I have serious doubts about the proposed readng *sw* on epigraphic and grammatical grounds: there does not seem to be sufficient space for the sign ⸸ (*sw*) before *w* ; the dependent pronoun should be introduced by a particle. As a result, I consider the reading highly problematic and abstain from drawing any inferences from it.

Nevertheless, some information can be gained from this highly fragmentary scene. The two participants, namely, the Horus-name as substitute for a king and Antef, are not in a harmonious relationship, but appear juxtaposed. Antef rather holds the staff in a determined fashion against the royal name, which can be interpreted that the man is acting vis-à-vis the royalty. As all action is assumed to

[46] *Wb.* I 328, 4-5.

emanate from the authority, the representation is indeed unusual. Its *raison d'être* can be surmised in the object held by Antef towards the royal name, i.e., towards the ruler. His is the earliest attestation, with a number of parallels dating from Thutmosis III to the early years of Amenophis IV.[47] Different from the representation here, they include the pictorial representation of the king seated in a kiosk on an elevated level. In two instances the staff is replaced by a "floral arrangement:[48] in one instance (Menkheperreʿ-seneb = TT 86) it serves as an introduction to the depiction of Syrian tribute.[49] Of particular interest is the depiction in the tomb of Ramose (TT 55) because of the lengthy texts it includes as annotation. Ramose is shown twice[50] in front of the enthroned Amenophis III. Once it shows him holding up towards the king a staff surmounted by a ram's head; the second case shows him holding in his raised hands something of presumably squarish shape. Although he is dressed basically the same way in both, the title varies as does the statement ascribed to him. In the first one he is denoted as "mayor and vizier"; in the second these titles are preceded by "mouth of Nekhen for the true priest." What is represented to the king is in both cases denoted as *ʿnḫ n ỉt.k*; the shape of the presented object differs as does the deity with which it is connected. The first is "[Amun-Reʿ] residing in *Ỉpt-swt*." the second is "Reʿ-Harakhte who is jubilated in the horizon in his name as Shu who is Aton." This *ʿnḫ* of the king's divine father consists of a series of intentions: "he will favor you, he will love you, he will make you last as lord of life, duration, luck and bravery, he will give to you [many years] on the great [throne], he will overthrow your enemies <unto> death, while you last on the throne of Horus of the living ones; all life-luck is with you, all health is with you as (with) your father Reʿ every day." The second statement, denoted as *ʿnḫ* of Harakhte runs in part parallel: "he will favor you, he will love you, he will make you last, he will give to you jubilant ones during the years of your annals and jubilee feasts with all (flat) lands under your feet. He will overthrow your enemies in death and in life; all joy is with you, all health is with you, all life is with you, while you last on the throne of Reʿ eternally."

In view of the introductory *ḏd-mdw* it is certain that Ramose in various priestly roles delivers a message to the king which purports to be divine. In other words, Ramose is the interpreter of divine messages. In its formulation the statements aré atemporal and thus can be taken as presently, and also as prospectively valid. Davies, op.cit., 31, had understood the statements in a hortative vein and thus rendered "may he praise thee, etc. . . ." Also hortative is Helck's[51] interpretation of the statements as "Er lobe dich, liebe dich . . ." The consequence of these interpretations is curious. The king is seen as not being in possession of divine grace; instead, the vizier is wishing it for the king, which is not particularly reassuring. Finally, it makes little sense that these wishes accompany the presentation to the king of an object associated with the deity. A closer nexus between deed and saying could, indeed, be expected.

[47]For their listing, see B. van de Walle, "Le pieu sacré d'Amon," Ar.Or. 20 (1952), 130 ff.; cf. also Helmut Satzinger, "Der heilige Stab als Kratquelle des Königs," *Jahrbuch der Kunsthistorischen Sammlungen in Wien* 77 (1982), 16 f.

[48]Johanna Dittmar, *Blumen und Blumensträuße als Opfergabe im alten Ägypten*, MÄS 43 (1986), 73 f.

[49]R. de Garis Davies, *The Tomb of Menkheperreseneb, Amenmose and another*, Theban Tomb Series, V (1933), pl. III.

[50]Davies, *The Tomb of the Vizier Ramose* (1941), pl. 23; 31.

[51]Wolfgang Helck, *Urkunden der 18. Dynastie, deutsch* (1961), 254.

The presented object is described as *ʿnḫ n it.k*, which Davies and Helck interpreted as "bouquet of flowers" ("Strauss"), a rendering which seems in accord with the presentation of an elaborately assembled bunch of flowers in some cases.[52]

However, neither the root *ʿnḫ* nor the determinative (𓏠) of the word points to a close connection with flowers. It rather seems that the object presented to the formally enthroned king is an accompaniment, while the main feature of the event is the relaying to the king of the message of a god and his intentions. These aspects make it doubtful that *ʿnḫ* denotes primarily the floral arrangement, which does not deny the possibility of its secondary extension to it. Word and determinative rather remind one of the term *ʿnḫ*, "oath," or of some form of formal written record.[53]That *ʿnḫ* is also used for "flower bouquet"[54] in no way affects the question of the origin of the practice. It appears that the flowery arrangement serves as a tangible demonstration of a promise or intention of formal nature. In the representation of Ramose it is quite clear that the vizier conveys a message, specifically a promise to the enthroned king. On this occasion he holds the heavy staff mounted by a ram's head towards the king. The inner nexus between the "promise" (*ʿnḫ*) and the presentation of the staff would make it seem that the latter is a physical symbol of the divine word. As the word for "staff" (*mdw*) is a homophon with *mdw*, "word," a nexus becomes discernible. The staff carried by the high official is thus a symbol for the "divine word" he bears, just as the bearing of a staff in earlier representation is an indication of the bearer's ability to "speak" (*mdw*) in a socio-juridical sense. This cannot be the place to pursue such a vast and coplex issue *in extenso.* However, Satzinger's notion[55] can be quoted here, that "im Amon-Stab wird der Aspekt Gottes sichtbar, der dem König sein Wirken ermöglicht." When one interprets the divine staff as a physical rendering of the "god's word," not only do the scenes in which the "staff" is presented towards the king become transparent, but also the numerous three-dimensional representations of either a king or a high official holding a large staff, which can be surmounted either by a divine symbol (ram, falcon) or by a king's head. The meaning of this rendering could be interpreted that the depicted one embraces and finds support in the divine or royal word.

Antef's presentation of the "divine staff" towards the ruler appears to be the earliest rendering of its kind. What inspired it cannot be determined, but despite the absence of a precedent it would seem a valid assumption that the meaning of the scene is the same as in later renderings. As a result, it can be assumed that the topic is Antef's conveying a divine message to the person in authority. Two aspects are noteworthy in this connection: first, Antef's position as "Great Herald" does not seem to carry political power of consequence; second, the "divine saying" does not seem to consist of a promise of support or grace for the ruling one. Although the words of the "divine message" are mostly obliterated, they would seem to concern "his (Antef's ?) lord" and also "the palace." With this fragmentary information it is, of course, difficult to establish the meaning with any degree of certainty. Nevertheless, I surmise that it has something to do with

[52]J. Dittmar, op. cit. 132.

[53]*Wb.* I 204, 17.

[54]*Wb.*, I 204, 3 f.

[55]Op. cit. 26 f.

the situation of Antef's lord, i.e., Thutmosis III, once he had reached an agrement with Hatshepsut. The message is apparently directed to the holder of authority in the country, as expressed by the Horus-name. I surmise that this reference applies to Hatshepsut. Because of the fragmentary state of preservation nothing more definite can be said about what appears to have great potential as historic information.

That Antef was a partisan of Thutmosis III during the years when he is oblivious in the historical record is also confirmed by his lengthy inscription, which was once set up in conjunction with his Theban tomb[56] and which provides further details. It is especially in the closing section that information usable for historical inquiry occurs. The larger part of the text consists of statements about Antef's high moral standards and the attitude he held in his official and private life. Although texts of the Eighteenth Dynasty are not oblivious to stating the moral precepts of a man, there is none as extensive as that of Antef. One gets the almost unavoidable impression of a highly egotistical personality, but some of the seemingly excessive self-esteem vanishes when the text is seen as the adaptation of a eulogy bestowed upon Antef on a specific occasion, possibly his funeral.

Even in the concluding section there is a striking emphasis on morality.[57] It seems difficult to envisage that someone could be so convinced of moral aptitude, giving the impression that the emphasis is actually a reaction to some unjust accusation which brought Antef great harm.

The text, which has received only limited attention, is highly structured. It is especially the culling of two sentences into one thought-unit which is striking in its pervasiveness. This particular stylistic device is especially a hallmark of classical wisdom writings, as John D. Foster has demonstrated.[58] Its use in this text gives the appearance of an emulation of the clasical form, but could, of course, also have very personal reasons. In order to demonstrate the particular structure of the text, the translation is arranged to reflect this formalism. The closing section, marked by an introductory "Antef, he says" consists of two parts, one dealing with the general moral conduct of the deceased, the other with his performance in the service of Thutmosis III:

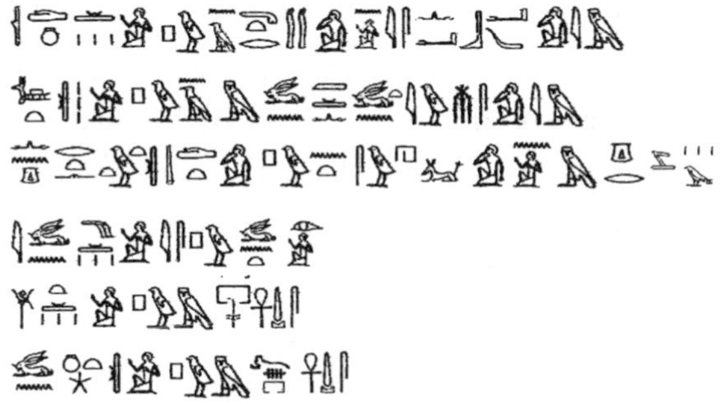

[56]*Urk.* IV 963-75.

[57]Henry J. Breasted, *Ancient Records*, II § 298; A. Hermann, op. cit. 117 ff.

[58]John D. Foster, *Thought Couplets and Clause Sequences in a Literary Text.* (1972).

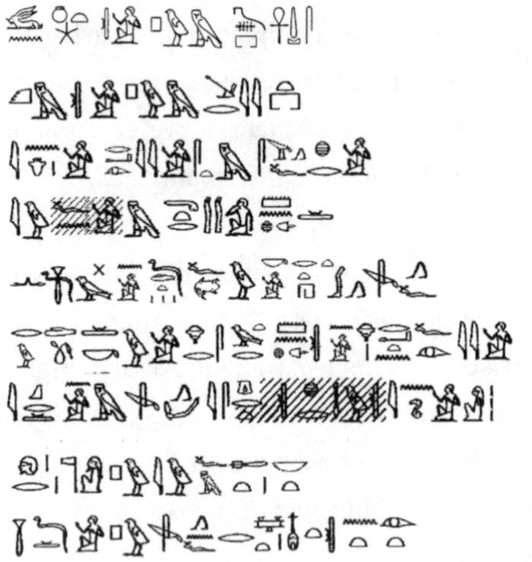

"My character trends are these, which are testified for me[a] without boasting therein.
"My marvels are these truly without an incorrectness therein.[b]
"It is not a smooothing over of the accusation that I have boasted with lies:[c]
My dispositon is that, that I acted[d]
be it in my offices in the royal house, l. p.h.
be it in my sevices in the court service, l.p.h.
be it in my final state in the guard house.[e]
"It is my heart which caused that I do it through its directive to me,
as it is an excellent witness for me.[f]
"I do not diminish whatever it (*scil.* the heart) says, as I am afraid to trespass its guidance.
"As I am very firm bccause of it, I was excellent because of what it caused that I do.[g]
I was trustworthy by its direction, so I am [vindicated} by men.[h]
It is god's pronouncement, as it is in every body.[i]
It is the fortunate one whom it guides to the proper path of action."[j]

a) *Mtr n.i* was taken by Breasted, *Ancient Records* II § 770 and by A. Burkhardt, et al., *Urkunden der 18. Dynastie, deutsch*, 359 as a *sḏmw.n.f* relative-form and thus rendered "which I have testified" and "die ich bezeugt habe." The specific meaning of *mtr* is "to testify," an activity which, however, cannot be done on one's own behalf, but rather for (*n*) someone. Consequently, I consider *mtr* a passive participle, i.e., the claims made by Antef are willingly corroborated by testimony on his behalf.

ʿbʿ "to brag" is a conspicuous concern in the period of Antef's acme: *Urk.* IV 101, 13 dates to Thutmosis I, while *Urk.* IV 368 is by Hatshepsut and *Urk.* IV 430, 1 is identical in date with Antef, except that Djehuty appears to have been a partisan of Hatshepsut.

b) Gardiner, *Egyptian Grammar*[3] § 130 rendered it "this is my character in reality." Although the rendering "character" is customary for *bỉ3t*,[59] in view of its apparent connection with the word *bỉ3t*, "marvel,"[60] the latter has been used here. It appears to denote less a person's "character" in the psychological or moral sense, but rather what is considered outstanding, either positive or negative.

Ỉwms is not so much a term for "lie" than one for "incorrectness," in the sense of lacking physical accuracy. It does not convey any moral condemnation as, e.g., *grg* does. Gardiner, op. cit., § 194 takes it as "untruth, misstatement," which disregards the negative parallel to it as *nn-ms*.

c) In the literary structure this statement serves as a summary of the two preceding ones, so that it does not have their bipartite structure.

A. Burkhardt, et. al., render "auch war es keine Beschönigung, dass ich mich etwa mit Lügen gerühmt hatte"; R.O. Faulkner, *Concise Dictionary* 253 lists *stwt mdt* as "smoothing of words—extenuation (?)," similar to *Wb*. IV 335, 13, "Beschönigung, o.ä."; for the construction, cf. also B. Gunn, *Studies in Egyptian Syntax*, 170. For the use of the *sḏm.n.f* after the genitival adjective, see Gardiner, op. cit. § 192. *Mdt* appears to have here the implication of "accusation," with its cause specified after it; that *mdt* has also specific juridical application transpires especially from *wḏ*ᶜ*-mdt*, "to investigate an accusation." The objectionable aspect is, of course, not the action denoted as *swh3* but the use of "lies" (*m grg*). The emphasis on boasting is curious and brings *Urk*. IV 751, 7, "I did not speak braggingly in order to boast of what I have done" to mind.

d) Gardiner discussed this passage,[61] rendering it "what I used to do was my (real) nature"; he considered "*wnt* is perf. participle and past habit is expressed." The translation offered by A. Burkhardt, "Das, was ich zu tun pflegte, war meine (wirkliche) Farbe (= Wesen)," follows this verbatim. While the grammatical analysis can be supported, though with some difficulty, the proposed rendering entails some problems. One is the apologetic reference to lies, which Antef admits to have promulgated, and which are not identified as to their nature. The other is the seeming contradiction between the claim that "what I used to do was my (real) nature" and the ensuing claim that Antef followed the guidance of his heart. This dichotomy results from the notion that *ỉwn* has here the extended use of "(true) nature." It rather appears that the motivation is assigned to the heart, while the preceding reference to *ỉwn* does not convey the depth of conviction detailed later. This would seem to imply that *ỉwn* does not refer to an inner but rather to an outer aspect in the moral behavior. As a result of these considerations I am inclined to see the meaning of *ỉwn* rather in the vein of "appearance" than "nature"; the basic meaning of *ỉwn* as "color" would seem to agree with a notion of superficiality.

For *ỉs pw* in an affirmative statement, see *CT* II 215-216 a. The resulting "My appearances are that, that I do!" is apparently the statement which was referred to before as having "boasted by lies."

e) The three parallel-formed non-verbal clauses serve as circumstantial indicators; for this use, see Gardiner, *Grammar* § 133. With the help of the three statements Antef refers to three consequential

[59] *Wb*.I 441, 16 ff.; cf. also G. Posener, *RdE* 16 (1964), 37 ff.
[60] *Wb*. I 440, 7 ff.
[61] *Eg. Gr.* § 473.3.

segments of his life, namely, his offices in the royal administration (*pr-nswt*), his service in the court, i.e., personal service for a ruler, and finally its completion. The particular formulation with the help of a non-verbal expression intends to indicate the lack of any vacillation during the different stages. *Kmt* was considered to mean "Pflicht" by A. Burkhardt, after Breasted conjectured a meaning "duty"; *Wb*. V 130, 4 lists it as "Dienst, Obliegenheit jemds.," with this occurrence as its only attestation. Instead of assuming here an otherwise unattested word, it seems better to associate *km.i* with the well documented verbal use "to complete, to end time"; see *Wb*. V 129. For *ʿrryt*, "guardhouse," cf. W. Helck, *Zur Verwaltung des Mittleren und Neuen Reiches* 65 ff.; cf. also the use of the term in reference to a place of judgment in Peasant B 1, 35 and especially *Urk*. IV 1107, 5. The *ʿrryt* is hardly a proper place for an esteemed official to end his career, but rather has the ring of political prosecution to it. It can only be political, since Antef enjoyed a formal burial place at Thebes, although it is difficult to establish precisely when he received it.

In other words, I understand the reference to Antef's "end in the guardhouse" as concerning the last stage of his life when he was under arrest and prosecuted. Even during this last stage he claims to have folllowed his moral principles despite the accusations which had been voiced against him.

f) The motivation for his actions Antef attributes to his heart. It is noteworthy that the actions performed in this way are not defined. The clause *iw.f [n.i] m mtr mnḫ*, "as it is an excellent witness," I link with the preceding clause. *Mtr*, according to the determinative, is the word for "witness" rather than "Zeugnis" (A. Burkhardt); cf. *Wb*. II 172, 9. It appears to be an allusion to the Osirian judgment.

The use of the preposition *ḫr* is somewhat surprising in this context, because *n* could be expected. It might be a way to indicate the continuity of the heart's directive to Antef, i.e., that it was in continuous close contact with him.

g) The anticipated and desired testimony on behalf of Antef is cast into a pair of chiastically arranged syntegmas, to which a third, similarly construed one is attached. In the opening pair a verbal clause is joined with a pseudo-verbal one in alternating order. Although intended as expressing the heart's testimony, it is formulated in the first person, thus giving the impression of being an indirect quote. A. Burkhardt has divided the section into separate sentences despite the differing grammatical formulations. Rather to be seen here is the kind of pairing of sentences which J.D. Foster has demonstrated first for the classical wisdom literature[62] The two sentence pairs not only mirror each other in their arrangement, but also complement each other. While the first expresses the adherence to the heart's "sayings," the second concerns the positive consequences of this conduct.

Ḥḏ has the specific connotation of diminishing something, here applied to the advice received; to put this in other words, Antef stresses that he fully embraced the teaching of his conscience, as which the "heart" is best understood here. Interesting is the corollary to it, namely, the fear of trespassing the heart's guidance. It seems to imply that Antef claims strict adherence, not only to not falling short of the moral precepts, but also not overstepping them in extensive application.

[62]Cf. note 58.

Despite the appearance, I doubt that **mnḫ.n.i* is to be read here, because it would limit its application to the past. A better meaning is attained by reading *mnḫ n.i* , i.e., "excellence belongs to me," which is the cause of this moral claim following it, introduced by the preposition *ḥr*. *Rwḏ.kwi* was rendered by A. Burkhardt "ich erreichte viel," but the Old Perfective would have a more general connotation than mere past. It should be kept in mind that Antef is speaking here of moral rather than material accomplishments, which makes one doubt the appropriateness of a limitation to the past. *Wb*. II 411, 13 gives for this occurrence of *rwḏ* the meaning "sich wohl befinden, gedeihen," while A. Burkhardt gives for it "ich erreichte viel." The text is, after all, part of a funerary statement, which makes the applicability of the Wörterbuch rendering doubtful. Since Antef appears to have ended his career under not particularly desirable circumstances, a claim "to have achieved much" would be quite out of place. It appears more appropriate to take *rwḏ* here in a more abstract sense, namely, "to be firm about something." The implied meaning I take to be that Antef claims conviction in his beliefs, which had as its consequence the fact *mnḫ n.i ḥr rdt.n.f iri.i*, "excellence belongs to me for that what it (the heart) caused that I do."

h) Again, the question is if *iqr* is here a *sḏm.n.f*, or if it would be better taken as a noun, followed by a dative expressing possession. The statement is clearly parallel to *mnḫ n.i* and I am inclined to the second option, because the implicit moral claim should have universal validity. According to the duplex structure pertinent otherwise in the text, it seems justified to assume that *iqr n.i* is the first part of a syntactical unit.

Unfortunately, a lacuna at this point mars the text. A. Burkhardt made the remains into "[Es ist wahr . . .] sagen die Menschen," which follows Breasted's "lo, . . . said the people." *In rmṯ* occurs earlier in the text (*Urk*. IV 972, 14), where it is used as an agent, a use most likely to prevail here as well. Although there is little to go to restore the lacuna, I am tempted to conjecture reading **is grt mꜣꜥ-ḫrw.i n.f*] *in rmṯ* "lo, I am vindicated for it] by men." The cause for which Antef claims vindication by men is taken up next, and identified as *tp-rꜣ nṯr* "god's pronouncement." The mention in Inana's biography (*Urk*. IV 67, 1), *ink is mꜣꜥ-ḫrw tp-tꜣ*, "Lo, I am vindicated on earth," is of particular interest in this connection. It appears that Antef claims recognition by his fellow men despite the adversity he faced in official circles.

i) The "god's pronouncement" is, indeed, what caused Antef to be vindicated by men. While "the god who is in men" denoting the conscience as a motivating force is well attested in the Eighteenth Dynasty,[63] I am not aware of a parallel to *tp-rꜣ-nṯr*. The use of *tp-rꜣ* as "god's creative word"[64] makes it seem tempting to surmise that *tp-rꜣ-nṯr* indicates here a divine message in the sense of a religious teaching.

The qualifying *iw.f m ḫt nb*, "it is in every body," could be taken to refer to conscience as the divine guidance present inside man; it is curious that it should be denoted here as *tp-rꜣ*, i.e., "the creative word." As a result, I am uncertain if *iw.f m ḫt nb* should be taken as an indication of general validity, i.e., "it is in every body," or rather an anticipated state, "it is to be in every body."

j) The emphasis on the significance of the "god's utterance" bespeaks more of a religious revelation

[63] *Wb*. II 359, 2; *Urk*. IV 119, 15; cf. Miriam Lichtheim, *Maat in Egyptian Autobiographies and Related Studies*, OBO 120 (1992), 52 ff.; idem, *Moral Values in Ancient Egypt*, OBO 155 (1997), 73.

[64] *Wb*. V 287, 9; the creator *qmꜣ nty nb m tp-rꜣ.f*, "who created all there is with his utterance."

than of a moral principle. The reference to "the fortunate one, whom it guides" is a clear indication that "god's utterance" is not universal, i.e., present in everybody, but its guidance is apparently limited to a selected group. What constitutes the guidelines is not detailed. Its aim, however, is specified as *wꜣt nfrt nt ỉrt*, "the good/proper path of action." It would seem that "the god's utterance" is a guidance for proper conduct for those who adhere to it, or who have received it.

While the first section consists of general statements about a specific form of divine guidance based on god's pronouncement, revealed not universally but only to specific persons, the second section concerns Antef's actions performed under the divine guidance. It transpires that he was one of those who had received or shared in the "god's utterance" without any further possible definition. That Antef's actions were seen by him as inspired by divine guidance results from the opening statement of this section, "Lo, I was one like it."[65] The comparison is with "the fortunate one, whom it (the god's utterance) guides to the good/proper path of action."

This proper path of action is described as follows:[l]

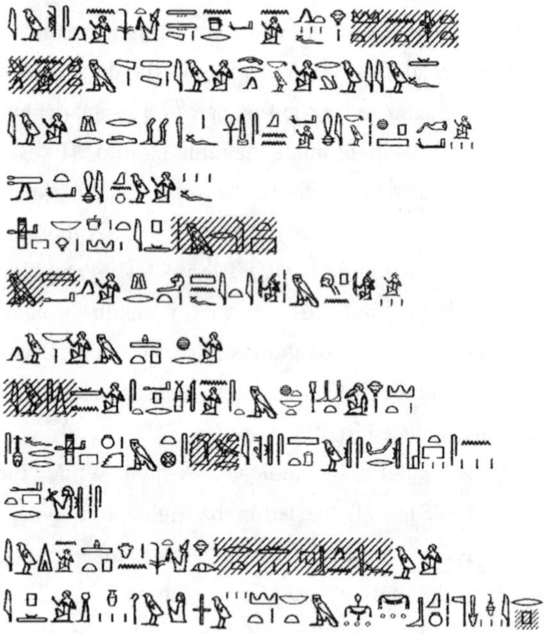

"As I followed the King of the Two Lands,

I accepted his travels on the desert [of the East].

I reached the forest land and the flat land

as I arrived at its end.[m]

As I was at the feet of his Majesty, l.p.h.,

[65] A. Burkhardt, et al., translated "Siehe, solch einer war ich."

I acted bravely like the holders-of-arms and I was accepted like his brave-ones.[n]

Every camp on the foreign land was readied as watch-tower,

as I marched ahead of the infantry as the first one of the 'army.'[o]

When even my lord comes successfully, I say,

as I have prepared it and I have furnished it with everything which one could wish in a foreign land:

'I shall beautify (it) more than the palace of Egypt.'[p]

[I] shall clean and purify the private part and I shall assign its halls, and [my] chamber according to its needs.[q]

As I had caused the heart of the king to be pleased about [my] doings,

[he sent] me, that I assess the trade-goods of the chief of those in various desert lands, consisting of gold, silver, oil, incense and wine."[r]

l) The description of Antef's activities is intertwined with his discourse about religious precepts, and culminates in his mention of the "god's utterance" whose adherence makes "the lucky one." Antef emphasizes as link between the two sections that he was a match of such a lucky one, as the "god's utterance" was in him. The application of this religious view is, however, not in the service of the deity, but rather in the service to the king. It is noteworthy that the latter is introduced here not as *ḥm.f*, "his Majesty," but rather with the somewhat unusual designation *nswt-tꜣwy*.[66] This is apparently chosen to emphasize the base of the kingship comprising "the Two Lands," i.e., Upper and Lower Egypt. Although no name is given, there can be no doubt that the reference concerns Thutmosis III. The same designation is used by Inana for Thutmosis III at the point of his ascent to the throne.[67] Antef's activity is described as *šms*, which can be taken here either literally as "to follow" or as the extended "to serve."

m) Antef's service or following for the "king of the Two Lands" provides the general frame, but the specific point is formulated as *nḏr.n.ỉ nmtwt.f*. The specific meaning of *nḏr* is "to grasp,"[68] which is difficult to reconcile with its object, namely, the movement on foot. The tenor appears to be the firmness of the association, i.e., Antef stuck closely to the king during his travel. The specification of this travel is unfortunately lost. Sethe restored it *ḥr ḫꜣst [rsyt mḥtt]*, which was accepted by A. Hermann and A. Burkhardt.[69] While such a restoration might seem tempting to consider in view of later claims by Thutmosis III,[70] at that particular point in the king's career no extensive travel had occurred, as far as is known. As a result it seems inappropriate to assume here a general reference to travels north and south. A more appropriate view is to assume a reference to a specific journey, a point supported by the fact that *ḫꜣst*,

[66] *Urk.* IV 59, 16; cf. also above p. 114 f.

[67] *Wb.* IV 482 f.

[68] *Wb.* II 382 f.; A. Burkhardt, et al., op.cit. 360, rendered "ich heftete mich an seine Schritte," after A. Hermann, op. cit. 129, had given for it "ich krallte mich an seine Schritte."

[69] The former translated "in dem südlichen und nördlichen Lande," the latter "in den [südlichen und nördlichen] Fremdländern."

[70] In his campaigns as full ruler Thutmosis reached the Euphrates in the Northeast and the Fifth Cataract in the South.

"foreign land," is indicated as a singular. The remaining words allow only to conclude that reference is made to a specific journey conducted by the young Thutmosis III, in which he was tenaciously accompanied by Antef. In view of the uncertainty caused by the lacuna any restoration can, of course, be only hypothetical. Nevertheless, I am tempted to conjecture as restoration *ḥr ḫ3st* [*nt i3btt*], "on the desert of the East," a suggestion made on the basis of the reference in the el-Arish inscription that Thutmosis III, named there in mythological disguise as Geb, traveled to the East.[71]

The lacuna marring the specification as to where Thutmosis III had traveled affects also the next statement. Because of the consistency in the arrangements in sentence pairs, one formulated with a *sḏm.n.f*, the other with a circumstantial *iw* introducing it, it can be taken for granted that the missing opening of the sentence was a *sḏm.n.f*, as Sethe had restored it. If *pḥ* is correct seems far from being certain. Two points have to be taken into consideration: first, the preceding restoration is, as has been pointed out, incorrect, which leaves somewhat more space than Sethe had envisaged; second, the object of Antef's action is not a word for "beginning" as has been assumed.

The circumstantial clause has *spr* as its predicate. According to the construction it can only be taken to state a completed act, circumstantial to the one stated in the preceding *sḏm.n.f*- clause.[72] It results that the arrival *r pḥwy.f* was the prerequisite for the action described before. The suffix *.f* can only refer to *t3*, because there is no other masculine word occurring here. In sum, Antef came first to the northern end of the region, from which he proceeded to finally reach a point denoted as *ḫtyw-t3*. The stress on the aspect of arrival implies that Antef, and the party which he accompanied, remained in this place for some time. Although the geographical definition is not too easy on the basis of the rather imprecise information provided, it would nevertheless seem necessary to locate the final destination south of the original point of contact with the region, i.e., Antef entered it from the North. This agrees principally with what can be established about the final point. *Ḫtyw*, lit. "woods,"[73] is a well-attested term especially in reference to Sinai and should be seen in parallel with Seïr ("forest") denoting Sinai, specifically the mining district of Wadi Maghara and Serabit el-Khadim.

The upshot of this indication in Antef's biographical summary comprises several historically significant points: first, Thutmosis III, denoted as "King-of-the-Two-Lands," traveled outside of Egypt. The choice of words speaks against a military undertaking and suggests rather some form of travel. This move is not specified so as to be aimed at a specific destination, but rather appears to have been a journey where the goal was not defined before the outset. Although a lacuna mars the possibility of defining the travel, it

[71]See my forthcoming study of the el-Arish text.

[72]A. Hermann and A. Burkhardt coordinated the *sḏm.n.f*-clause with the pseudo-verbal one, as if the different verb forms were mere stylistic fancy. They render "und bin zu seiner nördlichsten gelant" or "und gelangte bis zu ihrem Ende (= nördlichter Teil)."

[73]Henri Gauthier, "Le 'reposoir' du dieu Min," *Kêmi* 2 (1929), 41 ff., had emphasized the hilly locale on which trees grow, or the elevated aspect of wooden scaffolding. While this aspect is indeed pertinent, the root is instead to be seen in *ḫt* , "wood." *Ḫtyw* is a derivate plural and denotes first of all "woods," i.e., a closed stand of trees. The various extensions, such as *ḫtyw nyw ˁš*, "forest of the cedar" or *ḫtyw mfk3*, "turquoise forest," emphasize the presence of trees, something basically unfamiliar for Egyptians, rather than geographical features. While the former denotes the Lebanon (cf. Gardiner, *JEA* 35, 1949, 49), the latter applies to the (western ?) Sinai; cf. Jaroslav Černý, *Inscriptions of Sinai*, II (1953), 1; cf. also J.J. Clère, *JEA* 24 (1938), 125 f.

indicates an easterly direction. The point of entry into a geographically distinct area was from the north end of it and continued from there, remaining, however, confined to this one area. It is denoted as *ḫtyw*, "forest," and allows an identification with the Sinai Peninsula. Such an identification agrees also with the few details that are available, in particular its location to the East and the fact that it is entered from the North.

n) During the travels of "the King of the Two Lands" Antef accompanied his lord in close proximity. The travel was apparently not without hazards, because Antef, who himself was not a member of the military in any form, acted "bravely like the holders-of-arms." *Qnn*, "to be brave," has a strong militant connotation.[74] *Nb-ḫpš* follows the pattern well documented in classical literature to indicate someone as the possessor of something.[75] The rendering "wie die Besitzer von Kraft" (A. Hermann) or "wie die Kraftvollen" (A. Burkhardt) would imply that Antef considered himself a weakling, someone without strength; in order to make the comparison in any way meaningful a rendering "possessor of *ḫpš*" is necessary with *ḫpš* denoting a concrete object rather than an abstract. *Ḫpš* is attested as a term for a particular kind of sword, and it is probably in this vein that the mention here is to be understood.[76] If taken in this way it would imply that Antef behaved as courageously during the travel as the military ones participating in it. The implicit stress of this term suggests that the accompanying military were armed with *ḫpš*- swords, which, however, are not indigenous weapons. Their use as conspicuous equipment can thus be seen as an indication that those accompanying Thutmosis III in his early travel were not genuine Egyptians but rather foreigners in his service. The "sickle-sword" is a Levantine weapon in MB II,[77] and should be considered as such in this context.

It appears that Antef was particularly proud of his prowress during the difficulties accompanying the journey, militarily and otherwise. An indication of this attitude is the fact that in this case two main statements are intertwined with the circumstantial *iw*- clause. It is not clear to me if *iṯi.i* is active or passive. While *qnn* is apparently geminated, *iṯi* is not; for the sake of parallelism one would like to have identical verb-forms in parallel sentences. This is the reason why I favor a passive rendering, but this is at best tentative. An active "I (indeed) took hold like his brave ones" also makes good sense and could be taken as a reference to the acceptance of the adverse situation matching the military in the outlook.

o) Although all available copies appear to have **ʿḥ nb* "every palace,"[78] this reading makes no sense in the given context. *ʿḥ* is only attested denoting the residence of a king or a deity, neither one being very likely located "on the back of the desert." In view of the indicated locale no royal or similarly rated "palace" should be assumed here. The likelihood of established shrines is equally improbable. The

[74]For *qnw*, "brave ones," cf. *Wb.* V 41, 5; 44, 13; *Urk. IV* 894, 16; 895, 2.

[75]*Wb.* II 228 II.

[76]As late as the Amarna Period (*Urk*, IV 1561, 8) *ḫpš* is also used for the typically Egyptian battle-ax.

[77]Cf. *LÄ* III 819 ff; Manfred Bietak, *Avaris and Piramesse* (1979), pl. XXXVIb.

[78]In view of the improbability of numerous "palaces on the back of the desert," it seems feasible to consider the posibility of reading "lord's palace," although a more indicative spelling might be expected. The significance of the indication is connected with the rendering of *ḥr-sꜣ*, which could be taken as "over the back of the desert," i.e., beyond; see further below.

circumstances rather make one expect a mention of dwellings typical for the desert. As a result I suspect here a word for "camp," although a euphemistic use for dwelling in the mining region is also feasible. On the basis of the latter notion, I conjecture a rendering "any dwelling on the back of the desert was requisitioned as 'shelter' as a dwelling place for the emigree before the military."

This rendering deviates widely from earlier renderings, such as A. Hermann, "Jedes Schloss hinter den Bergländern wurde geprüft unter meiner Aufsicht"; A. Burkhardt, et al., "Jeder Palast hinter dem Bergland [wurde registriert . . ." neither one making much sense in the given context. As pointed out before, *ʿḥ* is attested only as "royal palace," and there is neither any information about royal (Egyptian) palaces "on the back of the desert" nor does it make sense to have residences of alien dignitaries "registered." Although the reading is still unsettled, it seems necessary to take **ʿḥ* as a term for a local dwelling place located at the area which Antef had finally reached, namely, the "forest-land." For reasons discussed earlier Antef's whereabouts at this point appear to be in western Sinai, specifically in the Serabit el-Khadim region. Installations of some type unquestionably had existed there before Antef's arrival, because mining activity had been going on for several centuries. Needless to say, those shelters were not palatial, but were of the most primitive kind.[79]

At present the word denoting the "abode" is uncertain; as there are no caves in this region, some form of simple structure, presumably huts made of stone, should be envisaged. Their location *ḥr s3 ẖ3st*, "on the ridge of the desert," gives the impression of being specific without allowing its appreciation. The location at the height of the gebel would seem curious for dwelling purposes and the notion has its appeal that the term denotes not a place or dwelling, but rather one for military surveillance. In this case a reading *mnw*, "watchtower," would be in place. For *ip m*, "to count as," see *Wb*. I 66. The lacuna can be restored only hypothetically for lack of any similar formulation. I surmise **ip m rsw iw mšʿ<.i> ḥr ẖ3t mnfyt* , "were readied as watchtowers as I travelled ahead before the army." Only 𓂝𓏏𓂻 is given by Sethe; A. Hermann considered the restoration *ẖry-st-ḥr.j*, "unter meiner Aufsicht." Antef at this point in time does not seem to be stationary, which makes it unlikely that something was "under his supervision."

The overall duplex structure of the syntax makes it likely that in the lacuna a new sentence begins introduced by *iw*. The restoration *mšʿ<.i >* suggested by A. Hermann and A. Burkhardt suits the context. The exact connotation is not entirely clear as Antef's movement does not seem to have been part of an organized military maneuver. *Mšʿ* appears to denote here land travel without any belligerent connotation. *Ḫr-ḥ3t mnfyt*, "before the army," is significant, as the compound preposition *ẖr-ḥ3t* has a more specific meaning than "in front of."[80] Its use in connection with *bh3*, "to flee," (*Urk*. IV 711, 2; Sinuhe R 87) shows that the term indicates not a position of leadership but rather the opposite, namely, the retreat "in front of" a hostile force. The latter can only be identified as *mnfyt*, i.e., "troops." Although the term is used quite commonly, it is still not clear what the specific features of this military body were. Faulkner, *JEA* 39, 1953,

[79]Very little is recorded about the settlements in which those working in Sinai, specifically in Serabit el-Khadim, lived.

[80]Faulkner, op. cit. 162; A. Hermann translated "Ich [marschierte (?)] an der Spitze der Abtailung als Erster des Heeres," while A. Burkhardt gave for it "Ich marschierte vor den Truppen an der Spitze des Heeres."

44 saw in it a loosely used term for "soldiery," while Alan R. Schulman, *Military Rank, Title and Organization in the Egyptian New Kingdom*, MÄS 6, 1964, 13 f., considered it a term for "infantry, the army, soldiers"; Vandersleyen[81] doubted any military connotation of *mnfyt* ; Andrea M. Gnirs, *Militär und Gesellschaft,* SAGA 17, 1996, 12 ff., insists on the military character of the term. As Antef apparently was moving before it, i.e., moving away from it, the notion seems justiified that *mnfyt* denotes here a military unit employed in the pursuit of Antef and his companions. Antef calls himself *tpy n mšꜥ* (?) which would ask for a rendering "first of the army." However, it should be noted that the sign of the squatting man with a feather on his head does not bear arms; thus it is unlikely to stand for a military body in action. *Mšꜥ* is also used as "journey," "expedition," "sojourn," which appears to be a more appropriate rendering here, because no military action is involved.

p) *Ꞽw nb.i m ḥtp* has been taken as a circumstantial statement to which *ḫr.i* was adjoined. A. Hermann rendered "wenn dann mein Herr bei mir in Frieden ankam," which was closely followed by A. Burkhardt. However, two points in these renderings have to be criticized. First, the *sḏm.f* is used here, which is unquestionably not a genuine narrative; the text is rather careful in using the *sḏm.n.f* when events of the past are being related. The second concerns the assumed occurrence of the preposition *ḫr*. The latter is in general a refined expression[82] and does not lose its basic meaning of "in the presence of/with." In view of the assumed personalities involved, namely, the royal lord on the one hand and his servant Antef on the other, the use of the preposition *ḫr* would seem most unlikely. As a basic rule of protocol, the royal lord does not arrive "at" a subaltern, because of the demeaning implication such a formulation would have. Arrival is only towards superiors, but not the other way. This stylistic point becomes even more weighty when taking the qualifying *m ḥtp*, "in peace/successful" into consideration. The king or any other lord cannot be labeled in this fashion for arriving at a subaltern. As a result, *ḫr.i* cannot be the preposition, but should rather be recognized as *ḫr.i*, "I say." The expression appears to be a colloquialism, but occurs already in the Letters to the Dead,[83] and becomes a common feature in Late Egyptian.[84] In other words, *ḫr.i* introduces the words Antef says to his lord, when the latter finally arrives.

The speech falls into two basic sections, the first stating what Antef had already accomplished, the second what he still intends to do. These two sections are again intertwined in the same fashion as the majority of duplex syntactic units in the text, namely, a circumstantial statement introduced by *ỉw* followed by what could be considered the main clause, here with a prospective outlook. Despite the relative ease in establishing the syntactic structure, there are nevertheless some problems in this section, caused by the ambiguity with which some personal pronouns are used. In the retrospective statements the neutral *st* occurs twice and it is not clear to what it refers. In the prospective part an even more puzzling *sn* occurs.

What Antef apparently claims to have achieved concerns the readying of some place, the exact nature

[81]C. Vadersleyen, *les Guerres d'Amosis* (1971), 188.

[82]Cf. Alexandre Varille, "Sur un emploi particulière de la préposition *kher*," *Kêmi* 4 (1931), 193 ff.

[83]Cf. A.H. Gardiner–K. Sethe, *Egyptian Letters to the Dead* (1935), 24.

[84]A. Erman, *Neuägyptische Grammatik*^{2} § 715.

of which is not apparent. Its mention was probably contained in the gap after *ip m*, "counted as," and might possibly be restored as **rswt*, i.e., a place to awaken. The way I understand it, Antef claims to his lord that he has done the best he could, but that he would like to do it so as to outshine any/the "palace" of Egypt. The latter is construed with a plural genitival adjective (*nyw*), which, if correct, could be the explanation of the subsequently used pronoun *sn*. Since the meaning of *ꜥḥ* is rather uncertain, just as its similar use was earlier, the remaining ambiguity is great. For *sspd*, "to prepare, to outfit," cf. *Wb*. IV 276, 1; Pap. Westcar 3, 7; 7, 9; 11, 20; *Urk*. IV 656, 2; 835, 17. For *ꜥpr* "to equip, to furnish," see *Wb*. I 180, 15. The imperfective passive participle *ꜣbb* appears to have here the connotation of "all that one can wish," i.e., it has implicit limitation.

q) *Snfr* and *swꜥb* had been taken as a participle,[85] but there is no antecedent they might qualiify. As a consequence I see here a change of outlook, namely, from telling what he had accomplished to what he would like to do, i.e., a change from *sḏm.n.f* to *sḏm.f*. Since it is still part of Antef's report to his lord, the omission of the suffix first person would be a reflection of the politeness appropriate for the occasion.

For *snfr* in regard to buildings, cf. *Wb*. IV 173, 1. Why the sentence lacks an object mystifies me. As already pointed out *ꜥḥ*, "palace," is apparently treated as a plural, as proposed by A. Hermann. If it implies "any palace" or if *ꜥḥ* is treated as a plural for other reasons cannot be decided because of the uncertainties associated with this term. The distinction between *swꜥb* and *twr* as purification by water and incense proposed by A. Hermann has great appeal. The object should be *sštꜣw* "secret" (part), which I surmise to denote the private part of the dwelling. This appears juxtaposed to the common parts, i.e., those used and accessible to everybody, which I see in *ḥwt*. Who is meant by *.sn* is unclear; there is no appropriate mention of a plural preceding it, except possibly *"ꜥḥ*. For *sḏsr*, "to make splendid a building," see *Wb*. IV 394, 7-8. *Ḥwt* has the basic meaning "enclosure"; how it is applied here is not clear, especially since it is impossible to decide to whom the qualifying *.sn* refers. Because of the uncertainty concerning *ḥwt.sn*, it is imposible to define *ꜥt*, "chamber," either. As it is not linked with any predicate, it seems necessary to see it as a second object of *sḏsr*. As *ḥwt* appears to be defined, I venture to assume that *ꜥt* was similarly defined; accordingly, I suggest restoring the suffix first person after it. A feasible interpretation of the passage appears to be that after mentioning the plans concerning the royal master's dwelling, Antef states his plans concerning the accommodation of the various members of the party and, at the end, also those for himself.

r) The final part of the text is again clear. It comprises once more a pair of clauses, the (first) one being introduced by *iw*, giving the condition for the second one. "After I had made content the heart of the king about the (my ?) doings, [he sent] me that I assess the gifts of the chief (shepherd) of those who are in various desert lands with silver, gold, oil, myrrh, and wine." The first part offers no particular problems; *rdi ḥtp ib*, corresponds to the more common causative *sḥtp ib*, apparently chosen here to stress Antef's participation. The mention of *ib-n-nswt* is somewhat surprising, although its basic meaning "wish/heart of

[85]It apparently goes back to Breasted's "made better than . . . purified, cleansed . . ." followed by A. Hermann, "indem es (zugleich) schöner gemacht war . . . gereinigt mit Wasser und mit [Räucherung] . . ." and A. Burkhardt "besser al . . . gereinigt und gesäubert . . ."

the king" is clear[86] because it emphasizes the formal aspect of the king after referring to him as *nb.i*, "my lord."

Ỉrt, "the deeds," would seem to require a connection with Antef, thus justifying a restoration of a suffix first person.[87] The ensuing lacuna offers some difficulty. At its end is , which I am taking as an object pronoun. This implies the mention of an action to which Antef was the object. Considering the preceding mention of the king, it would be most likely that the subject remains the same. *Ỉp.i* is clearly a *sḏm.f*-form and thus not a narrative as it was rendered by A. Hermann and A. Burkhardt. As the ciricumstantial *iw di.n.i* is clearly retrospective, a *sḏm.f* in this context allows only two explanations. It is either prospective, i.e., "I shall . . ." or it is used dependently. Since the first of the sentences has such a construction, I assume the same here, i.e., *ip.i* is not an independent main clause, but rather states the nature of an intended action instigated previously. As a result I suggest restoring the lacuna *irt* [*.i h3b.n.f*] (or *ḥsy.n.f*) *wi ip.i inw* " . . . my deeds, [he sent me] that I assess the goods . . ." For the construction, see Gardiner, *Egyptian Grammar*^{3} § 451.

What Antef is expected to do is indicated as *ip inw m*, "to assess the trade goods . . . consisting of . . ." *Ỉnw* is not "tribute"[88] but denotes rather things which are brought without any requirement; see David Lorton, *The Juridical Terminology of International Relations in Egyptian Texts through Dyn. XVIII*, 1974, 104. There is some ambiguity as to the partner in this business. A. Hermann and A. Burkhardt assumed a plural qualified by the nisbe adjective *imyw-ḫꜣst*. The prevailing orthography does not support their interpretation. It rather indicates a singular as far as *ḥqꜣw*, "sheikh," and *ḫꜣst* "(foreign) land" are concerned. It would thus seem appropriate to take *ḥqꜣw* as a reference to a specific "ruler"[89] and to take *imyw ḫꜣst-nbt* as denoting the objects of said "ruler." The term is unusual, but can be compared with *imyw-šꜥ*, "those in the sand." The listed goods are rather startling in their nature as well as in their sequence: "electrum, gold, oil, myrrh, wine." Two of them are too bulky to be of any significance, namely wine and oil. How they came to be traded is puzzling in the given setting, which does not seem to concern an area where they were produced.

Antef's long autobiographical text adds hitherto unknown facts to the intellectual and historical situation during the parallel reign of Hatshepsut and Thutmosis III. It is especially the intensity of religious orientation which transpires from it. Hatshepsut's devotion to Amun is extensively documented. It culminates in the divine oracle which brought her to power and in the promulgation of Amun's fatherhood of Hatshepsut. While these two could be considered focal points, they are indeed not exclusive, but are

[86]There is obviously no relation to *Wb*. I 59, 15.

[87]So also A. Burckhardt, although her rendering "(das) was ich getan habe" would require a relative form. For the noun, cf. *Wb*. I 113, 6-7.

[88]So A. Hermann and A. Burkhardt, who rendered *inw* as "Abgaben." There is no indication that Thutmosis III was at this time in a position to collect dues, especially not outside of Egypy's traditional borders. Edward Bleiberg, *The official Gift in Ancient Egypt* (1996), 122 does not discuss the passage in relation to his thesis that *inw* denotes an official gift.

[89]There are obviously no plural strokes following the somewhat puzzling determinative. The combination of the singular *ḥqꜣw* and the plural *imyw ḫꜣst nbt* points to some kind of social organization covering a large area.

surrounded by numerous other symptoms of Hatshepsut's piety.[90] It would seem simple to interpret her concern for Amun as political expediency, because the Amun priesthoood, especially, of course, Senenmut, was essential in her reach for power. That she utilized the aspirations of Theban parochialism does not entail an irreligious attitude on her part; on the contrary, the mixture of politics and religion seems pronounced. However, it appears that Hatshepsut was deeply motivated personally in her orientation towards Amun.

The religious fervor is less ubiquitous as far as Thutmosis III is concerned, but he not only carried out an extensive building program in Amun's temple at Karnak, but also dedicated some of the spoils of his military campaigns to it. How much of this capacity had political motives, i.e., to match Hatshepsut's support, is, indeed, hard to estimate in detail. However, it should be noted that Thutmosis III claims to have been Amun's choice when he was a very young man.[91] Of course, this divine interference in favor of Thutmosis III can also be suspected of political rather than religious aims, generated in competition with Hatshepsut's attitude.

While the depth of the religious convictions of Thutmosis III might be open to some scepticism, the religiosity of the Herald Antef is beyond reproach. It is a central theme of his lengthy autobiographical inscription and is claimed as the "good path of action." It is nevertheless a predominantly personal religiosity which he displays, and it could be described as individual consciousness. Although Antef emphasizes his thoroughly religious motivation, there is no name used to identify its object. "God" is rather mentioned as an anonymous power,[92] which is active in the individual's heart. There is no reference to Amun in Antef's autobiography despite its religious overtone. The conclusion is unavoidable that he did not adhere to the cult of Amun, but rather followed a different religious persuasion. To the latter he apparently clung with single-minded exclusiveness. It was apparently this religious conviction which had brought him into difficulties with the authorities of the time. Although their exact nature is not spelled out in detail, the scene depicting him with a "divine staff" in hand confronting a Horus-name limelights the problem. The latter serves as an indication of the most formal aspect of a ruler, while the juxtaposition, as discussed earlier, points to a discord.[93] Since Antef indicates repeatedly that he was a loyal partisan of Thutmosis III, the frictions would have to have been with Hatshepsut. The most important information to be gathered form Antef's text is the existence of religious issues as part of or aside from the political frictions between Hatshepsut and Thutmosis III.

Antef appears to have been a stubborn, outspoken man, who abstained from any reconciliation and rather insisted on his conscience. His "confrontations" with the authority are not described in detail but are

[90]Concerning Hatshepsut's religious fervor, cf. S. Ratié, op. cit., 318 ff.

[91]*Urk.* IV 156 ff. It has to be stressed that Thutmosis III announced the act of divine interference well after he had become sole ruler in the land. It is not entirely clear how much of the indicated devotion for Amun is personal and how much is part of the complex political maneuvering with the aim to reconcile the royal politics with those of Thebes.

[92]It is an old Egyptological issue if *nṯr* reflects an anonymous supreme divine power or denotes a specific theistic concept. The different attitude is of course a reflection of religious notion an not an Egyptological issue.

[93]See above p. 141.

only alluded to as his having "boasted with lies." It seems that his unbending rectitude brought Antef into serious trouble, if the mention of the "guardhouse" is, indeed, a reference to the setting of the latest stage in his career. The lengthy moralizing text, originally set up in the tomb's court, is so conspicuously apologetic that it makes sense only as a belated but emphatic effort to exonorate Antef. If this step occurred prior to or after his death is impossible to decide. It seems, however, that the final decoration of the tomb, and presumably also its use as a burial place, occurred while Hatshepsut was still alive. The recurrent mention of or allusion to Thutmosis III can be taken as an indication that the decoration was made during a time when it was possible for a partisan of Thutmosis III to display his loyalty, i.e., during the years immediately following the rapprochement between the two political antagonists which was formalized in the jubilee of the year 15. The allusions to this event among the tomb decorations support this notion and also provide a more specific chronological indicator. As discussed previously, the references to the "jubilee" mention this event as being in the offing, i.e., the inscriptions should be dated shortly before it occurred in year 15. On this basis it can be surmised that Antef profited personally from the reconciliation, or at least received an exonoration after having been persecuted for his political and religious stance.

While he makes no direct mention of any consequences he had to face aside from a possible allusion to ending his career in the "guardhouse," in the final section of his stela he provides some details about events in which he had participated and which brought him into the eye of the political storm raging at the time.

The lord he served is denoted as "King of the Two Lands," (*nswt t3wy*), which is a particularity of this time in its emphasis on the extent of authority.[94] It aims to convey the royal lord's claim to unrestricted control over all of Egypt, disputed or undermined by Hatshepsut since the death of Thutmosis I. Of particular importance is the specification that Antef's service for the king led him away from Egypt, i.e., the king left Egypt for reasons not detailed. There is no indication of belligerence, i.e., of an organized military campaign in the way recorded later for Thutmosis III. There is also no specific goal indicated for the journey, except that it was "on the desert," presumably of the East. This final point was reached coming from the North and is given as "forest-land," a designation of the western Sinai.[95]

The journey itself was apparently not without its hazards. This is indicated by the tenacity with which Antef "clung" to it. Antef was indeed not the only participant in the move, but possibly the only one of non-military background. That he compares himself with " the brave ones," i.e., professional soldiers, suggests that the gross of the participating people were of the latter. Antef appears to have acted as a quartermaster for the party and boasts about his efforts to provide as much comfort as was possible; he uses the occasion to declare what he would like to do, namely, outdoing any "palace of Egypt."[96] The reality seems to have

[94]The extent of the kingship is an issue only in the reigns of Hatshepsut and Thutmosis III. It is inicated in such formulation as *nswt w3ḥ* or *nswt* t3wy reflecting the struggle between the two antagonists. Despite it there is no indication that it took violent form during the many years it dominated Egypt's stage.

[95]See above, p. 152.

[96]See p. 155.

been quite different. It appears that the travel reached a final point, presumably in the only geographically specified area, namely in Sinai. There a kind of makeshift royal residence was established. Antef at this time was in charge of exchange with a local dignitary and it is not clear if he received or furnished goods for the royal presence.

How Antef's career came to an end is not detailed, nor is any information provided how his sojourn from Egypt ended. As he makes specific reference to the "jubilee" of "year 15" in which Hatshepsut and Thutmosis III partook, it would seem likely that he was not only active at this time, but that he had returned to Egypt to take part in it. If he physically participated cannot be decided, but it seems that he died around this very moment. It might be a demonstration of the spirit of collaboration which was to be kindled on this occasion that Antef received as significant a burial as he did. It appears to have been an attempt to compensate for the earlier political prosecution he had had to suffer.

His offense appears to have been partially in a religious vein by his insistence on following his personal conscience rather than religious practice. It is not clear if he originally held any specific political views. However, if seems that the prosecution he had to endure brought him to the camp of Thutmosis III in his controversy with Hatshepsut. While lacking details of the stance taken by Antef, either as an individual or as a member of a group of similarly inclined people, it is important to note the duplicity of tensions dominating the early years of Thutmosis III until Hatshepsut finally succeeded in gaining the upper hand. In other words, two controversial issues prevailed simultaneously. One was the struggle for political control, the other a question of religious orientation. In the wake of Hatshepsut's initial success the two groups, originally in all probability separate ones, appear to have joined forces.

Antef turns out to be one of the earliest, if not the earliest attested case of political prosecution. He was eventually vindicated, but only at the very end of his life. The prosecution led him to leave the country, and it was for this reason that he associated with Thutmosis III. Despite this hardship Antef appears to have retained his moral precepts. To judge from the decorations in his tomb, he did not mind defending his convictions, including his controvesy with Hatshepsut. At the same time he shows no bitterness. On the contrary, according to him, professional soldiers are rather to participate in producing red grape-juice—which as a metaphor for life that will eventually find a new role—than to shed blood.